True Ghost Stories

True Ghost Stories

Haunted Homes and Family Legends of Great Britain

by
John H. Ingram

SIENA

This edition published and distributed by Parragon, 1998

Parragon
13 Whiteladies Road
Clifton
Bristol
BS8 1PB

First published 1886

ISBN 0 75252 763 0

Cover photograph by Michael Trevillion,
courtesy of the Trevillion Picture Library

A copy of the British Library Cataloguing-in-Publication Data
is available from the British Library.

Printed and bound in the EC

PREFACE.

THIS collection of strange stories and weird traditions. has not been compiled with a view of creating *un frisson nouveau*, but to serve as a guide to the geography of Ghostland—a handbook to the Haunted Houses of Great. Britain. Many historic tales of apparitions and super- naturally disturbed dwellings are imbedded in British literature; are frequently alluded to in journalistic and other publications, and are known to everybody by name, but by name only. Most people have heard of "The Demon of Tedworth," "The Lord Lyttleton Ghost. Story," and other celebrated narratives of the *uncanny* kind, but it is rare to find anyone able to furnish particulars of them: to enable them to do this is the *raison d'être* of this work.

The number of dwellings reputed to be haunted is. much greater than is commonly supposed; and although.

steam-engines and speculative builders are rapidly diminishing these lingering relics of the past, Dr Mackay's words, in his *Extraordinary Popular Delusions*, anent this theme, are still applicable :—
"Who has not either seen or heard of some house, shut up and uninhabitable, fallen into decay, and looking dusty and dreary, whence, at midnight, strange sounds have been heard to issue—the rattling of chains, and the groaning of perturbed spirits ?—a house that people have thought it unsafe to pass after dark, and which has remained for years without a tenant, and which no tenant would occupy even were he paid to do so ? There are hundreds of such houses in England at the present day . . . . which are marked with the mark of fear—places for the timid to avoid, and the pious to bless themselves at, and ask protection from, as they pass—the abodes of ghosts and evil spirits. There are many such houses in London; and if any vain boaster of the march of intellect would but take the trouble to find them out and count them, he would be convinced that intellect must yet make some enormous strides before such old superstitions can be eradicated."

Although Dr. Mackay may not have exaggerated the number of places having the discredit of being haunted, particulars of the manner of the haunting is generally difficult to obtain : nearly every ancient castle, or time-worn hall, bears the reputation of being thus troubled, but in a very large majority of such cases no evidence is forthcoming—not even the ghost of a tradition! Guide-books, topographical works, even the loquacious custodian—where there is one—of the building, fail to furnish any details; were it otherwise, instead of one modest volume a many-tomed cyclopedia would be necessary.

To mention here separately the many sources whence the information contained in this compilation has been drawn would be impossible, and as in most instances the authority for each story has been specified under its respective heading, would be needless; but still thanks are due and are hereby tendered to those authors whose books have been made use of, and to those noblemen and gentlemen who have aided the work by their friendly information.

In conclusion, it should be remarked that authors and correspondents having, as far as possible, been allowed to tell their tales after their own fashion, the editor does not hold himself responsible for their opinions. Had he ever entertained any belief whatever in supernatural manifestations—as evidently many of his authorities do—the compilation of this work would have effectually cured him of such mental weakness; but, it must be added, no story has been included the incidents of which have been proved to have been the result of palpable deception, or for which any natural explanation has been found. Trusting that his *psychomanteum* will exercise no worse effect upon his readers than it has had upon its compiler, he leaves it to their judgment.

JOHN H. INGRAM.

CONTENTS.

APPENDIX TO FIRST SERIES

CONTENTS.

True Ghost Stories

THE HAUNTED HOMES

AND

FAMILY TRADITIONS

OF GREAT BRITAIN.

ALLANBANK.

In North Britain haunted castles, and hereditary apparitions, appear to have lingered more persistently and to have had longer leases of existence, than they have had in the less romantically inclined southern portion of the island. One of the most noted Scotch spirits attendant upon a certain family is that known as "Pearlin Jean," so called from a species of lace made of thread with which this spectre is bedecked. "Pearlin Jean's" continuous and demonstrative annoyances at Allanbank—a seat of the Stuarts, a family of Scotch baronets—are so thoroughly believed in and widely known, that it has been found difficult to obtain a tenant for the place.

Mr. Charles Kirkpatrick Sharpe, the antiquary, has furnished the following explanatory account of Pearlin Jean's hauntings at Allanbank, together with the cause of her doing so.

"In my youth," says Mr. Sharpe, "Pearlin Jean was the most remarkable ghost in Scotland, and my terror when a child. Our old nurse, Jenny Blackadder, had been a servant at Allanbank, and often heard her rustling in silks up and down stairs, and along the passages. She never saw her; but her husband did.

"She was a French woman, whom the first baronet of Allanbank,* then Mr. Stuart, met with at Paris, during his tour to finish his education as a gentleman. Some people said she was a nun; in which case she must have been a sister of Charity, as she appears not to have been confined to a cloister. After some time, young Stuart either became faithless to the lady or was suddenly recalled to Scotland by his parents, and had got into his carriage at the door of the hotel, when his Dido unexpectedly made her appearance, and stepping on the fore-wheel of the coach to address her lover, he ordered the postilion to drive. on; the consequence of which was that the lady fell, and one of the wheels going over her forehead, killed her.

"In a dusky autumnal evening, when Mr. Stuart drove under the arched gateway of Allanbank, he perceived Pearlin Jean sitting on the top, her head and shoulders covered with blood.

---

* Sir Robert Stuart was created a baronet in the year 1687.

"After this, for many years, the house was haunted; doors shut and opened with great noise at midnight · the rustling of silks and pattering of high-heeled shoes were heard in bed-rooms and passages. Nurse Jenny said there were seven ministers called in together at onc time to *lay* the spirit; 'but they did no mickle good, my dear.'

"The picture of the ghost was hung between those of her lover and his lady, and kept her comparatively quiet; but when taken away, she became worse-natured than ever. This portrait was in the present Sir J. G.'s possession. I am unwilling to record its fate.

"The ghost was designated Pearlin, from always wearing a great quantity of that sort of lace.

"Nurse Jenny told me that when Thomas Blackadder was her lover (I remember Thomas very well), they made an assignation to meet one moonlight night in the orchard at Allanbank. True Thomas, of course, was the first comer; and seeing a female figure in a light-coloured dress, at some distance, he ran forward with open arms to embrace his Jenny; when lo, and behold! as he neared the spot where the figure stood, it vanished; and presently he saw it again at the very end of the orchard, a considerable way off. Thomas went home in a fright; but Jenny, who came last, and saw nothing, forgave him, and they were married.

"Many years after this, about the year 1790, two ladies paid a visit at Allanbank—I think the house was then let—and passed the night there. They had never heard a word about the ghost; but they were disturbed

1 *

the whole night with something walking backwards and
forwards in their bed-chamber. This I had from the
best authority."

To this account may be added that a housekeeper,
called Betty Norrie, who, in more recent times, lived
many years at Allanbank, positively averred that she,
and many other persons, had frequently seen Pearlin
Jean; and, moreover, stated that they were so used to
her as to be no longer alarmed at the noises she made.

BAIR HALL.

THE communicator of the story hereafter detailed was
described in *Notes and Queries* as a well-informed
young lady, and as one who firmly believed what she
stated. Moreover, it was further remarked that, previous to her seeing the apparition she tells of, she had
heard nothing whatever of any story or legend that
could have put it into her mind or have caused her to
dream of it; whilst the corroborative evidence of her
hostess and her household, would put all idea of a
dream or hallucination out of the question. In consequence of the correspondence this story called forth, a
contributor to *Notes and Queries* made it fairly evident
that the "Bair Hall" visited by the narrator was
identical with Torisholme Hall, the property of J. Lodge
of Bare, in the county of Lancashire, Esquire.

"A short time ago," states the relater of this story, "I went with a friend to pay a visit to a family in the neighbourhood of Lancaster. We were very cordially received at Bair Hall by the hostess, who assigned to our use a spacious bed-room with old fashioned furniture, and we noticed particularly an old press. My companion and myself retired to bed, and enjoyed a good night's rest. I happened to awaken at about five o'clock, it being a bright summer's morning, broad daylight, and, to my great surprise, saw distinctly within a few feet of the old-fashioned bed, an old gentleman seated in an arm-chair, earnestly gazing at me with a pleasant expression of countenance. I was not alarmed, but surprised, as I had locked the door when I went to bed, and, considering it a mental delusion, I closed my eyes for a moment and looked again; in the interval the old gentleman had moved his chair, and placed its back against the chamber door; he was seated in it as before, and gazed at me with rather an amused expression. I turned round to look at my companion; she was fast asleep. I immediately awoke her, and requested her to look across the room at the door. She could see nothing, neither could I; the old gentleman had gone. When I told her what I had seen, she got out of bed in haste; we both quitted the room in great alarm, and went to the bed-room of our hostess, who admitted us, and there we remained until it was time to dress.

"The lady asked us if we had opened the old press wardrobe; it appeared we had. 'Oh!' said she, 'it is only James Bair, my uncle (or great-uncle) ; he does not like anyone but myself to examine his ancient clothes, or interfere with his press. He frequently joins me in the house, and some of the other members of the family also, but they don't like him. With me he often converses.'

" I found," concludes the narrator, who does not appear to have had any further encounter with James Bair's apparition, " if any of the rooms or closets were locked at night they were found open in the morning, and our hostess thought nothing of it."

BARBY.

DR LEE, in his work on *Glimpses of the Supernatural*, furnishes a curious account of the discovery of hidden treasure by the agency of an apparition. He does not appear to entertain the slightest doubts as to the correctness of his information in this case, and indeed declares, as will be seen later on by the reader, that the circumstances recorded were completely verified.

The events to which Dr. Lee refers are stated to have occurred at Barby, a village of between six and seven hundred inhabitants, in the county of Northampton, situated about eight miles from Rugby, and a little more than five miles from Daventry. A house in this small village was, until recently, reputed to be haunted and this in the following manner, according to the authority above referred to.

"An old woman of the name of Webb, a native of the place, and above the usual height, died on March 3rd, 1851, at 2 A.M., aged sixty-seven. Late in life she had married a man of some means, who having predeceased her, left her his property, so that she was in good circumstances. Her chief and notorious characteristic, however, was excessive penuriousness, she being remarkably miserly in her habits; and it is believed by many in the village that she thus shortened her days. Two of her neighbours, women of the names of Griffin and Holding, nursed her during her last illness, and her nephew, Mr. Hart, a farmer in the village, supplied her temporal needs; in whose favour she had made a will, by which she bequeathed to him all her possessions.

"About a month after the funeral, Mrs. Holding, who with her uncle lived next door to the house of the deceased (which had been entirely shut up since the funeral), was alarmed and astonished at hearing loud and heavy thumps against the partition wall, and especially against the door of a cupboard in the room wall, while other strange noises, like the dragging of furniture about the rooms, though all the furniture had been removed, and the house was empty. These were chiefly heard about two o'clock in the morning.

"Early in the month of April a family of the name of Accleton, much needing a residence, took the deceased woman's house—the only one in the village vacant—

and bringing their goods and chattels, proceeded to inhabit it. The husband was often absent, but he and his wife occupied the room in which Mrs. Webb had died, while their daughter, a girl of about ten years of age, slept in a small bed in the corner. Violent noises in the night were heard about two o'clock—thumps, tramps, and tremendous crashes, as if all the furniture had been collected together and then violently banged on to the floor. One night at 2 A.M. the parents were suddenly awakened by the violent screams of the child. 'Mother! mother! there's a tall woman standing by my bed, a shaking her head at me!' The parents could see nothing, so did their best to quiet and compose the child. At four o'clock they were awakened by the child's screams, for she had seen the woman again; in fact, she appeared to her no less than seven times on seven subsequent nights.

"Mrs. Accleton, during her husband's absence, having engaged her mother to sleep with her one night, was suddenly aroused at the same hour of two by a strange and unusual light in her room. Looking up, she saw quite plainly the spirit of Mrs. Webb, which moved towards her with a gentle appealing manner, as though it would have said 'Speak! speak!'

"This spectre appeared likewise to a Mrs. Radbourne, a Mrs. Griffiths, and a Mrs. Holding. They assert that luminous balls of light seemed to go up and towards a trap-door in the ceiling which led to the roof of the cottage. Each person who saw it testified likewise to hearing a low, unearthly moaning noise, 'strange and unnatural like,' but somewhat similar in character to the moans of the woman in her death-agony.

"The subject was of course discussed, and Mrs. Accleton suggested that its appearance might not impossibly be connected with the existence of money hoarded up in the roof—an idea which may have arisen from the miserly habits of the dead woman. The hint having been given to and taken by her nephew, Mr. Hart, the farmer, he proceeded to the house, and with Mrs. Accleton's personal help, made a search. The loft above was totally dark, but by the aid of a candle there was discovered, firstly, a bundle of old writings, old deeds, as they turned out to be, and afterwards a large bag of gold and bank-notes, out of which the nephew took a handful of sovereigns and exhibited them to Mrs. Accleton. But the knockings, moanings, strange noises, and other disturbances, did not cease upon this discovery. They did cease, however, when Mr. Hart, having found that certain debts were owing by her, carefully and scrupulously paid them. So much for the account of the haunted house at Barby."

The circumstances detailed were most carefully investigated by Sir Charles Isham and other gentlemen in the neighbourhood, and the conclusion they arrived at was that the above facts were completely verified by the evidence laid before them.

BEAMINSTER SCHOOL.

IN 1774 the *Gentleman's Magazine* printed the following narrative, prefacing it with these words : " The
following very singular story comes well authenticated."
In many respects the story may be deemed unique in
the history of the supernatural. The apparition appears
in broad daylight, and is seen by five children, one of
whom did not even know the individual it represented
when alive, and yet proved its identity by a wonderful
piece of circumstantial evidence. The intense pathos
of the unfortunate and evidently - murdered lad, re-
appearing amid the scenes of his childish occupations,
and where he had been wont to play with those boys
who now could only look upon him as a passing
shadow, is most suggestive.

The school of Beminster (Beaminster), says the
account, is held in a gallery of the parish church to
which there is a distinct entrance from the churchyard.
Every Saturday the key of it is delivered to the clerk
of the parish by one or the other of the schoolboys.
On Saturday, June the 22nd, 1728, the master had
dismissed his lads as usual. Twelve of them loitered
about in the churchyard to play at ball. It was just
about noon. After a short space, four of the lads
returned into the school to search for old pens, and
were startled by hearing in the church a noise which
they described as that produced by striking a brass pan.
They immediately ran to their playfellows in the church-

yard and told them of it. They came to the conclusion that someone was in hiding in order to frighten them, and they all went back into the school together to discover who it was, but could not find anyone. As they were returning to their sport, on the stairs that lead into the churchyard, they heard in the school a second noise. Terrified at that, they ran round the church, and when at the belfry, or west door, they heard what seemed to them the sound of someone preaching, which was succeeded by another sound as of a congregation singing psalms. Both of these noises lasted but a short time.

With the thoughtlessness of youth the lads soon resumed their sport, and after a short time one of them went into the school for his book, when he saw a coffin lying on one of the benches, only about six feet away. Surprised at this, he ran off and told his playfellows what he had seen, on which they all thronged to the school-door, whence *five* of the twelve saw the apparition of John Daniel, who had been dead more than seven weeks, sitting at some distance from the coffin, further in the school. *All* of them saw the coffin, and it was conjectured that why all did not see the apparition was because the door was so narrow they could not all approach it together. The first who knew it to be the apparition of their deceased schoolfellow was Daniel's half-brother, and he, on seeing it, cried out, "There sits our John, with just such a coat on as I have"— (in the lifetime of the deceased boy the half-brothers were usually clothed alike),—" with a pen in his hand,

and a book before him, and a coffin by him. I'll throw
a stone at him." The other boys tried to stop him, but
he threw the stone, as he did so saying, "Take it!"
upon which the apparition immediately disappeared.

The immense excitement this created in the place
may be imagined. The lads, whose ages ranged between
nine and twelve, were all magisterially examined by
Colonel Broadrep, and all agreed in their relation of the
circumstances, even to the hinges of the coffin; whilst
their description of the coffin tallied exactly with that
the deceased lad had been buried in. One of the lads
who saw the apparition was quite twelve years of age,
and was a quiet sedate lad for his age; he entered the
school after the deceased boy had left it (on account of
illness about a fortnight before his death), and had
never seen Daniel in his life-time. This lad, on examination, gave an exact description of the person of the
deceased, and took especial notice of one thing about
the apparition which the other boys had not observed,
and that was, it had a white cloth or rag bound round
one of its hands. The woman who laid out the corpse
of John Daniel for interment deposed on oath that she
took such a white cloth from its hand, it having been
put on the boy's hand (he being lame of it) about four
days or so before his death.

Daniel's body had been found in an obscure place in
a field, at about a furlong distant from his mother's
house, and had been buried without an inquest, in
consequence of his mother alleging that the lad had
been subject to fits. After the appearance of the

apparition the body was disinterred, a coroner's inquest held, and a verdict returned to the effect that the boy had been " strangled." This verdict appears to have been mainly arrived at in consequence of the depositions of two women " of good repute " that two days after the corpse was found they saw it, and discovered a " black list " round its neck; and likewise of the joiner who put the body into the coffin, and who had an opportunity of observing it, as the shroud was not put on in the usual way, but was in two pieces, one laid under and the other over the body. A " chirurgeon " who gave evidence could not or would not positively affirm to the jury that there was any dislocation of the neck. So far as can be learnt, no steps were taken to bring anyone to justice on account of the suggested death by violence of the lad.

BISHAM ABBEY.

BISHAM ABBEY, in Berkshire, was formerly the family seat of the Hobbys, and about the first half of the sixteenth century was in possession of Sir Thomas Hobby, or Hoby, a man of no slight reputation for learning in those days. He married Elizabeth, the third daughter of Sir Anthony Cooke, who shared the general fame of her family for intellectual qualifications. When Sir Thomas went to France as ambassador for

Queen Elizabeth his wife accompanied him, and on his death abroad in 1566 Lady Hoby brought his body home and had it interred in a mortuary chapel at Bisham. Subsequently she married John, Lord Russell.

By her first husband the Lady Hoby is said to have had a son who, when quite young, displayed the most intense antipathy to every kind of study; and such was his repugnance to writing, that in his fits of obstinacy he would wilfully and deliberately blot his writing-books. This conduct enraged his mother, whose whole family were noted for their scholastic attainments, and who, like her three sisters, Lady Burleigh, Lady Bacon, and Lady Killigrew, was not only an excellent classical scholar, but was also married to a man of literary note, that she chastised the unfortunate lad with all the violence at that period permitted to, and practised by, parents on their children. She beat him, according to the old legend, again and again on the shoulders and head, and at last so severely and unmercifully that he died.

It is commonly reported that, as a punishment for her unnatural cruelty, her spirit is doomed to haunt Bisham Abbey, the house where this cruel act of manslaughter was perpetrated. Several persons have seen the apparition, the likeness of which, both as regards feature and dress, to a pale portrait of her ladyship in antique widow's weeds still remaining at Bisham, is said to be exact and life-like. She is reported to glide through a certain chamber, in the act of washing blood-stains from her hands, and on some occasions her apparition is said to have been seen in the grounds of the old mansion.

A very remarkable occurrence in connection with this narrative took place some years ago, according to Dr. Lee, author of *Glimpses of the Supernatural*. "In taking down an old oak window-shutter of the latter part of the sixteenth century," he states that "*a packet o antique copy-books of that period were discovered pushed into the wall between the joists of the skirting, and several of these books on which young Hobby's name was written were covered with blots, thus supporting the ordinary tradition.*"

BOTATHEN.

In the second volume of Hitchen's *History of Cornwall* is given *in extenso* a most remarkable account of an apparition that is believed to have appeared in that county. The scene of its appearance was a place called Botaden, or Botathen, in the parish of South Petherwin, near Launceston. Various authors have alluded to this marvellous, and, all things considered, inexplicable story; but as Hitchen appears to have derived his account direct from one of the persons chiefly concerned—that is to say, from the Rev. John Ruddle, Head Master of the Grammar School at Launceston, Vicar of Alternon, and Prebendary of Exeter, it is better to follow him.

"Young Mr. Bligh," says Hitchen, "a lad of bright parts and of no common attainments, became on a sudden pensive, dejected, and melancholy. His friends, observing the change without being able to discover the cause, attributed his behaviour to laziness, an aversion to school, or to some other motive which they suspected he was ashamed to avow. He was, however, induced to inform his brother, after some time, that in a field through which he passed to and from school "—that is to say, to and from Launceston Grammar School, of which, as has already been observed, Mr. Ruddle was Head Master—"he was invariably met by the apparition of a woman, whom he personally knew while living, and who had been dead about eight years." Young Bligh is said to have been at this time about sixteen. "Ridicule, threats, and persuasions were alike used in vain by the family to induce him to dismiss these absurd ideas. Mr. Ruddle was, however, sent for, to whom the lad ingenuously communicated the time, manner, and frequency of this appearance. It was in a field called Higher Broomfield. The apparition, he said, appeared dressed in female attire, met him two or three times while he passed through the field, glided hastily by him, but never spoke. He had thus been occasionally met about two months before he took any particular notice of it; at length the appearance became more frequent, meeting him both morning and evening, but always in the same field, yet invariably moving out of the path when it came close to him. He often spoke, but could never get any reply. To avoid this unwelcome visitor he forsook the field, and went to school and returned from it through a lane, in which place, between the quarry pack and nursery, it always met him. Unable to disbelieve the evidence of his own senses, or to obtain credit with any of his family, he prevailed upon Mr. Ruddle to accompany him to the place.

" 'I arose,' says this clergyman, 'the next morning, and went with him. The field to which he led me I guessed to be about twenty acres, in an open country, and about three furlongs from any house. We went into the field, and had not gone a third part before the spectrum, in the shape of a woman, with all the circumstances he had described the day before, so far as the suddenness of its appearance and transition would permit me to discover, passed by.

" 'I was a little surprised at it, and though I had taken up a firm resolution to speak to it, I had not the power, nor durst I look back ; yet I took care not to show any fear to my pupil and guide, and therefore, telling him that I was satisfied in the truth of his statement we walked to the end of the field and returned— nor did the ghost meet us that time but once.

" 'On the 27th July, 1665, I went to the haunted field by myself, and walked the breadth of it without any encounter. I then returned and took the other walk, and then the spectre appeared to me, much about the same place in which I saw it when the young gentleman was with me. It appeared to move swifter than before, and seemed to be about ten feet from me

2

on my right hand, insomuch that I had not time to
speak to it, as I had determined with myself beforehand.
The evening of this day, the parents, the son, and
myself, being in the chamber where I lay, I proposed to
them our going all together to the place next morning.
We accordingly met at the stile we had appointed;
thence we all four walked into the field together. We had
not gone more than half the field before the ghost made
its appearance. It then came over the stile just before
us, and moved with such rapidity that by the time we had
gone six or seven steps it passed by. I immediately
turned my head and ran after it, with the young man by
my side. We saw it pass over the stile at which we
entered, and no farther. I stepped upon the hedge at
one place and the young man at another, but we could
discern nothing; whereas I do aver that the swiftes
horse in England could not have conveyed himself out
of sight in that short space of time. Two things I
observed in this day's appearance: first, a spaniel dog,
which had followed the company unregarded, barked
and ran away as the spectrum passed by; whence it is
easy to conclude that it was not our fear or fancy which
made the apparition. Secondly, the motion of the
spectrum was not *gradatim* or by steps, or moving of
the feet, but by a kind of gliding, as children upon ice,
or as a boat down a river, which punctually answers the
description the ancients give of the motion of these
Lamures. This ocular evidence clearly convinced, but
withal strangely affrighted, the old gentleman and his
wife. They well knew this woman, Dorothy Durant, in

her life-time; were at her burial, and now plainly saw her features in this apparition.

"'The next morning, being Thursday, I went very early by myself, and walked for about an hour's space in meditation and prayer in the field next adjoining. Soon after five I stepped over the stile into the haunted field, and had not gone above thirty or forty paces before the ghost appeared at the further stile. I spoke to it in some short sentences with a loud voice; whereupon it approached me, but slowly, and when I came near it moved not. I spoke again, and it answered in a voice neither audible nor very intelligible. I was not in the least terrified, and therefore persisted until it spoke again and gave me satisfaction; but the work could not be finished at this time. Whereupon the same evening, an hour after sunset, it met me again near the same place, and after a few words on each side it quietly vanished, and neither doth appear now, nor hath appeared since, nor ever will more to any man's disturbance. The discourse in the morning lasted about a quarter of an hour.

"' 'These things are true,' concludes the Rev. John Ruddle, 'and I know them to be so, with as much certainty as eyes and ears can give me; and until I can be persuaded that my senses all deceive me about their proper objects, and by that persuasion deprive me of the strongest inducement to believe the Christian religion, I must and will assert that the things contained in this paper are true.'"

BOWOOD.

In the popular *Memoirs* of Mrs. Schimmelpenninck, the well-known authoress, a curious story connected with Bowood, the seat of the Marquis of Lansdowne, is related as having occurred whilst the celebrated Dr. Priestley was librarian there to Lord Shelburn.

"One day," says Mrs. Schimmelpenninck, "Mr. Petty, the precocious and gifted youth, sent for Dr. Priestley (Lord Shelburn, Mr. Petty's father, being then absent, I think, in London). When the doctor entered, Mr. Petty told him he had passed a very restless night, and had been much disturbed by uncomfortable dreams, which he wished to relate to Dr. Priestley, hoping that, by so doing, the painful impression would pass away.

"He then said he dreamed he had been very unwell, when suddenly the whole household was in preparation for a journey. He was too ill to sit up, but was carried lying down in the carriage. His surprise was extreme in seeing carriage after carriage in an almost interminable procession. He was alone, and could not speak; he could only gaze in astonishment. The procession at last wound slowly off. After pursuing the road for many miles towards London, it at last appeared to stop at the door of a church. It was the church at High Wycombe, which is the burial-place of the Shelburn family. It seemed, in Mr. Petty's dream, that he entered, or rather was carried into the church. He looked back; he saw the procession which followed him was in black, and that the carriage from which he had been taken bore the semblance of a hearse. Here the dream ended, and he awoke.

"Dr. Priestley told him that his dream was the result of a feverish cold, and that the impression would soon pass off. Nevertheless, he thought it best to send for the family medical attendant. The next day Mr. Petty was much better; on the third day he was completely convalescent, so that the doctor permitted him to leave his room; but as it was in January, and illness was prevalent, he desired him on no account to leave the house, and, with that precaution, took his leave. Late the next afternoon the medical man was returning from his other patients; his road lay by the gates of Bowood, and as Lord Shelburn was away, he thought he might as well call to see Mr. Petty and enforce his directions. What was his surprise, when he had passed the lodge, to see the youth himself, without his hat, playfully running to meet him! The doctor was much astonished, as it was bitterly cold and the ground covered with snow. He rode towards Mr. Petty to rebuke him for his imprudence, when suddenly he disappeared—whither he knew not, but he seemeh instantaneously to vanish. The doctor thought it very extraordinary, but that probably the youth had not wished to be found transgressing orders, and he rode on to the house. There he learnt that Mr. Petty had just expired."

THE BRISTOL VICARAGE.

In 1846 certain strange doings were reported to be
going on in an ancient residence in Bristol. The papers
found the matter exciting such interest that they felt
bound to notice it, but did so in a half-serious, half-
sarcastic spirit, as the following excerpt from the *Bristol
Times* will show. Under the heading of " A Ghost at
Bristol," the journal named made this statement :—

"We have this week a ghost story to relate. Yes, a
real ghost story, and a ghost story without, as yet, any
clue to its elucidation. After the dissolution of the
Calendars, their ancient residence, adjoining and almost
forming a part of All Saints' Church, Bristol, was
converted into a vicarage-house, and it is still (in 1846)
called by that name, though the incumbents have for
many years ceased to reside there. The present occupants are Mr. and Mrs. Jones, the sexton and sextoness
of the church, and one or two lodgers; and it is to the
former and their servant-maid that the strange visitor
has made his appearance, causing such terror by his
nightly calls, that all three have determined upon
quitting the premises, if indeed they have not already
carried their resolution into effect. Mr. and Mrs.
Jones's description of the disturbance as given to the
landlord, on whom they called in great consternation,
is as distinct as any ghost story could be. The nocturnal visitor is heard walking about the house when
the inhabitants are in bed ; and Mr. Jones, who is a

man of by no means nervous constitution, declares he
has several times seen a light flickering on one of the
walls. Mrs. Jones is equally certain that she has heard
a man with creaking shoes walking in the bed-room
above her own, when no man was on the premises (or at
least ought not to be), and 'was nearly killed with the
fright.' To the servant-maid, however, was vouchsafed
the unenvied honour of seeing this restless night
visitor; she declares she has repeatedly had her bed-
room door unbolted at night, between the hours of
twelve and two o'clock—the period when such beings
usually make their promenades—by something in human
semblance. She cannot particularise his dress, but
describes it as something antique, and of a fashion
'lang syne gane,' and to some extent corresponding to
that of the ancient Calendars, the former inhabitants of
the house. She further says, he is ' a whiskered gentleman' (we give her own words), which whiskered
gentleman has gone the length of shaking her bed,
and, she believes, would have shaken herself also, but
that she invariably puts her head under the clothes
when she sees him approach. Mrs. Jones declares she
believes in the appearance of the whiskered gentleman,
and she had made up her mind the night before she
called on her landlord to leap out of the window (and
it is not a trifle that will make people leap out of the
windows) as soon as he entered the room. The effect
of the 'flickering light' on Mr. Jones was quite terrific,
causing excessive trembling, and the complete doubling
up of his whole body into a round ball, like."

As far as can be ascertained no elucidation of this mysterious affair was ever forthcoming. Mrs. Crowe—to whose knowledge the account was brought—subsequently wrote to the editor of the *Bristol Times*, and received a reply that "the whole affair remains wrapped in the same mystery as when chronicled in the pages of" the paper, and this statement was subsequently confirmed by Mrs. Jones.

CAMBRIDGE.

IN the narrative about to be recited, the appearance of the apparition, and the coincidence of the date of death with its appearance, differ in no way from the usual records of such things. But the wonderful series of events by which the discrepancies between the official report and the spectral visit were ultimately explained, render this story one of the most marvellous known. It is related by Robert Dale Owen, in his famous *Footfalls*, wherein he declares that although in accordance with the wishes of the family some of the names are merely represented by initials, they are all known to him. As, however, the name of the officer subsequently appeared in print, we shall not be committing any breach of courtesy or of good feeling in stating that Captain German Wheatcroft is the name in full. The story taken as a whole is so truly marvellous, that it is deemed but just that it should be given *verbatim* from Owen's record, not abridging or altering a single foot-note, nor omitting aught save a spiritual episode which does not affect the general narrative. The tale runs thus :—

"In the month of September, 1857, Captain German Wheatcroft, of the 6th (Inniskilling) Dragoons, went out to India to join his regiment.

"His wife remained in England, residing at Cambridge. On the night between the 14th and 15th of November, 1857, towards morning, she dreamed that she saw her husband, looking anxious and ill; upon which she immediately awoke, much agitated. It was bright moonlight: and, looking up, she perceived the same figure standing by her bed-side. He appeared in his uniform, the hands pressed across the breast, the hair dishevelled, the face very pale. His large dark eyes were fixed full upon her; their expression was that of great excitement, and there was a peculiar contraction of the mouth, habitual to him when agitated. She saw him, even to each minute particular of his dress, as distinctly as she had ever done in her life ; and she remembers to have noticed between his hands the white of the shirt-bosom, unstained, however, with blood. The figure seemed to bend forward, as if in pain, and to make an effort to speak; but there was no sound. It remained visible, the wife thinks, as long as a minute, and then disappeared.

"Her first idea was to ascertain if she was actually awake. She rubbed her eyes with the sheet, and felt that the touch was real. Her little nephew was in bed with her; she bent over the sleeping child and listened to its breathing: the sound was distinct, and she became convinced that what she had seen was no dream. It need hardly be added that she did not again go to sleep that night.

"Next morning she related all this to her mother, expressing her conviction, though she had noticed no marks of blood on his dress, that Captain Wheatcroft was either killed or grievously wounded. So fully impressed was she with the reality of that apparition, that she thenceforth refused all invitations. A young friend urged her soon afterwards to go with her to a fashionable concert, reminding her that she had received from Malta, sent by her husband, a handsome dress cloak, which she had never yet worn. But she positively declined, declaring that, uncertain as she was whether she was not already a widow, she would never enter a place of amusement until she had letters from her husband (if indeed he still lived) of a later date than the 14th of November.

"It was on a Tuesday, in the month of December, 1857, that the telegram regarding the actual fate of Captain Wheatcroft was published in London. It was to the effect that he was killed before Lucknow on the *fifteenth* of November.

"This news, given in the morning paper, attracted the attention of Mr. Wilkinson, a London solicitor, who had in charge Captain Wheatcroft's affairs. When at a later period this gentleman met the widow, she informed him that she had been quite prepared for the melancholy news, but that she had felt sure her husband could not have been killed on the 15th of November, inasmuch as it was during the night between the 14th and 15th that he appeared to her.*

"The certificate from the War Office, however, which it became Mr. Wilkinson's duty to obtain, confirmed the date given in the telegram, its tenor being as follows:—

"'No. $\frac{9572}{1}$ WAR OFFICE,
                                          30th January, 1858

"'These are to certify that it appears, by the records in this office, that Captain German Wheatcroft, of the 6th Dragoon Guards, was killed in action on the 15th of November, 1857.†

"'(Signed)   B. HAWES.'

"Mr. Wilkinson called at the office of Messrs. Cox and Greenwood, the army agents, to ascertain if there were no mistake in the certificate. But nothing there appeared to confirm any surmise of inaccuracy. Captain Wheatcroft's death was mentioned in two separate despatches of Sir Colin Campbell, and in both the date corresponded with that given in the telegram.

"So matters rested, until, in the month of March,

---

* "The difference of longitude between London and Lucknow being about five hours, three or four o'clock A.M. in London would be eight or nine o'clock A.M. at Lucknow. But it was in the *afternoon*, not in the morning, as will be seen in the sequel, that Captain Wheatcroft was killed. Had he fallen on the 15th, therefore, the apparition to his wife would have appeared several hours before the engagement in which he fell, and while he was yet alive and well.—R. D. OWEN."

† "Into this certificate, of which I possess the original, an error has crept. Captain German Wheatcroft was of the 6th (Inniskilling) Dragoons, not of the 6th Dragoon Guards.—R. D. OWEN."

1858, the family of Captain Wheatcroft received from Captain G—— C——, then of the Military Train, a letter dated near Lucknow, on the 19th of December, 1857. This letter informed them that Captain Wheatcroft had been killed before Lucknow, while gallantly leading on the squadron, not on the 15th of November, as reported in Sir Colin Campbell's despatches, but on the *fourteenth, in the afternoon.* Captain C—— was riding close by his side at the time he saw him fall. He was struck by a fragment of shell in the breast, and never spoke after he was hit. He was buried at the Dilkoosha; and on a wooden cross, erected by his friend, Lieutenant R—— of the 9th Lancers, at the head of his grave, are cut the initials ' G. W.,' and the date of his death, the ' 14th of November, 1857.' *

"The War Office finally made the correction as to the date of death, but not until more than a year after the event occurred. Mr. Wilkinson, having occasion to apply for an additional copy of the certificate in April, 1857, found it in exactly the same words as that which I have given, only that the 14th of November had been substituted for the 15th.†

---

* "It was not in his own regiment, which was then at Meerut, that Captain Wheatcroft was serving at the time of his death. Immediately on arriving from England at Cawnpore, he had offered his services to Colonel Wilson, of the 64th. They were at first declined, but finally accepted; and he joined the Military Train then starting for Lucknow. It was in their ranks that he fell.—R. D. OWEN."

† "The originals of both these certificates are in my possession: the first bearing date 30th January, 1858, and certifying, as already shown, to the 15th; the second, dated 5th April, 1859, and testifying to the 14th.—R. D. OWEN."

" This extraordinary narrative was obtained by me direct from the parties themselves," says Owen. " The widow of Captain Wheatcroft kindly consented to examine and correct the manuscript, and allowed me to inspect a copy of Captain C——'s letter, giving the particulars of her husband's death. To Mr. Wilkinson, also, the manuscript was submitted, and he assented to its accuracy so far as he is concerned. I have neglected no precaution, therefore, to obtain for it the warrant of authenticity.

"It is, perhaps," concludes Owen, " the only example on record where the appearance of what is usually termed a ghost proved the means of correcting an erroneous date in the despatches of a Commander-in-Chief, and of detecting an inaccuracy in the certificate of a War-Office."

CAMBRIDGE UNIVERSITY.

INNUMERABLE stories are related of various rooms in the colleges of Oxford and Cambridge being haunted. One of the most circumstantial is given in Howitt's *History of the Supernatural*, as related to him by Wordsworth, on his return from paying a visit to his brother, Dr. Christopher Wordsworth, then Master of Trinity College, Cambridge. According to the poet's account, as detailed by Howitt, a young man, having just come to enter himself a student at Trinity, brought with him a letter of introduction to Dr. Wordsworth. Upon presenting his introductory epistle, the student asked the Master if he could recommend comfortable quarters to him, and Dr. Wordsworth mentioned some that were at that time vacant. The young man took them.

A few days after this, Dr. Wordsworth, seeing the collegian, asked him how he liked his new quarters. He replied that the rooms themselves were very comfortable, but that he should be obliged to give them up. Upon being asked what was his reason for doing so, the young freshman replied, Dr. Wordsworth might think him fanciful, but that the rooms were haunted, and that he had been awakened every night by the apparition of a child, which wandered about the rooms moaning, and, strange to say, with the palms of its hands turned outwards; that he had searched his rooms, and on each occasion found them securely locked, and that he was convinced nothing but an apparition could have traversed them. Dr. Wordsworth said he would now be candid with him, and confess that these rooms had been repeatedly abandoned by students on the plea that they were haunted, but that, having a perfect reliance on his judgment and veracity, from what he had heard of him, he was desirous of seeing whether he would confirm the story, having had no intimation of it beforehand. "Whether," says Howitt, very pertinently, " the young man thanked the

Master for his recommendation of such lodgings, does not appear."

In *The Night Side of Nature* is given another instance of the appearance of an apparition in one of the colleges at Cambridge, but, unfortunately, the name of the college is not given, and only the initial of the ghost-seer's name. The story is that three young men, students at the university, after having been out hunting, met and dined together in the apartments of one of them. After dinner the host and one of his guests, fatigued with their heavy exercise, fell asleep; but the third person present, Mr. M——, remained awake. After a time Mr. M—— beheld the door open, and an elderly gentleman enter and place himself behind the sleeping owner of the rooms. Having stood there for about a minute, the stranger moved away, and proceeded into the "gyp" room, a small inner chamber, whence there was no other means of exit than through the door he had entered. As the stranger did not come out again from the "gyp" room, Mr. M—— woke his host, and told him that somebody had gone into the room, remarking, "I don't know who it can be."

The young man rose and looked into the "gyp" room, but as there was no one there, he very naturally accused Mr. M—— of having been dreaming; but he was quite positive that he had not been asleep. He then gave a description of the visitor's appearance, describing him as dressed like a country squire, with gaiters, and so forth. "Why, that's like my father," said the host, and at once instituted inquiry as to whether the old gentleman had been there, and had contrived to slip out again unobserved. He had not been seen ; and an early post brought the intelligence of his death, which had occurred about the time he was seen at Cambridge.

CANTERBURY.

In his celebrated *Athenæ Oxonienses*, Anthony à Wood, the learned antiquary, states that Dr. Jacob, a well-known medical man, told him the following marvellous relation of an apparition that visited his house at Canterbury. "This very story," records à Wood, " Dr. Jacobs told me himself, being then at Lord Teynham's, in Kent, where he was then physician to my eldest son, whom he recovered from a fever." Dr. Jacob also repeated the relation in a letter which Aubrey, the antiquary, alludes to in his *Miscellanies*. The story is that " the learned Henry Jacob," a fellow of Merton College, Oxford, died at Dr. Jacob's house at Canterbury.

About a week after Henry Jacob's death, the doctor being in bed and awake, and the moon shining bright into his room, he beheld his deceased cousin standing by the bedside in his shirt, with a white cap on his head, and his " mustachoes turning up, as when he was alive." The doctor pinched himself to be assured that he was awake, and turned to the other side away from the apparition. After some time he plucked up courage to turn towards it again, and Henry Jacob stood there still. The doctor would have spoken to him, but could not, for which he has been sorry ever since. In some little time the apparition disappeared.

Not long after this incident the cook-maid, going out to the wood-pile one evening to fetch some wood for the kitchen fire, averred that she saw the apparition of Mr. Henry in his shirt, standing on the pile of wood.

This spectre does not seem to have troubled the doctor any more; but it is stated that when dying Henry Jacob would fain have told his cousin something, but was not able to. It is imagined, says Aubrey, that he would have informed Dr. Jacob with what person he had deposited the manuscripts of his own writings, which were all the riches he had, and which, it was strongly suspected, fell into the hands of a certain person who printed them under his own name. If anything could bring an author's spirit back to this sphere, certainly such an outrage on his memory would.

CAWOOD CASTLE.

ANYONE conversant with the less-known judicial records of the past, is well aware that supernatural evidence frequently formed an important factor in ancient crimi

nal trials. One of these curious cases is recorded in
Aubrey's *Miscellanies*, that medley of useful and useless matters, as having taken place in the immediate
vicinity of Cawood Castle, Yorkshire. The depositions
made at the trial, but for one extraordinary and all-
important piece of evidence, were of common-place type.
According to the circumstances brought out in the
course of investigation, the facts were these :—

On Monday, the 14th of April, 1690, William Barwick was out walking with his wife, Mary Barwick, close
to Cawood Castle. From motives not divulged at the
trial, although shrewdly guessed at by Aubrey, he determined to murder her, and finding a pond conveniently
at hand, he threw her in. Deeming, doubtless, that the
body would soon be discovered where it was, he went
the next day to the place, procured a huge spade, and,
getting the corpse out of the water, made a grave close
by, and buried it.

Apparently satisfied that no one had witnessed his
ghastly deed, Barwick actually went on the day he had
committed the murder to his wife's sister, and informed
her husband, Thomas Lofthouse, that he had taken his
wife to a relative's house in Selby, and left her there.
Lofthouse, however, according to his deposition on
oath, averred that on the Tuesday after the visit of
Barwick, " about half an hour after twelve of the clock,
in the day-time, he was watering quickwood, and as he
was going for the second pail, there appeared, walking
before him, an apparition in the shape of a woman.
Soon after she sat down over against the pond, on a

green hill. He walked by her as he went to the pond, and as he came with the pail of water from the pond, looking sideways to see if she sat in the same place, which he saw she did." The witness then observed that the apparition was dandling "something like a white bag" on her lap, evidently suggestive, indeed, of her unborn babe that was slain with her. Lofthouse now emptied his pail of water, so he averred, and then stood in the yard of his house, to see if he could still see the woman's figure, but she had disappeared. He described her attire as exactly similar to that worn by his sister-in-law at the time of her murder, but remarked that she looked extremely pale, and that her teeth were visible, " her visage being like his wife's sister."

Notwithstanding the horror of this apparition, Lofthouse, according to Aubrey's account, did not mention anything about it to his wife till night-time, when, at his family duty of prayers, the thoughts of the apparition were so overpowering, that they interrupted his devotion. After he had made an end of his prayers, therefore, he told the whole story of what he had seen to his wife, "who, laying the whole circumstances together, immediately inferred that her sister was either drowned or otherwise murdered, and desired her husband to look after her the next day, which was Wednesday in Easter week." Lofthouse now recalled to mind what Barwick had told him about having left his wife at his uncle's at Selby, and therefore went to him and made inquiries, and found that neither the man nor his wife had been seen or heard of there. This information, coupled with the appearance of the apparition, increased his suspicions against Barwick to such a degree, that he went before the Lord Mayor of York, and obtained a warrant for the arrest of his brother-in-law.

The culprit, when arrested, confessed the crime, and the body of the murdered woman being disinterred, was found dressed in clothing similar, apparently, to that worn by the apparition. Ultimately Barwick suffered the extreme penalty of the law for his crime.

CHEDWORTH.

ACCORDING to an anecdote related by Mrs. Crawford, in the *Metropolitan Magazine* for 1836, Chedworth, the seat of Lord Chedworth, in Gloucestershire, has not escaped the fate common to the residences of most noble families; that is to say, it has a story of an apparition attached to it. The account of this circumstance is stated to have been told to Mrs. Crawford by Miss Wright, the adopted child of Lord Chedworth, and daughter of a sister of his. The story, as told by his niece, was, that Lord Chedworth had great doubts as to the existence of the soul in another world, doubts which were equally shared by a gentleman for whom he had a very great friendship.

One morning Miss Wright remarked, when her uncle joined her at the breakfast-table, that he was very thoughtful, had no appetite, and was unusually silent,

At last he said, " Molly "—for thus he was accustomed to call his niece—"I had a strange visitor last night. My old friend B—— came to me."

" What ! " said Miss Wright, " did he come after I went to bed ? "

" *His spirit did,*" said Lord Chedworth, solemnly.

" Oh, my dear uncle ! how could the spirit of a living man appear ? " said she, smiling.

" He is dead, beyond doubt," replied his lordship; " listen, and then laugh as much as you please. I had not entered my bedroom many minutes when he stood before me. Like you, I could not believe but that I was looking on the living man, and so accosted him; but he (the spirit) answered, ' Chedworth, I died this night at eight o'clock. I came to tell you there is another world beyond the grave : there is a righteous God that judgeth all ! ' "

" Depend upon it, uncle, it was only a dream; " but even as Miss Wright was still speaking, a groom on horseback rode up the avenue, and immediately afterwards delivered a letter to Lord Chedworth, announcing the sudden death of his friend.

CHESHUNT.

IN Mrs. Crowe's *Night Side of Nature* is a remarkable account of a haunted dwelling, stated to be " in the neighbourhood of the metropolis." Mrs. Crowe neither

mentions the name of the locality, nor furnishes more
than the initial of the " gentleman engaged in business
in London," whose family suffered from the "hauntings"
at this residence; but in Howitt's *History of the Supernatural* these omitted particulars are supplied. According to Mr. Howitt, the old-fashioned house referred to
by Mrs. Crowe was at Cheshunt, and belonged to Sir
Henry Meux; and the account given by the authoress
was taken down from the recital of Mr. and Mrs. Charles
Kean, the well-known actors, who also furnished the
same particulars to Mr. Howitt. A comparison of the
statements given by Mrs. Crowe and Mr. Howitt enables
us to give the following details:—

Mr. Chapman, the brother-in-law of Mr. Kean, and
apparently the well-known publisher, had been induced,
by the unusually low rental, to purchase the seven years'
lease of a large old-fashioned house at Cheshunt. The
house was a good country residence, was furnished, and
had a considerable quantity of land attached to it, including a garden and pleasure-ground. The family
removed into the place, and Mr. Chapman joined them
once or twice a week, as his business engagements
permitted.

"They had been some considerable time in the house,"
says Mrs. Crowe, " without the occurrence of anything
remarkable, when one evening, towards dusk, Mrs.
Chapman, on going into what was called the oak bed-
room, saw a female figure near one of the windows; it
was apparently a young woman with dark hair hanging
over her shoulders, a silk petticoat, and a short white

robe, and she appeared to be looking eagerly through the window, as if expecting somebody. Mrs. Chapman clapped her hands upon her eyes, ' as thinking she had seen something she ought not to have seen,' and when she looked again the figure had disappeared.

"Shortly after this, a young girl, who filled the situation of under nursery-maid, came to her in great agitation, saying that she had had a terrible fright, from seeing a very ugly old woman looking in upon her as she passed the window in the lobby. The girl was trembling violently, and almost crying, so that Mrs. Chapman entertained no doubts of the reality of her alarm. She, however, thought it advisable to laugh her out of her fear, and went with her to the window, which looked into a closed court, but there was no one there, neither had any of the other servants seen such a person. Soon after this the family began to find themselves disturbed with strange and frequently very loud noises during the night. Among the rest, there was something like the beating of a crowbar upon the pump in the above-mentioned court, but, search as they would, they could discover no cause for the sound.

"One day, when Mr. Chapman had brought a friend from London to stay the night with him, Mrs. Chapman thought proper to go to the oak bed-room, where the stranger was to sleep, for the purpose of inspecting the arrangements for his comfort, when, to her great surprise, someone seemed to follow her up to the fire-place, though, on turning round, there was nobody to be seen. She said nothing about it, however, and returned below, where her husband and the stranger were sitting. Présently one of the servants (not the one mentioned above) tapped at the door, and requested to speak with her, and Mrs. Chapman going out, she told her, in great agitation, that in going up-stairs to the visitor's room a footstep had followed her all the way to the fire-place, although she could see nobody. Mrs. Chapman said something soothing, and that matter passed, she herself being a good deal puzzled, but still unwilling to admit the idea that there was anything extra-natural in these occurrences. Repeatedly after this these footsteps were heard in different parts of the house, when nobody was to be seen; and often whilst she was lying in bed she heard them distinctly approach her door, when, being a very courageous woman, she would start out with a loaded pistol in her hand, but there was never anyone to be seen. At length it was impossible to conceal from herself and her servants that these occurrences were of an extraordinary nature, and the latter, as may be supposed, felt very uncomfortable. Amongst other unpleasant things, whilst sitting all together in the kitchen, they used to see the latch lifted, and the door open, though no one came in that they could see; and when Mr. Chapman himself watched for these events, although they took place, and he was quite on the alert, he altogether failed in detecting any visible agent.

"One night, the same servant who had heard the footsteps following her to the bed-room fire-place, happening to be asleep in Mrs. Chapman's chamber, she became much disturbed, and was heard to murmur, 'Wake me! Wake me!' as if in great mental anguish. Being aroused, she told her mistress a dream she had had, which seemed to throw some light upon these mysteries. She thought she was in the oak bed-room, and at one end of it she saw a young female in an old-fashioned dress, with long dark hair; whilst in another part of the room was a very ugly old woman, also in old-fashioned attire. The latter, addressing the former, said, 'What have you done with the child, Emily? What have you done with the child?' To which the younger figure answered, ' Oh, I did not kill it. He was preserved, and grew up, and joined the —— Regiment, and went to India.' Then, addressing the sleeper, the young lady continued, 'I have never spoken to mortal before, but I will tell you all. My name is Miss Black, and this old woman is nurse Black. Black is not her name, but we call her so because she has been so long in the family.' Here the old woman interrupted the speaker by coming up and laying her hand on the dreaming girl's shoulder, whilst she said something; but she could not remember what; for, feeling an excruciating pain from the touch, she had been so far aroused as to be sensible she was asleep, and to beg to be wholly awakened.

"As the old woman seemed to resemble the figure that one of the other servants had seen looking into the window, and the young one resembled that she had herself seen in the oak chamber, Mrs. Chapman naturally concluded that there was something extraordinary about this dream; and she consequently took an early opportunity of inquiring in the neighbourhood what was known as to the names or circumstances of the former inhabitants of this house; and after much investigation she learnt that, about seventy or eighty years before, it had been in the possession of a Mrs. Ravenhall, who had a niece named Miss Black living with her. This niece, Mrs. Chapman supposed, might be the younger of the two persons who had been seen. Subsequently she saw her again in the same room, wringing her hands, and looking with a mournful significance to one corner. They had the boards taken up on that spot, but nothing was found.

"One of the most curious incidents connected with this story remains to be told. After occupying the house three years, they were preparing to quit it—not on account of its being haunted, but for other reasons—when, on awaking one morning, a short time before their departure, Mrs. Chapman saw, standing at the foot of her bed, a dark-complexioned man, in a working dress, a fustian jacket, and red comforter round his neck, who, however, suddenly disappeared. Mr. Chapman was lying beside her at the time, but asleep. This was the last apparition that was seen; but the strange thing is, that a few days after this, it being necessary to order in a small quantity of coals, to serve till their removal, Mr. Chapman undertook to perform the commission on his way to London. Accordingly, the next day she mentioned to him that the coals had arrived; which he said was very fortunate, since he had entirely forgotten to order them. Wondering whence they had come, Mrs.

Chapman hereupon inquired of the servants, who none of them knew anything about the matter; but, on interrogating a person in the village by whom they had frequently been provided with this article, he answered, that they had been ordered by a dark man, in a fustian jacket and a red comforter, who had called for the purpose!"

After this last event Mr. Chapman quitted the house, and when he had given up possession found that several previous tenants had been under the necessity of doing so, on account of annoyances similar to those his household had suffered from. However, he kept the cause of his removal quiet, and managed to sell his lease to a clergyman who kept a school, but he, in his turn, was compelled to give up the house for the same cause, and for years it stood empty. Ultimately, it was partly pulled down and re-built: and it would seem as if this alteration had broken the spell, for it has been inhabited since, and reported, said Mr. Howitt, in 1863, free from hauntings.

CORBY CASTLE, CUMBERLAND.

THE apparition of a "Radiant Boy," as it is called, is not uncommon in the history of haunted buildings, as various sections of this work will show. Dr. Kerner, the great German authority on spectral affairs, cites an instance of one of these apparitions which was believed to appear only once in seven years, and to be connected in some way with the murder of a child by its mother. Mrs. Crowe, in her *Night Side of Nature*, refers to the well-known tradition that C(orby?) Castle, Cumberland, is haunted by a spirit of this description. A friend of the family owning this ancient dwelling is authority for the following account of an appearance of the ghostly visitant: it is copied from a manuscript volume, and it is dated C—— Castle, December 22nd, 1824 :—

"In order to introduce my readers to the haunted room, I will mention that it forms part of the old house, with windows looking into the court, which, in early times, was deemed a necessary security against an enemy. It adjoins a tower built by the Romans for defence; for C—— was, properly, more a border tower than a castle of any consideration. There is a winding staircase in this tower, and the walls are from eight to ten feet thick.

"When the times became more peaceable, our ancestors enlarged the arrow-slit windows, and added to that part of the building which looks towards the river Eden ; the view of which, with its beautiful banks, we now enjoy. But many additions and alterations have been made since that.

"To return to the room in question; I must observe that it is by no means remote or solitary, being surrounded on all sides by chambers that are constantly inhabited. It is accessible by a passage cut through a wall eight feet in thickness, and its dimensions are twenty-one by eighteen. One side of the wainscoting is covered with tapestry, the remainder is decorated with old family pictures, and some ancient pieces of embroidery, probably the handiwork of nuns. Over a press, which has doors of Venetian glass, is an ancient oaken figure, with a battle-axe in his hand, which was one of those formerly placed on the walls of the city of Carlisle, to represent guards. There used to be also an old-fashioned bed and some dark furniture in this room; but so many were the complaints of those who slept there, that I was induced to replace some of these articles of furniture by more modern ones, in the hope of removing a certain air of gloom, which I thought might have given rise to the unaccountable reports of apparitions and extraordinary noises which were constantly reaching us. But I regret to say I did not succeed in banishing the nocturnal visitor, which still continues to disturb our friends.

"I shall pass over numerous instances, and select one as being especially remarkable, from the circumstance of the apparition having been seen by a clergyman well known and highly respected in this county, who, not six weeks ago, repeated the circumstances to a company of twenty persons, amongst whom were some who had previously been entire disbelievers in such appearances.

"The best way of giving you these particulars, will be by subjoining an extract from my journal, entered at the time the event occurred.

"Sept. 8, 1803.—Amongst other guests invited to

C—— Castle, came the Rev. Henry A. of Redburgh, and rector of Greystoke, with Mrs. A., his wife, who was a Miss S., of Ulverstone. According to previous arrangements, they were to have remained with us some days ; but their visit was cut short in a very unexpected manner. On the morning after their arrival we were all assembled at breakfast, when a chaise and four dashed up to the door in such haste that it knocked down part of the fence of my flower-garden. Our curiosity was, of course, awakened to know who could be arriving at so early an hour ; when, happening to turn my eyes towards Mr. A., I observed that he appeared extremely agitated. ' It is our carriage ! ' said he : ' I am very sorry, but we must absolutely leave you this morning.'

"We naturally felt and expressed considerable surprise, as well as regret, at this unexpected departure ; representing that we had invited Colonel and Mrs. S., some friends whom Mr. A. particularly desired to meet, to dine with us on that day. Our expostulations, how- ever, were vain ; the breakfast was no sooner over than they departed, leaving us in consternation to conjecture what could possibly have occasioned so sudden an alteration in their arrangements. I really felt quite uneasy lest anything should have given them offence ; and we reviewed all the occurrences of the preceding evening, in order to discover, if offence there was, whence it had arisen. But our pains were vain ; and after talking a great deal about it for some days, other circumstances banished the matter from our minds.

" It was not till we some time afterwards visited the part of the county in which Mr. A. resides, that we learnt the real cause of his sudden departure from C——. The relation of the fact, as it here follows, is in his own words :—

" ' Soon after we went to bed, we fell asleep : it might be between one and two in the morning when I awoke. I observed that the fire was totally extinguished; but although that was the case, and we had no light, I saw a glimmer in the centre of the room, which suddenly increased to a bright flame. I looked out, apprehending that something had caught fire; when, to my amazement, I beheld a beautiful boy, clothed in white, with bright locks resembling gold, standing by my bedside, in which position he remained some minutes, fixing his eyes upon me with a mild and benevolent expression. He then glided gently towards the side of the chimney, where it is obvious there is no possible egress, and entirely disappeared. I found myself again in total darkness, and all remained quiet until the usual hour of rising. I declare this to be a true account of what I saw at C—— Castle, upon my word as a clergyman.' "

Mrs. Crowe, in alluding to this story in her above-mentioned book, remarks that she was acquainted with some of the family and several of the friends of the Rev. Henry A——, who, she continues, " is still alive, though now an old man; and I can most positively assert that his own conviction with regard to the nature of this appearance has remained ever unshaken. The circumstance made a lasting impression upon his mind,

and he never willingly speaks of it; but when he does,
it is always with the greatest seriousness, and he never
shrinks from avowing his belief that what he saw admits
of no other interpretation than the one he then put
upon it."

As a pendant to this narrative it will be appropriate
to relate the story of "The Radiant Boy," so well
known in traditionary lore as having appeared to the
second Marquis of Londonderry, better known as Lord
Castlereagh, whilst on a visit to a gentleman resident
in the north of Ireland. The time of this visit would
appear to have been about the end of the last century.
The story has been variously detailed by different writers,
but in the following account, derived from Mrs. Crowe's
Ghost Stories, it is less romantically told than usual,
and, consequently, has a greater air of *vraisemblance*.
In this form it is stated to have been obtained from a
member of the Marquis's family:—

"Captain Stewart, afterwards Lord Castlereagh,"
reads the account, "when he was a young man,
happened to be quartered in Ireland. He was fond of
sport, and one day the pursuit of game carried him so
far that he lost his way. The weather, too, had become
very rough, and in this strait he presented himself at
the door of a gentleman's house, and, sending in his
card, requested shelter for the night. The hospitality
of the Irish country gentry is proverbial; the master of
the house received him warmly, said he feared he could
not make him so comfortable as he could have wished,
his house being full of visitors already—added to which,

some strangers, driven by the inclemency of the night, had sought shelter before him; but that such accommodation as he could give he was heartily welcome to: whereupon he called his butler, and, committing his guest to his good offices, told him he must put him up somewhere, and do the best he could for him. There was no lady, the gentleman being a widower.

"Captain Stewart found the house crammed, and a very jolly party it was. His host invited him to stay, and promised him good shooting if he would prolong his visit a few days; and, in fine, he thought himself extremely fortunate to have fallen into such pleasant quarters.

"At length, after an agreeable evening, they all retired to bed, and the butler conducted him to a large room almost divested of furniture, but with a blazing peat fire in the grate, and a shake-down on the floor, composed of cloaks and other heterogeneous materials. Nevertheless, to the tired limbs of Captain Stewart, who had had a hard day's shooting, it looked very inviting; but, before he lay down, he thought it advisable to take off some of the fire, which was blazing up the chimney in what he thought an alarming manner. Having done this, he stretched himself upon the couch, and soon fell asleep.

"He believed he had slept about a couple of hours when he awoke suddenly, and was startled by such a vivid light in the room that he thought it was on fire; but on turning to look at the grate he saw the fire was out, though it was from the chimney the light proceeded.

4

He sat up in bed, trying to discover what it was, when he perceived, gradually disclosing itself, the form of a beautiful naked boy, surrounded by a dazzling radiance. The boy looked at him earnestly, and then the vision faded, and all was dark. Captain Stewart, so far from supposing what he had seen to be of a spiritual nature, had no doubt that the host, or the visitors, had been amusing themselves at his expense, and trying to frighten him. Accordingly, he felt indignant at the liberty; and, on the following morning, when he appeared at breakfast, he took care to evince his displeasure by the reserve of his demeanour, and by announcing his intention to depart immediately. The host expostulated, reminding him of his promise to stay and shoot. Captain Stewart coldly excused himself, and, at length, the gentleman seeing something was wrong, took him aside and pressed for an explanation; whereupon Captain Stewart, without entering into particulars, said that he had been made the victim of a sort of practical joking that he thought quite unwarrantable with a stranger.

"The gentleman considered this not impossible amongst a parcel of thoughtless young men, and appealed to them to make an apology; but one and all, on their honour, denied the impeachment. Suddenly a thought seemed to strike him; he clapt his hand to his forehead, uttered an exclamation, and rang the bell. 'Hamilton,' said he to the butler, 'where did Captain Stewart sleep last night?'

"'Well, Sir,' replied the man, in an apologetic tone,

'you know every place was full—the gentlemen were lying on the floor three or four in a room—so I gave him the *Boy's Room*; but I lit a blazing fire to keep him from coming out.'

"'You were very wrong,' said the host; 'you know I have positively forbidden you to put anyone there, and have taken the furniture out of the room to insure its not being occupied.' Then retiring with Captain Stewart, he informed him very gravely of the nature of the phenomenon he had seen; and at length, being pressed for further information, he confessed that there existed a tradition in his family that whomever the *Radiant Boy* appeared to would rise to the summit of power, and when he had reached the climax, would die a violent death; 'and I must say,' he added, 'the records that have been kept of his appearance go to confirm this persuasion.'"

It is scarcely necessary to remind the reader that subsequently Lord Castlereagh became head of the Government, and, finally, perished by his own hand.

CORTACHY CASTLE.

OF all the haunted castles in Great Britain, none, probably, has acquired a greater amount of notoriety than that of Cortachy Castle, the seat of the Earl of Airlie. This ancient stronghold is haunted by the spirit of a

4 *

drummer, and whenever his drum is heard it may be
accepted, according to the popular belief, as a token of
the speedy death of a member of the Ogilvie family.
The origin of this tradition is that either the drummer,
or some officer whose emissary he was, had excited the
jealousy of a former Lord Airlie, and that, in consequence, he was put to death by being thrust into his
own drum, and flung from the window of the tower in
which is situated the chamber where his music is,
apparently, chiefly heard.   It is said that he threatened
to haunt the family if his life were taken ; and he would
appear to be as good, or rather as bad, as his word,
the strain of his invisible drum having been heard several
times even in the memory of living persons, and once,
notoriously, quite recently.

The authoress who gives the following account of a
somewhat recent occasion when the drummer was heard
performing upon his ill-omened instrument, introduces
it by the remark that about Christmas, 1844, a letter
just received from a member of a distinguished Perth-
shire family was sent to her for perusal.   The sender,
an eminent literary man, accompanied the communication with the remark, "Read the enclosed ; and we shall
now have an opportunity of observing if any event
follow the prognostic."

The information afforded by the letter was to the
following effect :—

"Miss Dalrymple, a relative of the present Lady
C——, who had been staying some time with the Earl
and Countess at their seat, near Dundee, was invited to

spend a few days at Cortachy Castle, with the Earl and Countess of Airlie. She went, and whilst she was dressing for dinner, the first evening of her arrival, she heard a strain of music under her window, which finally resolved itself into a well-defined sound of a drum. When her maid came upstairs, she made some inquiries about the drummer that was playing near the house, but the maid knew nothing on the subject. For the moment the circumstance passed from Miss Dalrymple's mind ; but recurring to her again during the dinner, she said, addressing Lord Airlie, ' My Lord, who is your drummer ? ' upon which his lordship turned pale, Lady Airlie looked distressed, and several of the company, who all heard the question, embarrassed ; whilst the lady, perceiving that she had made some unpleasant allusion, although she knew not to what their feelings referred, forebore further inquiry till she reached the drawing-room, when, having mentioned the circumstance again to a member of the family, she was answered, ' What! have you never heard of the drummer-boy ? ' ' No,' replied Miss Dalrymple, ' who in the world is he?' 'Why, replied the other, 'he is a person who goes about the house playing his drum whenever there is a death impending in the family. The last time he was heard was shortly before the death of the last Countess (the Earl's former wife); and that is why Lord Airlie became so pale when you mentioned it. The drummer is a very unpleasant subject in this family, I assure you ! '

" Miss Dalrymple was naturally much concerned, and

indeed, not a little frightened at this explanation, and her alarm being augmented by hearing the sounds on the following day, she took her departure from Cortachy Castle, and returned to Lord C.'s, stopping on her way to call on some friends, where she related this strange circumstance to the family through whom the information reached me.

"This affair was very generally known in the north, and we awaited the event with interest. The melancholy death of the Countess about five or six months afterwards, at Brighton, sadly verified the prognostic. I have heard that a paper was found on her desk after her death, declaring her conviction that the drum was for her; and it has been suggested, that probably the thing preyed upon her mind and caused the catastrophe; but in the first place, from the mode of her death, that does not appear to be the case; and, in the second, even if it were, the fact of the verification of the prognostic remains unaffected; besides which, those who insist upon taking refuge in this hypothesis, are bound to admit, that before people living in the world, like Lord and Lady Airlie, could attach so much importance to the prognostic as to entail such fatal effects, they must have had very good reasons for believing in it."

The incidents just narrated took place, it will be recollected, in 1844. Five years later, or, to be more precise, on the evening of the 19th of August 1849, a young English gentleman was on his way to the Tulchan, a shooting-lodge belonging to the Earl of Airlie. He was mounted on a stout pony, having a stalwart High-

lander for his guide across the wild Forfarshire moor.
For about two hours darkness had fallen upon the
scenes, that is to say, it was about half-past eight in the
evening, when the welcome lights, issuing from the
windows of the Tulchan, met our traveller's anxious
gaze. At the same moment a swell of faint music smote
suddenly upon his ear. The sound was as that of a
distant band accompanied by the drum, and appeared to
emanate from the low ridge of ground below the hunting-
lodge in front of him. As it was wafted in louder
accents across the moor, he could not forbear from feeling
that it had something of an eerie and unearthly character
about it. Astonished at such an unaccountable occurrence in a spot where the Tulchan was the only house
within many miles, and where bracken, brown heath,
and morass stretched far and wide upon every side of
him, the young man called the attention of his guide to
the strange burst of music which he had just heard.
Muttering that such sounds were "no canny," and professing that to him they were inaudible, the Highlander
urged on his pony to as great a speed as the weary beast
could exert after a journey of twenty-five miles, and in a
little while the two riders drew rein at the hospitable
door of the lodge.

Upon descending from his pony the Englishman
learnt that his friend and host, Lord Ogilvie (afterwards
tenth Earl of Airlie), had been summoned to London
on account of his father's dangerous illness. On the
following day the ninth Earl of Airlie breathed his last
in Regent Street, London, thus affording another testi-

mony to the truth of the old tradition, that weird music
and the sound of the drum haunt the dwellings of the
Ogilvies prior to the death of a member of the family.

CRESLOW MANOR HOUSE.

CRESLOW, in Buckinghamshire, like so many ancient
English manor-houses, has its family ghost. According
to Dr. Lee, the old residence is haunted by the restless
spirit of a lady long since deceased : she frequents
a certain sleeping-chamber in the most ancient portion
of the building. She has not often been seen, yet has
but too frequently been heard, and only too distinctly, by
those who have ventured to sleep in or to enter after
midnight the room she appears to deem hers. She is
said to come up from the old groined crypt, and always
appears to enter by the door at the top of the nearest
staircase. After entering the chamber she is heard to
walk about it, sometimes in a stately manner, with her
long silk train sweeping the floor, and at other times
with a quick and hurried motion, with her silken dress
rustling violently, as if she were engaged in a desperate
struggle. The fact that the whole of this time the lady
and her accessories are invisible adds in no slight degree
to the horror of the affair.

This haunted chamber, although furnished as a bed-
room, is rarely used, and it is said that it cannot be

entered, even in the day-time, without trepidation and awe. However, some persons have been found bold enough to dare the harmless noises of the mysterious intruder; and many are the traditions current in Buckinghamshire respecting the results to these people of the adventure.

The following will suffice as a specimen, and may, according to Dr. Lee, be depended on as authentic :—

" About the year 1850, a gentleman, not many years ago High Sheriff of the county, who resides some few miles distance from Creslow, rode over to a dinner party; and, as the night became exceedingly dark and rainy, he was urged to stay over the night if he had no objection to sleep in the haunted chamber. The offer of a bed in such a room, so far from deterring him, induced him at once to accept the invitation. He was a strong-minded man of a powerful frame and undaunted courage, and, like so many others, entertained a sovereign contempt for all haunted chambers, ghosts and apparitions. The room was prepared for him. He would neither have a fire nor a night-light, but was provided with a box of lucifers that he might light a candle if he wished. Arming himself in jest with a cutlass and a brace of pistols, he took a serio-comic farewell of the family and entered his formidable dormitory.

" In due course morning dawned ; the sun rose, and a most beautiful day succeeded a very wet and dismal night. The family and their guests assembled in the breakfast room, and every countenance seemed cheered and brightened by the loveliness of the morning.

They drew round the table, when the host remarked that Mr. S——, the tenant of the haunted chamber, was absent. A servant was sent to summon him to breakfast, but he soon returned, saying he had knocked loudly at his door, but received no answer, and that a jug of hot water left there was still standing unused. On hearing this, two or three gentlemen ran up to the room, and, after knocking and receiving no answer, opened it and entered. It was empty. Inquiry was made of the servants; they had neither seen nor heard anything of him. As he was a county magistrate, some supposed that he had gone to attend the Board which met that morning at an early hour.

" But his horse was still in the stable, so that could not be. While they were at breakfast, however, he came in, and gave the following account of his last night's experiences:—' Having entered my room,' said he, ' I locked and bolted both the doors, carefully examined the whole room, and satisfied myself that there was no living creature in it but myself, nor any entrances but those which I had secured. I got into bed, and, with the conviction that I should sleep soundly as usual till six in the morning, was soon lost in a comfortable slumber. Suddenly I was awakened, and, on raising my head to listen, I certainly heard a sound resembling the light soft tread of a lady's footstep, accompanied with the rustling as of a silk gown. I sprang out of bed, and, having lighted a candle, found that there was nothing either to be seen or heard. I carefully examined the whole room. I looked under the bed, into the fire-place, up the chimney, and at both the doors, which were fastened just as I had left them. I then looked at my watch, and found it was a few minutes past twelve. As all was now perfectly quiet again, I put out the candle, got into bed, and soon fell asleep. I was again aroused. The noise was now louder than before. It appeared like the violent rustling of a stiff silk dress. A second time I sprang out of bed, darted to the spot where the noise was, and tried to grasp the intruder in my arms. My arms met together, but enclosed nothing. The noise passed to another part of the room, and I followed it, groping near the floor to prevent anything passing under my arms. It was in vain, I could do nothing. The sound died at the doorway to the crypt, and all again was still. I now left the candle burning, though I never sleep comfortably with a light in my room, and went to bed again, but certainly felt not a little perplexed at being unable to detect the cause of the noise, nor to account for its cessation when the candle was lighted.'"

DAINTREE.

In the Rev. John Mastin's *History of Naseby*, is cited a story of an apparition that was supposed to have appeared to Charles the First at Daintree, near Naseby, previous to the famous battle of that name.

The army of Charles, says the historian, consisting of less than 5,000 foot, and about as many horse, was ordered to Daintree, whither the King went with a thorough resolution of fighting. The next day, however, to the surprise of Prince Rupert and all the rest of the army, this design was given up, and the former one of going to the north resumed. The reason of this alteration in his plans was alleged to be some presages of ill-fortune which the King had received, and which were related to me, says Mr. Mastin's authority, by a person of Newark, at that time in His Majesty's horse. About two hours after the King had retired to rest, said the narrator, some of his attendants hearing an uncommon noise in his chamber, went into it, where they found His Majesty sitting up in bed and much agitated, but nothing which could have produced the noise they fancied they had heard. The King, in a tremulous voice, inquired after the cause of their alarm, and told them how much he had been disturbed, apparently by a dream, by thinking he had seen an apparition of Lord Strafford, who, after upbraiding him for his cruelty, told him he was come to return him good for evil, and that he advised him by no means to fight the Parliament army that was at that time quartered at Northampton, for it was one which the King could never conquer by arms. Prince Rupert, in whom courage was the predominant quality, rated the King out of his apprehensions the next day, and a resolution was again taken to meet the enemy. The next night, however, the apparition appeared to him a second time, but with looks of anger assuring him that would be the last advice he should be permitted to give him, but that if he kept his resolution of fighting he was undone. If His Majesty had taken the advice of the friendly ghost, and marched northward the next day, where the Parliament had few English forces, and where the Scots were becoming very discontented, his affairs might, perhaps, still have had a prosperous issue, or if he had marched immediately into the west he might afterwards have fought on more equal terms. But the King, fluctuating between the apprehensions of his imagination and the reproaches of his courage, remained another whole day at Daintree in a state of inactivity. The battle of Naseby, fought 14th June, 1645, put a finishing stroke to the King's affairs. After this he could never get together an army fit to look the enemy in the face. He was often heard to say that he wished he had taken *the warning*, and not fought at Naseby; the meaning of which nobody knew but those to whom he had told of the apparition which he had seen at Daintree, and all of whom were, subsequently, charged to keep the affair secret.

DUNFERMLINE.

On the 31st May 1847, Sir Joseph Noel Paton, the celebrated artist, wrote a letter to Mrs. Crowe, which she subsequently published in her eerie work, *The*

Night Side of Nature. This letter, although it only
recites a dream, is of a marvellous character when
it is considered how numerous were the coincidences
required in order to accomplish its prophetic symbolism,
if one may so term it. The vision is so clearly por-
trayed in Sir Joseph's own letter, and it is obviously, in
citations of this kind, so far preferable to give the
original words of an authority, that we print the letter
intact.

"That dream of my mother's was as follows," says
Sir Joseph. "She stood in a long, dark, empty gallery:
on one side was my father, and on the other my eldest
sister, Amelia; then myself, and the rest of the family
according to their ages. At the foot of the hall stood
my younger sister, Alexes, and above her my sister
Catherine—a creature, by the way, in person and mind
more like an angel of heaven than an inhabitant of earth.
We all stood silent and motionless. At last *It* entered
—the unimagined *something* that, casting its grim
shadow before, had enveloped all the trivialities of the
preceding dream in the stifling atmosphere of terror. It
entered, stealthily descending the three steps that led
from the entrance down into the chamber of horror, and
my mother *felt It was Death.* He was dwarfish, bent,
and shrivelled. He carried on his shoulder a heavy
axe; and had come, she thought, to destroy 'all her
little ones at one fell swoop.' On the entrance of the
shape my sister Alexes leapt out of the rank, interposing
herself between him and my mother. He raised his
axe and aimed a blow at Catherine, a blow which, to her

horror, my mother could not intercept, though she had snatched up a three-legged stool, the sole furniture of the apartment, for that purpose. She could not, she felt, fling the stool at the figure without destroying Alexes, who kept shooting out and in between her and the ghastly thing. She tried in vain to scream; she besought my father, in agony, to avert the impending stroke; but he did not hear, or did not heed her, and stood motionless, as in a trance. Down came the axe, and poor Catherine fell in her blood, cloven to 'the white halse bane.' Again the axe was lifted by the inexorable shadow, over the head of my brother, who stood next in the line. Alexes had somewhere disappeared behind the ghastly visitant, and with a scream my mother flung the footstool at his head. He vanished, and she awoke.

"This dream left on my mother's mind a fearful apprehension of impending misfortune, 'which would not pass away.' It was *murder* she feared, and her suspicions were not allayed by the discovery that a man some time before discarded by my father for bad conduct, and with whom she had, somehow, associated the *Death* of her dream, had been lurking about the place, and sleeping in an adjoining outhouse on the night it occurred, and for some nights previous and subsequent to it. Her terror increased; sleep forsook her, and every night, when the house was still, she arose and stole, sometimes with a candle, sometimes in the dark, from room to room, listening, in a sort of waking night-mare, for the breathing of the assassin, who, she imagined, was lurking in some one of them. This could not last. She reasoned with herself, but her terror became intolerable, and she related her dream to my father, who, of course, called her a fool for her pains—whatever might be his real opinion of the matter.

"Three months had elapsed, when we children were all of us seized with scarlet fever. My sister Catherine died almost immediately—sacrificed, as my mother in her misery thought, to her (my mother's) over-anxiety for Alexes, whose danger seemed more imminent. The dream-prophecy was in part fulfilled. I also was at death's door—given up by the doctors, but not by my mother : she was confident of my recovery, but for my brother, who was scarcely considered in danger at all, but on whose head *she had seen* the visionary axe impending, her fears were great, for she could not recollect whether the blow had, or had not, descended when the spectre vanished. My brother recovered, but relapsed, and barely escaped with life. But Alexes did not; for a year and ten months the poor child lingered, and almost every night I had to sing her asleep; often, I remember, through bitter tears ; for I knew she was dying, and I loved her the more as she wasted away. I held her little hand as she died, I followed her to the grave—the last thing that I have *loved* on earth. And *the dream was fulfilled.*

"Truly and sincerely yours,

"J. NOEL PATON."

EDGE HILL.

In Lord Nugent's *Memorials of John Hampden* is cited, from a pamphlet of Charles the First's time, one of the most, if not the most, marvellous account of two entire armies of apparitions on record. Somewhat similar, but more distant and weakly testified to phantoms, are averred to have been seen in various times and climes, but, as Lord Nugent points out, this wonderful story is " attested upon the oath of three officers, men of honour and discretion, and of three other gentlemen of credit, selected by the King as commissioners to report upon these prodigies, and to tranquillise and disabuse the alarms of a country town ; adding, moreover, in confirmation, their testimony to the identity of several of the illustrious dead, as seen among the unearthly combatants who had been well-known to them, and who had fallen in the battle." " A well supported imposture," adds Lord Nugent, " or a stormy night on the hill-side might have acted on the weakness of a peasantry in whose remembrance the terrors of the Edge Hill fight were still fresh ; * but it is difficult to imagine how the minds of officers, sent there to correct the illusions, could have been so imposed upon. It will, also, be observed, that no inference is attempted by

* The battle of Edge Hill, between the forces of the King and those of the Parliament, had been fought about two months previous to the first appearance of these apparitions.

the witnesses to assist any notion of a judgment or
warning favourable to the interests or passions of
their own party."

The pamphlet referred to by Lord Nugent was printed
immediately after the events it records, on the 23rd of
January 1642. It narrates the appearance of the late
apparitions, and records the particulars of the PRO-
DIGIOUS NOISES OF WAR AND BATTLE, at Edge Hill,
near Keinton, in Northamptonshire, and its truth is
certified to by " William Wood, Esquire and Justice for
the Peace for the same county, and Samuel Marshall,
Preacher of God's Word in Keinton, and other persons
of quality."

Omitting the introductory matter, which merely refers
to the antiquity of, and the great mass of evidence in
favour of the reality of apparitions, and modernizing
the spelling, this strongly accredited pamphlet reads
thus :—

" Edge Hill, in the very confines of Warwickshire,
near unto Keynton, in Northamptonshire, a place, as
appears by the sequel, destined for civil wars and battles;
as where King John fought a battle with his barons, and
where, in defence of the kingdom's laws and liberty, was
fought a bloody conflict between His Majesty's and the
Parliament's forces. At this Edge Hill, at the very
place where the battle was fought, have since, and doth
appear, strange and portentous apparitions of two
jarring and contrary armies, as I shall in order deliver,
it being certified by men of most credit in those parts,
as William Wood, Esquire, Samuel Marshall, Minister,

and others, on Saturday, which was in Christmas time
. . . Between twelve and one o'clock in the morning,
was heard by some shepherds, and other countrymen,
and travellers, first the sound of drums afar off, and the
noise of soldiers, as it were, giving out their last groans;
at which they were much amazed, and amazed stood
still, till it seemed, by the nearness of the noise, to
approach them; at which, too much affrighted, they
sought to withdraw as fast as possibly they could; but
then, on the sudden, whilst they were in their cogita-
tions, appeared in the air the same incorporeal soldiers
that made those clamours, and immediately, with
ensigns displayed, drums beating, muskets going off,
cannons discharged, horses neighing, which also to these
men were visible, the alarum or entrance to this game
of death was, one army, which gave the first charge,
having the King's colours, and the other the Parliament's
at their head or front of the battle, and so pell-mell to
it they went. The battle, that appeared to the King's
forces seeming at first to have the best, but afterwards
to be put into apparent rout. But till two or three in the
morning in equal scale continued this dreadful fight, the
clattering of arms, noise of cannons, cries of soldiers,
so amazing and terrifying the poor men, that they could
not believe they were mortal, or give credit to their
eyes and ears; run away they durst not, for fear of
being made a prey to these infernal soldiers, and so
they, with much fear and affright, stayed to behold the
success of the business, which at last suited to this
effect. After some three hours' fight, that army which

5 *

carried the King's colours withdrew, or rather appeared
to fly; the other remaining, as it were, masters of the
field, stayed a good space triumphing, and expressing
all the signs of joy and conquest, and then, with all
their drums, trumpets, ordnance, and soldiers, vanished.
The poor men, glad that they were gone that had so
long stayed them there against their wills, made with all
haste to Keinton, and there knocking up Mr. Wood, a
Justice of Peace, who called up his neighbour, Mr.
Marshall, the Minister, they gave them an account of
the whole passage, and averred it upon their oaths to be
true.   At which affirmation of theirs, being much
amazed, they should hardly have given credit to it, but
would have conjectured the men to have been either mad
or drunk, had they not known some of them to have
been of approved integrity; and so, suspending their
judgments till the next night about the same hour, they,
with the same men, and all the substantial inhabitants
of that and the neighbouring parishes drew thither;
where, about half an hour after their arrival, on Sunday,
being Christmas night, appeared in the same tumultuous
warlike manner, the same two adverse armies, fighting
with as much spite and spleen as formerly; and so
departed the gentlemen and all the spectators, much
terrified with these visions of horror, withdrew themselves to their houses, beseeching God to defend them
from those hellish and prodigious enemies. The next
night they appeared not, nor all that week, so that the
dwellers thereabout were in good hope they had for ever
departed. But on the ensuing Saturday night, in the

same place, and at the same hour, they were again seen with far greater tumult, fighting in the manner aforementioned, for four hours, or very near, and then vanished. Appearing again on Sunday night, and performing the same actions of hostility and bloodshed, so that Mr. Wood and others, whose faith, it should seem, was not strong enough to carry them out against these delusions, forsook their habitations thereabout, and retired themselves to other more secure dwellings; but Mr. Marshall stayed, and some other; and so successively the next Saturday and Sunday the same tumults and prodigious sights and actions were put in the state and condition they were formerly. The rumour whereof coming to His Majesty at Oxford, he immediately dispatched thither Colonel Lewis Kirke, Captain Dudley, Captain Wainman, and three other gentlemen of credit, to take full view and notice of the said business, who, at first hearing the true attestation and relation of Mr. Marshall and others, stayed there till the Saturday night following, wherein they heard and saw the fore-mentioned prodigies, and so on Sunday, distinctly knowing divers of the apparitions, or incorporeal substances, by their faces, as that of Sir Edmund Varney, and others that were there slain, of which upon oath they made testimony to His Majesty. What this doth portend God only knoweth, and time perhaps will discover; but doubtlessly it is a sign of His wrath against this land, for these civil wars, which He in His good time finish, and send a sudden peace between His Majesty and Parliament."

EDINBURGH: CANONGATE.

ABOUT the beginning of the eighteenth century stood a grand mansion near the head of the Canongate, the site of which now, however, is covered with buildings of a very different character. With this old mansion is connected a tale of terror, the circumstances of which were well known and talked about no longer ago than the beginning of the present century. A friend of Sir Walter Scott, in whose early life the story was still current, furnished him with the account from which the following version of the tradition is derived.

At the period referred to, a divine of great sanctity was summoned in the middle of a certain night, to come and pray with a person at the point of death. This was no unusual summons, but the consequences which followed were very terrifying. He was forced into a sedan chair, and, after having been carried for a considerable distance, was set down in a remote part of the city, where, at the muzzle of a cocked pistol, he was compelled to submit to being blindfolded. In the course of the discussion which his remonstrances caused, he heard enough, and, indeed, saw enough of their garb, to make him conjecture that the chairmen were greatly above the menial position they had assumed.

After many turnings and windings the sedan was carried up-stairs into an apartment, where the bandage was removed from his eyes, and whence he was conducted into a bed-chamber, where he found a lady recently delivered of an infant. He was commanded by one of those who had brought him to this place to say such prayers by the lady's bed-side as were suitable for a person not expected to survive a mortal disorder. The divine ventured to remonstrate, observing that the lady's appearance warranted a more hopeful condition. He was sternly commanded to obey his instructions, and so, but with much difficulty, recollected himself sufficiently to acquit himself of the duty enjoined him.

As soon as his ministrations were deemed performed, the divine was again blindfolded; replaced in the chair, and hurried off, but, as he was being carried down-stairs, he heard the ominous report of a fire-arm. He was taken home safely, and a purse of gold forced upon him; but, at the same time, he was warned that the least allusion to the affair which had just transpired would cost him his life. He betook himself to his bed-chamber, but was speedily aroused by his servant with the information that a most furious fire had just broken out in the house of . . . , near the head of the Canongate, and that the proprietor's daughter, a lady eminent for her beauty and accomplishments, had perished in the flames.

Our divine had his suspicions, but to have made them public would have availed nothing but to jeopardise his own safety. He was timid, and the family was one of power and distinction, so he soothed himself with the reflection that the deed was done and could not be undone. Time passed on, and with it carried away

some of his fears. He became unhappy at being the
sole custodian of so dark a secret, and, therefore,
gradually told it to some of his brother clergy, so that
by degrees the whole story leaked out.

In due course the divine died, and his terrible tale
had become nearly forgotten, when it so happened that a
fire broke out again on the very same site where the
house of . . . had formerly stood, but where now stood
buildings of an inferior style. When the flames were
at their height, the tumult which usually attends such
a scene, was suddenly suspended by a marvellous apparition. A beautiful female, in an extremely rich, but
very antique style of night-dress, appeared in the very
midst of the fire, and in an awful voice uttered these
terrifying words:—" Once burned! twice burned! the
third time I will scare you all!"

" The belief in this story," says our authority, " was
formerly so strong, that on a fire breaking out, and
seeming to approach the fatal spot, there was a good
deal of anxiety testified lest the apparition should make
good her denunciation."

EDINBURGH: GILLESPIE HOSPITAL.

On the site where Gillespie Hospital now stands,
formerly stood an ancient mansion that some years
after the conclusion of the American War of Inde-

pendence, was used by the late Lieutenant-General Robertson of Lawers, who had served through the whole of the said war, as his town residence. The General, on his return to Europe, brought with him a negro called "Black Tom," who remained in his service as a servant. Tom's own particular room was on the ground floor of the residence, and he was frequently heard to complain that he could not rest in it, for every night the figure of a headless woman, carrying a child in her arms, rose up from the hearth and frightened him terribly.

No one paid much attention to poor Tom's trouble, although the apartment had an uncanny reputation, as it was supposed to be the result of dreams caused by intoxication, the negro's character for sobriety not being very remarkable. But a strange thing happened when the General's old residence was pulled down to make way for James Gillespie's Hospital. There under the hearthstone which had caused "Black Tom" so many restless nights, was discovered a box containing the body of a woman, from which the head had been severed, and beside her lay the remains of an infant, wrapt in a pillow-case trimmed with lace. The unfortunate lady appeared to have been murdered without any warning; she was fully dressed, and her scissors were yet hanging by a ribbon to her side, and her thimble was also in the box, having apparently dropped from the shrivelled finger of the corpse.

EDINBURGH: TRINITY.

ONE of the most curious law suits of recent years occurred at Edinburgh in 1835, concerning the ghost disturbances in a dwelling-house at Trinity, about two miles or so from Edinburgh. This law-suit lasted for two years, and during its progress, Mr. Maurice Lothian, (afterwards Procurator Fiscal for the county), the advocate employed by Mr. Webster, the plaintiff, spent many hours in examining the numerous witnesses, several of whom were military officers, and gentlemen of good social position, but without obtaining any solution of the mysterious affair. The account furnished by Mr. Lothian himself is this :—

"Captain Molesworth took the house of a Mr. Webster, who resided in the adjoining one, in May or June 1835, and when he had been in it about two months, he began to complain of sundry extraordinary noises, which, finding it impossible to account for, he took it into his head, strangely enough, were made by Mr. Webster. The latter naturally represented that it was not probable he should desire to damage the reputation of his own house, or drive his tenant out of it, and retorted the accusation. Still, as these noises and knockings continued, Captain Molesworth not only lifted the boards in the room most infected, but actually made holes in the wall which divided his residence from Mr. Webster's, for the purpose of detecting the delinquent—of course without success. Do what they would, the thing went on just the same; footsteps of invisible feet, knockings, scratchings, and rustlings, first on one side, and then on the other, were heard daily and nightly. Sometimes this unseen agent seemed to be knocking to a certain tune, and if a question were addressed to it which could be answered numerically, as 'How many people are there in this room?' for example, it would answer by so many knocks. The beds, too, were occasionally heaved up, as if somebody were underneath, and where the knockings were, the wall trembled visibly, but, search as they would, no one could be found. Captain Molesworth had had two daughters, one of whom, named Matilda, had lately died; the other, a girl between twelve and thirteen, called Jane, was sickly, and generally kept her bed; and as it was observed that wherever she was these noises most frequently prevailed, Mr. Webster, who did not like the *mala fama* that was attaching itself to his house, declared that she made them, whilst the people in the neighbourhood believed that it was the ghost of Matilda warning her sister that she was soon to follow. Sheriff's officers, masons, justices of the peace, and the officers of the regiment quartered at Leith, who were friends of Captain Molesworth, all came to his aid, in hopes of detecting or frightening away his tormentor, but in vain. Sometimes it was said to be a trick of somebody outside the house, and then they formed a gordon round it; and next, as the poor sick girl was suspected, they tied her up in a bag, but it was all to no purpose.

"At length, ill and wearied out by the annoyances and the anxieties attending the affair, Captain Molesworth quitted the house; and Mr. Webster brought an action against him for the damages committed by lifting the boards, breaking the walls, and firing at the wainscot, as well as for the injury done to his house by saying it was haunted, which prevented other tenants taking it."

Miss Molesworth died soon after "the haunted house" was quitted, hastened out of the world, so people declared, by the severe measures to which she was subjected whilst she was an object of suspicion. At any rate, the house became quiet after the Captain and his family left it, and the persons who have since inhabited it, so it is said, have not experienced any repetitions of the disturbances.

ENFIELD CHACE.

Mr. T. WESTWOOD, from whose most attractive communication to *Notes and Queries* on the subject of "Ghosts and Haunted Houses," an excerpt is made in another portion of this work, gives the following account of a most singular and, as far as our knowledge of such things extends, unique experience. According to Mr. Westwood's narrative, which no one has as yet appeared to question, he on one occasion was directly and personally "under ghostly influences," or what appeared to be such. His story is, that "in a lonely neighbourhood on the verge of Enfield Chace, stands an old house, much beaten by wind and weather. It was inhabited when I knew it," states Mr. Westwood, "by two elderly people, maiden sisters, with whom I had. some acquaintance, and who once invited me to dine with them, and meet a circle of local guests. I well remember my walk thither. It led me up a steep ascent of oak avenue, opening out at the top on what was called the 'ridge-road' of the Chace.

"It was the close of a splendid autumn afternoon · through the mossy boles of the great oaks I saw

> . . . The golden autumn woodland reel
> Athwart the smoke of burning flowers . . .

"On reaching my destination, the sun had already dipped below the horizon, and the eastern front of the house projected a black shadow at its foot. What was there in the aspect of the pile that reminded me of the corpse described by the poet—the corpse that

> Was calm and cold, as it did hold
> Some secret, glorying ?

I crossed the threshold with repugnance.

"Having some changes to make in my attire, a servant led the way to an upper chamber, and left me. No sooner was he gone than I became conscious of a peculiar sound in the room—a sort of shuddering sound in the room, as of suppressed dread. It seemed close to me. I gave little heed to it at first, setting it down for the wind in the chimney, or a draught from the half open door; but moving about the room, I perceived that the sound moved with me. Whichever way I turned it followed me. I went to the furthest extremity of the chamber—it was there also. Beginning to feel uneasy, and being quite unable to account for the singularity, I completed my toilet in haste, and descended to the drawing-room, hoping I should thus leave the uncomfortable sound behind me, but not so. It was on the landing, on the stair, it went down with me, always the same sound of shuddering horror, faint, but audible, and always close at hand. Even at the dinner-table, when the conversation flagged, I heard it unmistakably several times, and so near, that, if there was an entity connected with it, *we were two on one chair*. It seemed to be noticed by nobody else, but t ended by harassing and distressing me, and I was relieved to think that I had not to sleep in the house that night.

" At an early hour, several of the guests having far to go, the party broke up, and it was a satisfaction to me to breathe the fresh, wholesome air of the night, and feel rid at last of my shuddering incubus.

" When I saw my hosts again, it was under another and unhaunted roof. On my telling them what had occurred to me, they smiled and said it was perfectly true, but added they were so used to the sound it had ceased to perturb them. Sometimes, they said, it would be quiet for weeks, at others it followed them from room to room, from floor to floor, pertinaciously, as it had followed me. They could give me no explanation of the phenomenon. It was a sound, no more, and quite harmless.

"Perhaps so, but of what strange horror," demands Mr. Westwood, "not ended with life, but perpetuated in the limbo of invisible things, was that sound the exponent?"

EPSOM: PITT PLACE.

THE story of Lord Lyttleton's "warning," as it is termed, has been frequently told, and almost as frequently attempts have been made to explain it away. Up to the present time, however, it must be confessed that all the evidence, circumstantial though it be, is in favour of the original tellers of the tale. Well known though the story be, it must not be omitted from this collection.

Thomas, the second Lord Lyttleton, had long led a life of dissipation. As he lay in bed one night at Pitt Place, Epsom, he was awakened out of his sleep, according to his own account, by a noise like the fluttering of a bird about the curtains. On opening his eyes he saw the apparition of a woman, who was, it is generally supposed, Mrs. Amphlett, the mother of a lady he had seduced, and who had just died of a broken heart. Dreadfully shocked, he called out, "What do you want?"

"I have come to warn you of your death," was the reply.

"Shall I not live two months?" he asked.

"No; you will die within three days," was the response.

The following day Lord Lyttleton was observed to be much agitated in his mind, and when questioned as to the cause, informed several persons of the apparition. By the third day, which was a Saturday, he was observed to have grown very thoughtful, but he attempted to carry it off by saying to those about him, "Why do you look so grave? Are you thinking about the ghost? I am as well as ever I was in my life."

He invited company to dinner, doubtless expecting in the midst of society to get rid of unwelcome thoughts. In the evening he said to his guests, "A few hours more and I shall jockey the ghost." At eleven o'clock he retired to his bed-room, and after a time began to undress himself. Meanwhile his servant was preparing a rhubarb draught for him, according to custom; but, having nothing to mix it with, went out of the room for a spoon. By the time he returned Lord Lyttleton was getting into bed, but before the man could give him the draught, he reclined his head back on the pillow, fell into convulsions, and died. The servant's cries aroused the household, they hastened to his assistance, but it was useless, for all was over.

The sequel to this story is as singular, but is less generally known, although quite as well testified to, as reference to the preface to Croker's edition of Boswell's

Life of Johnson will show. Mr. Miles Peter Andrews, the intimate friend of Lord Lyttleton, lived at Dartford, about thirty miles off. Mr. Andrews was entertaining a large company at his place, and expected a visit from Lord Lyttleton, whom he had just left, apparently in good health. Disturbed, however, by the impressive message he had received from the apparition, the nobleman, without giving Mr. Andrews any intimation of his intention, had determined to postpone his visit.

On the evening of the Saturday, Mr. Andrews finding Lord Lyttleton did not arrive, and feeling somewhat indisposed, retired to bed somewhat early, leaving one of his guests to do the honours of the supper-table on his behalf. He went to bed in a somewhat feverish condition, but had not been lying down long when the curtains at the foot of his bed were drawn open, and he beheld his friend standing before him, in a large-figured bed-gown which was always kept in the house for Lord Lyttleton's exclusive use. Mr. Andrews at once imagined that his friend had arrived after he had retired to rest, as he had so positively promised to come that day, and knowing how fond the nobleman was of practical joking, cried out to him, "You are at some of your tricks ; go to bed, or I will throw something at you." The reply to which was "*It's all over with me, Andrews.*"

Still deeming it was Lord Lyttleton joking with him, Mr. Andrews stretched his arm out of the bed, and, seizing one of his slippers, the nearest thing he could get hold of, he flung it at the figure, which then retreated

to the dressing-room, whence there was no means of
egress. Upon this Mr. Andrews jumped out of bed,
intending to follow and punish his friend for startling
him, but could find nobody in that room, nor in his
bed-room, the bolt of which was in its place. He rang
his bell, and inquired of the servants where Lord Lyttleton was; but no one had seen him, and the nightgown,
when sought for, was found in its usual place. Mr.
Andrews, getting annoyed, and unable to solve the
mystery, ordered that no bed was to be given to the
nobleman, who might find one at the inn for serving
him such a trick.

The next morning, Mrs. Pigou, the guest who had
headed Mr. Andrew's table when he retired, departed
early for London, and on arriving there heard of Lord
Lyttleton's death; she sent an express to Dartford to
inform Mr. Andrews, who, when he received the news,
was so shocked that he swooned away, and, to use his
own words, "was not his own man again, for three years."

EPWORTH PARSONAGE.

IN 1716, the Rev. Samuel Wesley, father of the
famous John Wesley, the founder of Methodism, was
rector of Epworth, in Lincolnshire. During the months
of December 1716, and January 1717, the parsonage
was haunted in a most unpleasant fashion. The rector
kept a diary in which the disturbances were recorded,
and which eventually formed the basis of the narrative

afterwards compiled by his well-known son, for the *Arminian Magazine.* This account, supplemented by personal inquiries, and carefully written statement of each member of the household, forms not only one of the most marvellous, but also one of the best authenticated cases of haunted houses on record. The famous Dr. Priestley, and the equally well-known Dr. Adam Clark, both furnish voluminous particulars of the affair, the latter devoting forty-six pages of his *Memoirs of the Wesley Family* to the narrative. In his *Life of Wesley* Southey, in reproducing the accounts of the mysterious disturbances, remarks that, "An author who, in this age, relates such a story and treats it as not utterly incredible and absurd, must expect to be ridiculed ; but the testimony upon which it rests is far too strong to be set aside because of the strangeness of the relation."

It is needless to reproduce anything like a complete account of the disturbances at Epworth Parsonage, so the reader must be content to have in a somewhat abridged form the narrative drawn up by John Wesley, supplemented by a few additional *data* gathered from other equally reliable sources.

"On December 2, 1716," says John Wesley, "while Robert Brown, my father's servant, was sitting with one of the maids, a little before ten at night, in the dining-room which opened into the garden, they both heard someone knocking at the door. Robert rose and opened it, but could see nobody. Quickly it knocked again and groaned. 'It is Mr. Turpine,' said Robert, 'he used to groan so.' He opened the door again twice or thrice,

6 *

the knocking being twice or thrice repeated; but still
seeing nothing, and being a little startled, they rose up
and went to bed. When Robert came to the top of the
garret stairs, he saw a handmill, which was at a little
distance, whirled about very swiftly. When he related
this he said, 'Nought vexed me but that it was empty.
I thought if it had been but full of malt he might have
ground his hand out for me.' When he was in bed, he
heard as it were the gobbling of a turkey-cock close to
the bed-side, and soon after the sound of one stumbling
over his shoes and boots; but there was none there,
he had left them below. The next day he and the maid
related these things to the other maid, who laughed
heartily, and said, 'What a couple of fools you are!
I defy anything to fright me!' After churning in the
evening, she put the butter in the tray, and had no
sooner carried it into the dairy than she heard a knocking on the shelf where several puncheons of milk stood,
first above the shelf, then below. She took the candle
and searched both above and below, but, being able to
find nothing, threw down butter, tray, and all, and ran
away for life.

"The next evening, between five and six o'clock, my
sister Molly, then about twenty years of age, sitting
in the dining-room reading, heard as if it were the door
that led into the hall open, and a person walking in that
seemed to have on a silk nightgown, rustling and trailing
along. It seemed to walk round her, and then to the
door, then round again; but she could see nothing.
She thought, 'It signifies nothing to run away; for,

whatever it is, it can run faster than me.' So she rose, put her book under her arm, and walked slowly away. After supper, she was sitting with my sister Sukey (about a year older than her), in one of the chambers, and telling her what had happened. She made quite light of it, telling her, 'I wonder you are so easily frightened. I would fain see what would frighten me.' Presently a knocking began under the table. She took the candle and looked, but could find nothing. Then the iron casement began to clatter. Next the catch of the door moved up and down without ceasing. She started up, leaped into the bed without undressing, pulled the bed-clothes over her head, and never ventured to look up until next morning.

"A night or two after, my sister Hetty (a year younger than my sister Molly) was waiting as usual between nine and ten, to take away my father's candle, when she heard someone coming down the garret stairs, walking slowly by her, then going slowly down the best stairs, then up the back stairs and up the garret stairs, and at every step it seemed the house shook from top to bottom. Just then my father knocked, she went in, took his candle, and got to bed as fast as possible. In the morning she told it to my eldest sister, who told her, 'You know I believe none of these things; pray let me take away the candle to-night, and I will find out the trick.' She accordingly took my sister Hetty's place, and had no sooner taken away the candle, than she heard a noise below. She hastened down-stairs to the hall, where the noise was, but it was then in the kitchen. She ran into the kitchen, when it was drum‹ ming on the inside of the screen. When she went round it was drumming on the outside, and so always on the side opposite to her. Then she heard a knocking at the back kitchen door. She ran to it, unlocked it softly, and, when the knocking was repeated, suddenly opened it, but nothing was to be seen. As soon as she had shut it, the knocking began again. She opened it again, but could see nothing. When she went to shut the door, it was violently knocked against her; but she set her knee and her shoulder to the door, forced it to, and turned the key. Then the knocking began again; but she let it go on, and went up to bed. However, from that time she was thoroughly convinced that there was no imposture in the affair.

"The next morning, my sister telling my mother what had happened, she said, 'If I hear anything myself, I shall know how to judge.' Soon after she begged her mother to come into the nursery. She did, and heard, in the corner of the room, as it were the violent rocking of a cradle; but no cradle had been there for some years. She was convinced it was preter-natural, and earnestly prayed it might not disturb her in her own chamber at the hours of retirement; and it never did. She now thought it was proper to tell my father. But he was extremely angry, and said, 'Sukey, I am ashamed of you. These boys and girls frighten one another; but you are a woman of sense, and should know better. Let me hear of it no more.'

"At six in the evening he had family prayers as

usual. When he began the prayer for the King, a knocking began all round the room, and a thundering knock attended the *Amen*. The same was heard from this time every morning and evening while the prayer for the King was repeated. As both my father and mother are now at rest, and incapable of being pained thereby, I think it my duty to furnish the serious reader with a key to this circumstance.

"The year before King William died, my father observed my mother did not say *Amen* to the prayer for the King. She said she would not, for she did not believe the Prince of Orange was King. He vowed he would never cohabit with her until she did. He then took his horse and rode away, nor did she hear anything of him for a twelvemonth. He then came back and lived with her as before. But I fear his vow was not forgotten before God."

"Being informed that Mr. Hoole, the vicar of Haxey," resumes John Wesley, "could give me some further information, I walked over to him. He said," referring to the bygone disturbances at Epworth Parsonage, "Robert Brown came over to me and told me your father desired my company; when I came, he gave me an account of all that had happened, particularly the knocking during family prayer. But that evening (to my great satisfaction) we heard no knocking at all. But between nine and ten a servant came in and said, 'Old Jeffrey is coming (that was the name of one that had died in the house), for I hear the signal.' This, they informed me, was heard every night about a quarter before ten. It was towards the top of the house, on the outside, at the north-east corner, resembling the loud creaking of a saw, or rather that of a windmill, when the body of it is turned about in order to shift the sails to the wind. We then heard a knocking over our heads, and Mr. Wesley, catching up a candle, said, ' Come, Sir, now you shall hear for yourself.' We went up-stairs, he with much hope, and I (to say the truth) with much fear. When we came into the nursery, it was knocking in the next room : when we went there, it was knocking in the nursery ; and there it continued to knock, though we came in, and particularly at the head of the bed (which was of wood) in which Miss Hetty and two of her younger sisters lay. Mr. Wesley, observing that they were much affected,—though asleep, sweating, and trembling exceeding,—was very angry, and, pulling out a pistol, was going to fire at the place whence the sound came. But I snatched him by the arm and said, ' Sir, you are convinced that this is something preternatural. If so, you cannot hurt it, but you give it power to hurt you.' He then went close to the place and said, sternly : ' Thou deaf and dumb devil ! why dost thou fright these children who cannot answer for themselves ! Come to me, in my study, that am a man ! ' Instantly it knocked his knock (the particular knock which he always used at the gate), as if it would shiver the board to pieces, and we heard nothing more that night."

Commenting upon this portion of the narrative, as furnished by the Rev. Mr. Hoole, John Wesley remarks :

"Till this time my father had never heard the least disturbance in his study. But the next evening, as he attempted to go into his study (of which none had the key but himself), when he opened the door it was thrust back with such violence as had like to have thrown him down. However, he thrust the door open, and went in. Presently there was a knocking, first on one side, then on the other, and, after a time, in the next room, wherein my sister Nancy was. He went into that room, and, the noise continuing, adjured it to speak, but in vain. He then said, 'These spirits love darkness: put out the candle, and perhaps it will speak.' She did so, and he repeated the adjuration; but still there was only knocking, and no articulate sound. Upon this he said, 'Nancy, two Christians are an overmatch for the devil. Go all of you down-stairs, it may be when I am alone he will have courage to speak.' When she was gone, a thought came into his head, and he said, 'If thou art the spirit of my son Samuel, I pray knock three knocks, and no more.' Immediately all was silence, and there was no more knocking at all that night. I asked my sister Nancy (then fifteen years old), whether she was not afraid when my father used that adjuration. She answered she was sadly afraid it would speak when she put out the candle, but she was not at all afraid in the day-time, when it walked after her, only she thought when she was about her work, he might have done it for her and saved her the trouble."

"By this time," continues John Wesley, "all my sisters were so accustomed to these noises, that they gave them little disturbance. A gentle tapping at their bed-head usually began between nine and ten at night. They then commonly said to each other, 'Jeffrey is coming; it is time to go to sleep.' And if they heard a noise in the day, and said to my youngest sister, 'Hark, Kezzy, Jeffrey is knocking above,' she would run upstairs, and pursue it from room to room, saying she desired no better diversion.

"My father and mother had just gone to bed," says Wesley, citing another instance of these mysterious disturbances, "and the candle was not taken away, when they heard three blows, and a second and a third three, as it were with a large oaken staff, struck upon a chest which stood by the bedside. My father immediately arose, put on his nightgown, and, hearing great noises below, took the candle and went down; my mother walked by his side. As they went down the broad stairs, they heard as if a vessel full of silver was poured upon my mother's breast and ran jingling down to her feet. Quickly after, there was a sound as if a large iron bell were thrown among many bottles under the stairs; but nothing was hurt. Soon after, our large mastiff dog came, and ran to shelter himself between them. While the disturbances continued he used to bark and leap, and snap on one side and the other, and that frequently before any person in the room heard any noise at all. But after two or three days he used to tremble, and creep away before the noise began. And by this the family knew it was at hand; nor did the observation ever fail.

"A little before my father and mother came into the hall," says Wesley, resuming the thread of his story, "it seemed as if a very large coal was violently thrown upon the floor, and dashed all in pieces; but nothing was seen. My father then cried out, ' Sukey, do you not hear? all the pewter is thrown about the kitchen.' But when they looked all the pewter stood in its place. Then there was a loud knocking at the back door. My father opened it, but saw nothing. It was then at the front door. He opened that, but it was still lost labour, After opening first the one, then the other, several times, he turned and went up to bed. But the noises were so violent all over the house that he could not sleep till four in the morning.

"Several gentlemen and clergymen now earnestly advised my father," concludes Wesley, "to quit the house. But he constantly answered, ' No : let the devil flee from me ; I will never flee from the devil.' But he wrote to my eldest brother, at London, to come down. He was preparing so to do, when another letter came informing him the disturbances were over, after they had continued (the latter part of the time day and night), from the 2nd of December to the end of January."

The elder Wesley's diary fully confirms all the more remarkable portions of John Wesley's *Narrative*, and even mentions some curious incidents not given by the son : for instance, the Rev. Samuel says, "I have been thrice pushed by an invisible power, once against the corner of my desk in the study, a second time against the door of the matted chamber, a third time against the right side of the frame of my study-door, as I was going in."

On the 25th December he records, " Our mastiff came whining to us, as he did always after the first night of its coming ; for then he barked violently at it, but was silent afterwards, and seemed more afraid than any of the children."

John Wesley, also, received several lengthy letters from various members of the family, corroborating the various details already given, but these communications are too lengthy to cite, besides being frequently but repetitions of the same, or similar stories. From a letter written by Emily Wesley (afterwards Mrs. Harper), some extracts, however, may be given. "A whole month was sufficient to convince anybody," she writes, "of the reality of the thing. . . . I shall only tell you what I myself heard, and leave the rest to others.

"My sisters in the paper-chamber had heard noises, and told me of them, but I did not much believe till one night, about a week after the first groans were heard, which was the beginning. Just after the clock struck ten, I went down-stairs to lock the doors, which I always do. Scarce had I got up the west stairs, when I heard a noise like a person throwing down a vast coal in the middle of the fore kitchen. I was not much frighted, but went to my sister Sukey, and we together went all over the lower rooms, but there was nothing out of order. Our dog was fast asleep, and our only cat in the other end of the house. No sooner was I got up-stairs and undressing for bed, but I heard a noise

. . . This made me hasten to bed. But my sister, Hetty, who sits always to wait on my father, going to bed, was still sitting on the lowest step of the garret stairs, the door being shut at her back, when, soon after, there came down the stairs behind her something like a man in a loose night-gown trailing after him, which made her fly rather than run to me in the nursery." Emily Wesley, the writer of these words, it may be added, appeared to believe herself followed by this manifestation through life. When writing to her brother John, thirty-four years after the Epworth disturbances had taken place, she alludes to "that wonderful thing called by us Jeffrey" as calling upon her before any extraordinary new affliction.

In summing up the general circumstances attendant upon the disturbances in their household, John Wesley remarks :

"Before it came into any room, the latches were frequently lifted up, the windows clattered, and whatever iron or brass was about the chamber rung and jarred exceedingly.

"When it was in any room, let them make what noise they would, as they sometimes did, its dead hollow note would be clearly heard above them all.

"The sound very often seemed in the air in the middle of a room ; nor could they ever make any such themselves, by any contrivance.

"It never came by day till my mother ordered the horn to be blown. After that time scarce anyone could go from one room into another but the latch of the room they went to was lifted up before they touched it.

"It never came into my father's study till he talked to it sharply, calling it a deaf and dumb devil, and bid it cease to disturb the innocent children, and come to him in his study if it had anything to say to him.

"From the time of my mother desiring it not to disturb her from five to six, it was never heard in her chamber from five till she came down-stairs, nor at any other time when she was employed in devotion."

No satisfactory explanation of these remarkable circumstances has ever, so far as we can discover, been afforded.

ESHER.

MISS ANNA MARIA PORTER, the authoress, and sister of the still better known writer, Jane Porter, authoress of *The Scottish Chiefs*, at one period of her life resided at Esher, in Surrey. An aged gentleman of her acquaintance, who lived in the same place, was accustomed to visit at her house almost daily, generally making his appearance in the evening, when he would take a cup of tea and read the paper.

One evening Miss Porter saw him enter the room as usual, and seat himself at the table, but without saying a word. She addressed some remark to him, but received no reply, and, after a few seconds, was surprised to see him rise and leave the room without uttering a word.

Fearing that he might have been taken ill suddenly, Miss Porter sent a servant to his house to make inquiries. She sent at once, but the answer the servant brought back was that the old gentleman had died suddenly about *an hour before*.

Miss Anna Maria, it is avowed, believed that she had seen an apparition, and was herself the authority for this story.

ETON.

SEVERAL writers of a past generation, including Joseph Glanvill, were fond of relating the story of Major Sydenham and his friend, Captain William Dyke, but it appears to have escaped the researches of modern commentators on the Supernatural. Shortly after the death of Major Sydenham, Dr. Thomas Dyke called on his cousin, Captain William Dyke, of Skilgate, in the county of Somersetshire, and agreed to pass the night with him. At the captain's request, Dr. Dyke agreed to sleep in the same bed with his cousin, but previous to composing himself to sleep, the Doctor was aroused by his companion calling up a servant and bidding the man bring him two of the largest candles he could obtain, and have them lighted.

The Doctor naturally inquired what these were

intended for, to which the Captain answered :—"You know, cousin, what disputes the Major and I have had touching the immortality of the soul, on which point we could never yet be resolved, though we so much desired it. And, therefore, it was at length fully agreed between us, that he who died first should, the third night after his funeral, between the hours of twelve and one, come to the little house which is here in the garden, and there give a full account touching these matters to the survivor, who should be sure to be present there at the set time, and so receive a full satisfaction. And this," says the Captain, "is the very night, and I am come on purpose to my present lodging to fulfil my promise."

The Doctor advised him not to follow strange counsels, for which he could have no warrant. The Captain replied, "that he had solemnly engaged," and that nothing should discourage him; and added, "that if the Doctor should wake awhile with him, he would shake him, if not, he might compose himself to rest; but, for his own part, he was resolved to watch, that he might be sure to be present at the hour appointed." To that purpose he set his watch by him, and as soon as he perceived that it was half an hour past eleven, he arose, and taking a candle in each hand, went out by a back door, of which he had before got the key, and walked into the garden house, where he continued two hours and a half. At his return he declared he had neither seen nor heard anything more than usual. "But I know," said he, "that the Major would surely have come had he been able."

About six weeks after, the Captain rode to Eton, to place his son a scholar there, when the Doctor went thither with him. They lodged at the sign of the " Christopher," and tarried two or three nights, not lying together now, as before at Dulverton, but in two several chambers. The morning before they went away, the Captain stayed in his chamber longer than usual, before he called the Doctor. At length he came into the chamber, but with his body shaking and trembling. Whereat the Doctor, wondering, presently demanded, " What is the matter ? " The Captain replied, " I have seen the Major." The Doctor seeming to smile, the Captain said, " If ever I saw him in my life, I saw him but now," and then related to the Doctor what had passed. " This morning, after it was light," said he, " one came to my bedside, and suddenly drawing back the curtains, called, ' Captain ! Captain ! ' To whom I replied, ' What, Major ? ' To which he returned, ' I could not come at the time appointed, but I am new come to tell you, *That there is a God, and a very just and terrible one, and if you do not turn over a new leaf* (the very expression the Doctor punctually remembered) *you shall find it so.*' " The Captain proceeded :—" On the table there lay a sword which the Major had formerly given me, and after the apparition had walked a turn or two about the chamber, he took up the sword, drew it, and finding it not so bright as it ought to be, cried, ' Captain ! Captain ! this sword did not use to be kept after this manner when it was mine.' After which he presently disappeared."

7

The Captain was not only thoroughly persuaded of the truth of what he had seen and heard, but was from that time observed to have become quite an altered man. And it was judged, by those who were well acquainted with his conversation, that the remembance of this passage stuck close to him; and that those words of his dead friend were frequently sounding in his ears during the remainder of his life; which was something more than two years.

GLAMIS CASTLE.

ONE of our ancient castles that has long had a reputation for the hauntings and the apparitions that trouble it is Glamis or Glammis Castle, in Forfarshire, the seat of Lord Strathmore. Although the whole pile of buildings appears to suffer under the ban, there is one particular chamber which is especially known as "the Haunted Room." Access to this ominous chamber is said to be now cut off by a stone wall, and none are supposed to be acquainted with its locality save Lord Strathmore, his heir, and the factor of the estate. This wall is alleged to have been erected some few years ago by order of the late proprietor, in consequence of certain mysterious sights and sounds which he had both seen and heard.

"There is no doubt," writes a correspondent of Dr. Lee, " about the reality of the noises at Glamis Castle. On one occasion, some years ago, the head of the family, with several companions, was determined to investigate the cause. One night, when the disturbance was greater, and more violent and alarming than usual—and, it should be premised, strange, weird, and unearthly sounds had often been heard, and by many persons, some quite unacquainted with the ill-repute of the the castle—his lordship went to the Haunted Room, opened the door with a key, and dropped back in a dead swoon into the arms of his companions; nor could he ever be induced to open his lips on the subject afterwards."

A well-known antiquary furnishes the following local legend connected with the old stronghold, to account for the sights and noises heard about it. He states that the tradition is that in olden time, during one of the constant feuds between the Lindsays and the Ogilvies, a number of the latter clan, flying from their enemies, came to Glamis Castle and begged hospitality of the owner. He did not like to deny them the shelter of his castle walls, and therefore admitted them, but, on the plea of hiding them, so it is averred, he secured them all in a large out-of-the-way chamber—that afterwards known as the *haunted* one—and there left them to starve. Their bones lie there till this day, according to the common tradition, their bodies never having been removed. It has been suggested that it was the sight of these which so startled the late Lord Strathmore on entering the room, and which caused him, subsequently, to have it walled up. The scene is believed to have been particularly horrifying, some of the unfortunate

7 *

captives having died apparently in the act of gnawing the flesh from their arms.

Thus much for the tradition that accounts for the weird disturbances which, if Dr. Lee's correspondent may be credited, were still in a state of activity not very long ago. Among other strange instances, the writer states that " on one occasion a lady and her child were staying for a few days at the castle. The child was asleep in an adjoining dressing-room, and the lady, having gone to bed, lay awake for awhile. Suddenly a cold blast stole into the room, extinguishing the night-light by her bedside, but not affecting the one in the dressing-room beyond, in which her child had its cot. By that light she saw a tall mailed figure pass into the dressing-room from that in which she was lying. Immediately thereafter there was a shriek from the child. Her maternal instinct was aroused. She rushed into the dressing-room and found the child in an agony of fear. It described what it had seen as a giant, who came and leant over its face."

We are unable to learn when this disturbing apparition appeared, but it is to be hoped not since Lord Strathmore had the Haunted Room walled up; that, it is most devoutly to be hoped, shut in all unpleasant sights, even if it could not quite suppress the sounds.

GLASGOW : THE HELL CLUB.

THERE is a somewhat well-known story, of an extremely startling character, related by Mrs. Crowe, under the title of the "Glasgow Hell Club," in that chapter of *The Night Side of Nature* styled "The Future that Awaits us." The story, notwithstanding its sensationalism, is declared to be a relation of facts, of which a contemporary account was published, but was bought up by the family of the chief actor in the drama. As usual in such cases, a few copies escaped destruction, and the narrative was reprinted and widely diffused. Mrs. Crowe's version of this "undoubted and well attested fact," is as follows :—

" Some ninety years ago, there flourished in Glasgow a club of young men, which, from the extreme pro-fligacy of its members and the licentiousness of their orgies, was commonly called the ' Hell Club.' Besides these nightly or weekly meetings, they held one grand annual saturnalia, in which each tried to excel the other in drunkenness and blasphemy ; and on these occasions there was no star amongst them whose lurid light was more conspicuous than that of young Mr. Archibald B., who, endowed with brilliant talents and a handsome person, had held out great promise in his boyhood, and raised hopes, which had been com-pletely frustrated by his subsequent reckless dissi-pations.

"One morning, after returning from this annual festival, Mr. Archibald B., having retired to bed, dreamt the following dream :—

"He fancied that he himself was mounted on a favourite black horse that he always rode, and that he was proceeding towards his own house, then a country seat embowered by trees, and situated upon a hill, now entirely built over and forming part of the city, when a stranger, whom the darkness of night prevented his distinctly discerning, suddenly seized his horse's reins, saying, 'You must go with me!'

"'And who are you?' exclaimed the young man, with a volley of oaths, whilst he struggled to free himself.

"'That you will see by and by,' returned the other, in a tone that excited unaccountable terror in the youth, who, plunging his spurs into his horse, attempted to fly. But in vain : however fast the animal flew, the stranger was still beside him, till at length, in his desperate efforts to escape, the rider was thrown, but instead of being dashed to the earth, as he expected, he found himself falling—falling—falling still, as if sinking into the bowels of the earth.

"At length, a period being put to this mysterious descent, he found breath to inquire of his companion, who was still beside him, whither they were going : 'Where am I? where are you taking me?' he exclaimed.

"'To hell!' replied the stranger, and immediately

interminable echoes repeated the fearful sound, 'To hell! to hell! to hell!'

"At length a light appeared, which soon increased to a blaze; but instead of the cries and groans, and lamentings the terrified traveller expected, nothing met his ear but sounds of music, mirth and jollity; and he found himself at the entrance of a superb building, far exceeding any he had seen constructed by human hands. Within, too, what a scene! No amusement, employment, or pursuit of man on earth, but was here being carried on with a vehemence that excited his unutterable amazement. 'There the young and lovely still swam through the mazes of the giddy dance! There the panting steed still bore his brutal rider through the excitement of the goaded race! There, over the midnight bowl, the intemperate still drawled out the wanton song or maudlin blasphemy! The gambler plied for ever his endless game, and the slaves of Mammon toiled through eternity their bitter task; whilst all the magnificence of earth paled before that which now met his view!'

"He soon perceived that he was amongst old acquaintances whom he knew to be dead, and each, he observed, was pursuing the object, whatever it was, that had formerly engrossed him; when, finding himself relieved of the presence of his unwelcome conductor, he ventured to address his former friend, Mrs. D., whom he saw sitting as had been her wont on earth, absorbed at loo, requesting her to rest from the game, and intro duce him to the pleasures of the place, which appeared to him to be very unlike what he had expected and, indeed, an extremely agreeable one. But with a cry of agony, she answered, that there was no rest in hell; that they must ever toil on at those very pleasures; and innumerable voices echoed through the interminable vaults, 'There is no rest in hell!' Whilst, throwing open their vest, each disclosed in his bosom an ever-burning flame! These, they said, were the pleasures of hell; their choice on earth was now their inevitable doom! In the midst of the horror this scene inspired, his conductor returned, and, at his earnest entreaty, restored him again to earth; but as he quitted him, he said, 'Remember; in a year and a day we meet again!'

"At this crisis of his dream the sleeper awoke feverish and ill; and whether from the effects of the dream, or of his preceding orgies, he was so unwell as to be obliged to keep his bed for several days, during which period he had time for many serious reflections, which terminated in a resolution to abandon the club and his licentious companions altogether.

"He was no sooner well, however, than they flocked around him, bent on recovering so valuable a member of their society; and having wrung from him a confession of the cause of his defection, which, as may be supposed, appeared to them eminently ridiculous, they soon contrived to make him ashamed of his good resolutions. He joined them again, resumed his former course of life, and when the annual saturnalia came round, he found himself with his glass in his hand, at the table, when the president, rising to make the accustomed speech, began by saying, ' Gentlemen : this being leap-year it is a year and a day since our last anniversary,' &c. &c. The words struck upon the young man's ear like a knell ; but ashamed to expose his weakness to the jeers of his companions, he sat out the feast, plying himself with wine even more liberally than usually, in order to drown his intrusive thoughts ; till, in the gloom of a winter's morning he mounted his horse to ride home. Some hours afterwards, the horse was found with his saddle and bridle on, quietly grazing by the road-side, about half-way between the city and Mr. B's house ; whilst a few yards off lay the corpse of his master."

Comment on this weird tale is needless on our part, unless it be to remark that it would " point a moral " in a far more emphatic manner were the real names given of the young man whose fate is supposed to be described.

GRAYRIGG HALL.

IN *Ducketiana* it is stated by Sir G. B. Duckett, that not a vestige remains of those extensive foundations which, a hundred years ago, attested the solidity and importance of the Westmoreland Ducketts' residence, the Manor House known formerly as Grayrigg Hall. A strange story is told of the last member of this opulent family, who inhabited this fine old English mansion ere it was dismantled. The narrative has been detailed with great similarity in various works, such as Ferguson's *Early Cumberland and Westmoreland Friends*, and Backhouse's *Life of Howgill*, and is popularly known as "The Quaker's Curse and its Fulfilment." .

Francis Howgill, a noted member of the Society of Friends, resided at Todthorne, near Grayrigg, in Westmoreland, about the middle of the seventeenth century. At one time he travelled about the south of England preaching, and when he visited Bristol, in company with his compatriot, John Camm, his preaching was made the occasion of great rioting. In 1663 he returned to his own neighbourhood, whither his reputation had apparently preceded him, for, upon arriving at the market-place of Kendal, he was summoned to appear before the Justices, who were holding a court in a tavern. They tendered Howgill the oath of allegiance when he came before them, and as he refused to take it they committed him to confinement in Appleby jail. It may be pointed out, as a matter of history, that in the earliest days of the brotherhood, members of the Society of Friends were often subjected to severe penalties and much persecution for their refusal to conform to the taking of judicial oaths. At Appleby the judges of Assizes also tendered Howgill the same oath and, on his refusal to swear it, ordered him to be indicted at the next Assizes. Meanwhile they offered to release him from custody if he would give a bond for his good behaviour in the interim, but this he refused to do, and therefore was re-committed to prison.

During his imprisonment a curious incident happened. Howgill was allowed by the magistrates to go home to Grayrigg for a few days on private affairs, and in the course of the time he was at liberty the Quaker felt himself compelled to visit a justice of the name of Duckett, residing at Grayrigg Hall, who was a great persecutor of the Quakers, and was, also, one of the magistrates concerned in committing him to prison. Francis Howgill, on this occasion, was accompanied by a friend who, over the initials " J. D." would appear to have left a written report of the interview. Justice Duckett expressed much surprise at seeing Howgill, and said to him, "What is your wish now, Francis? I thought you had been in Appleby jail." Howgill replied to this effect, " No, I am not, but I am come with a message from the Lord. Thou hast persecuted the Lord's people, but His hand is now against thee, and He will send a blast upon all that thou hast, and thy name shall rot out of the earth, and this thy dwelling shall become desolate, and a habitation for owls and jackdaws." When Howgill had delivered this message, the Justice trembled, and said, " Francis, are you in earnest? " To which Howgill responded, " Yes, I am in earnest, it is the word of the Lord to thee, and there are many now living who will see it."

This prediction by the Quaker appears to have been remarkably fulfilled ; for, according to the testimony of James Wilson, who was a minister among the Friends,

and who lived at one time at Grayrigg Foot, in Westmoreland, this Justice Duckett had several children, and
all those children died without leaving any issue, whilst
some of them came to poverty.   James Wilson himself
had repeatedly given alms at his door to a woman, the
last of the Duckett family, who begged her bread from
door to door.   Grayrigg Hall passed into the possession of the Lowther family, was dismantled, fell into
ruins, and in 1777 little more than its extensive foundations were visible.   After having long been the habitation of " owls and jackdaws," the ruins were entirely
removed, and a farmhouse erected upon the site of the
old Hall.   And thus the Quaker's curse was fulfilled.

HACKWOOD HOUSE.

In April, 1862, one of those stories of haunted houses,
which are continually " cropping up," both in print and
in private conversation, went the usual round of the
press.   The London correspondent of *Saunders's News
Letter*, having read the comments of his contemporaries,
told the tale in his own fashion, as below.   It should be
premised that the " Mr. R——" of the story is Mr.
Henry Phillip Roche, the friend of Lord Westbury, and,
thanks to that friendship, was by him appointed one of
the Registrars of the London Court of Bankruptcy.

    " Really, what with Mr. Home, Mr. Forster, and Sir

Bulwer Lytton's *Strange Story*," says the correspondent, "London Society seems just now affected with a general phantom mania. The last new phase of the malady is a ghost story which has lately obtained extensive currency in what are called the 'upper circles,' and which claims for its believers two counsel learned in the law, and the Lord High Chancellor himself. I don't pretend to vouch that the story can pretend to the 'ghost' of a foundation for its existence, I merely testify that it is being talked of by 'everybody,' and that the first question asked at most dinner-tables is, 'Have you heard of Lord Westbury's ghost?'

"The story runs thus :—Lord Westbury lately purchased Hackwood House, an old mansion near Basingstoke, the property of Lord Bolton. Snatching a spare day or two to obtain a more minute inspection of his investment, he took with him two of the gentlemen belonging to his official establishment, both members of the learned profession. On separating for the night, the bedroom destined for one of them, a Mr. R——, was found to be on the opposite side of the hall to those of the other gentlemen; he therefore shook hands and said 'good-night' in the hall, leaving the others talking there. He had not been very long asleep before he 'felt' himself awoke, but could neither hear nor perceive anything. By degrees, however, he became conscious of something luminous on the side of the room opposite his bed, which gradually assumed the appearance of a woman clothed in grey. He at first thought it was an optical illusion, next that his companions were playing him some phosphoric trick, and then, turning round, he composed himself to sleep again.

" Further on in the night he was awoke again, and then at once he saw the same figure brilliantly conspicuous on the wall. Whilst he was gazing at it, it seemed to leave the wall and advance into the middle of the apartment. He immediately jumped out of bed, rushed to it, and, of course, found—nothing. He was so impressed with the power of the delusion, that he found it impossible to seek any more sleep, and, as the day was beginning to break, he dressed and made his way into the grounds, where he walked for some time, pondering over the illusion so forcibly produced upon him.

" On his return to his room he wrote out an exact account of what he thought he had seen, it being then quite clear to him that it was no trick played by others, but simply an hallucination of his own brain. At the breakfast-table, however, he began to fancy that he had been cleverly imposed on by his friends, as they commenced at once bantering him on his night's rest, broken sleep, and so forth. Wishing to detect them if possible, he pretended unconsciousness and utter ignorance of their meaning, when, to his horror, one of them exclaimed, ' Come, come, don't think we didn't see one of the women in grey follow you into your room last night.' He rushed up-stairs, produced his written account, which he gave them to read, and the consternation became general. On inquiry, of course, they found the legend of a murder done in the days of yore, and the Lord Chancellor is supposed to be exceedingly vexed at an incident which has decidedly shut up one room in his house for ever, if not, in all probability, tabooed the mansion altogether. Thus much do the 'upper ten thousand' aver—how truly is quite another question."

HANLEY.

IN August, 1864, the *Spiritual Magazine*, published an account stated to have been related to the *Staffordshire Sentinel* in the previous year, of an apparition that had appeared to Mr. William Ridgway, a well-known pottery owner, of Hanley, Staffordshire. It is a curious circumstance that the manufacturer should have concealed the story from all his family and friends, and, after so many years of silence, have revealed it to an apparent stranger. The editor of the newspaper in question does not, and, of course, in the circumstances, cannot produce any corroborative evidence of Mr. Ridgway's belief that he had seen the apparition of his deceased mother, nor does he state why the story was held back until three months after Mr. Ridgway's death. However, it is not our present purpose to question the editor's narrative but to cite it.

"For many years the family of the Ridgways," remarks our authority, "have held a high and influential position in the commercial world. Their name will go down to

posterity as promoters of the beautiful art which gives
wealth and fame to the Staffordshire potteries. William
was in partnership with his elder brother, John, and was
esteemed for his manly courage, untiring energy, and
great probity of character ; no man doubted the word
of William Ridgway ; it is, therefore, of great value
in the support of the belief in and reality of apparitions to have the testimony of such a man, and I am
able to give a well-authenticated story from the columns
of the *Staffordshire Sentinel*, where a memoir of this
much-respected gentleman appeared, about the time of
his death in April last.   The story is thus related :—

" The two brothers became partners with their father
at the same time, when Mr. William was twenty-one
years' old, and on equal terms, and their own partnership continued many years after his death.

" Immediately after this event they had a dispute
which of the two should have the paternal mansion.
Mr. John maintained the right of the elder, Mr. William
the claim of an increasing family. The controversy
threatened to culminate in a quarrel, when, about
ten o'clock on a light evening, William beheld the
apparition of his deceased mother, near to the side of
the entrance of the house.

" The appearance was perfect as life, and she
addressed him audibly and distinctly, saying, ' William,
my dear, let your brother have the house, and God will
make it right with you.'   The next morning he simply
said to his brother, ' John, you shall have the house.'
But he never divulged the reason why he said this,

either to his brother, or his wife, or to any human being, until he related it to us in the month of June 1863.

"The superstitious may regard this statement in one aspect, and the philosophical in another, but all must admit that its truth is simply a question of credibility. No one would doubt Mr. Ridgway's word, and few will believe that the eyes and ears of the then young man were deceived by an illusion. Happily, the friendship of the two brothers was uninterrupted, and it continued unbroken through life."

HEANOR, DERBYSHIRE.

IN that remarkable work, *Footfalls on the Boundary of Another World*, Robert Dale Owen publishes an interesting account of an apparition, supposed to have appeared about the time of the death of the person it represented. This account was supplied by Mr. William Howitt, the well-known author, it having happened in his own family; and in accordance with our usual custom of giving as nearly as possible the original narrator's own words—the only proper course in such cases—the story referred to above shall be told as Mr. Howitt tells it in his letter dated Highgate, March 28, 1859.

8

" The circumstance you desire to obtain from me is one which I have many times heard related by my mother. It was an event familiar to our family and the neighbourhood, and is connected with my earliest memories ; having occurred about the time of my birth, at my father's house at Heanor, Derbyshire, where I was born.

"My mother's family name, Tantum, is an uncommon one, which I do not recollect to have met with except in a story of Miss Leslie's. My mother had two brothers, Francis and Richard. The younger, Richard, I knew well, for he lived to an old age. The elder, Francis, was, at the time of the occurrence I am about to report, a gay young man, about twenty, unmarried, handsome, frank, affectionate, and extremely beloved by all classes throughout that part of the country. He is described, in that age of powder and pig-tails, as wearing his auburn hair flowing in ringlets on his shoulders, like another Absolom, and was much admired, as well for his personal grace as for the life and gaiety of his manners.

" One fine calm afternoon my mother, shortly after a confinement, but perfectly convalescent, was lying in bed, enjoying from her window the sense of summer beauty and repose ; a bright sky above, and the quiet village before her. In this state she was gladdened by hearing footsteps, which she took to be those of her brother Frank, as he was familiarly called, approaching the chamber door. The visitor knocked and entered. The foot of the bed was towards the door, and the curtains at the foot, notwithstanding the season, were drawn, to prevent any draught. Her brother parted them, and looked in upon her. His gaze was earnest and destitute of its usual cheerfulness, and he spoke not a word. ' My dear Frank,' said my mother, ' how glad I am to see you! Come round to the bedside, I wish to have some talk with you.'

" He closed the curtains, as if complying; but instead of doing so, my mother, to her astonishment, heard him leave the room, close the door behind him, and begin to descend the stairs. Greatly amazed, she hastily rang, and when her maid appeared she bade her call her brother back. The girl replied that she had not seen him enter the house. But my mother insisted, saying, ' He was here but this instant, run! Quick! Call him back! I must see him!'

" The girl hurried away, but, after a time, returned, saying that she could learn nothing of him anywhere; nor had anyone in or about the house seen him either enter or depart.

" Now, my father's house stood at the bottom of the village, and close to the high road, which was quite straight; so that anyone passing along it must have been seen for a much longer period than had elapsed. The girl said she had looked up and down the road, then searched the garden, a large, old-fashioned one, with shady walks; but neither in the garden nor on the road was he to be seen. She had inquired at the nearest cottages in the village, but no one had noticed him pass.

"My mother, though a very pious woman, was far from superstitious; yet the strangeness of this circumstance struck her forcibly. While she lay pondering upon it, there was heard a sudden running and excited talking in the village street. My mother listened, it increased, though up to that time the village had been profoundly still; and she became convinced that something very unusual had occurred. Again she rang the bell, to inquire the cause of the disturbance. This time it was the monthly nurse who answered it. She sought to tranquillize my mother, as a nurse usually does a patient. 'Oh, it is nothing particular, ma'am,' she said, 'some trifling affair,' which she pretended to relate, passing lightly over the particulars. But her ill-suppressed agitation did not escape my mother's eye. 'Tell me the truth,' she said, 'at once. I am certain something very sad has happened.' The woman still equivocated, greatly fearing the effect upon my mother in her then situation; and at first the family joined in the attempt at concealment. Finally, however, my mother's alarm and earnest entreaties drew from them the terrible truth that her brother had just been stabbed at the top of the village and killed on the spot.

"The melancholy event had thus occurred. My uncle, Francis Tantum, had been dining at Shipley Hall with Mr. Edward Miller Mundy, Member of Parliament for the county. Shipley Hall lay off to the left of the village as you looked up the main street from my father's house, and about a mile distant *f o n* it; while

Heanor Fall, my uncle's residence, was situated to the right; the road from the one country seat to the other crossing nearly at right angles the upper portion of the village street, at a point where stood one of the two village inns, the 'Admiral Rodney,' respectably kept by the widow H——ks. I remember her well—a tall, fine-looking woman, who must have been handsome in her youth, and who retained, even past middle age, an air superior to her condition. She had one only child, a son, then scarcely twenty. He was a good-looking, brisk, young fellow, and bore a very fair character. He must, however, as the event showed, have been of a very hasty temper.

"Francis Tantum, riding home from Shipley Hall after the early country dinner of that day, somewhat elated, it may be, with wine, stopped at the widow's inn, and bade the son bring him a glass of ale. As the latter turned to obey, my uncle, giving the youth a smart switch across the back with his riding-whip, cried out, in his lively joking way, ' Now, be quick, Dick; be quick ! '

"The young man, instead of receiving the playful stroke as a jest, took it as an insult. He rushed into the house, snatched up a carving-knife, and darting back into the street, stabbed my uncle to the heart as he sat on his horse, so that he fell dead, on the instant, in the road.

"The sensation throughout the quiet village may be imagined. The inhabitants, who idolised the murdered man, were prevented from taking summary vengeance

on the homicide only by the constables carrying him
off to the office of the nearest magistrate.

"Young H——ks was tried at the next Derby
Assizes; but (justly, no doubt, taking into view the
sudden irritation caused by the blow) he was convicted
of manslaughter only; and, after a few months imprisonment, returned to the village; where, notwithstanding the strong popular feeling against him, he
continued to keep the inn, even after his mother's
death. He is still present to my recollection, a quiet,
retiring man, never guilty of any other irregularity of
conduct, and seeming to bear about with him the
constant memory of his rash deed—a silent blight
upon his life.

" So great was the respect entertained for my uncle,
and such the deep impression of his tragic end, that so
long as that generation lived the church bells of the
village were regularly tolled on the anniversary of his
death.

"On comparing the circumstances and the exact
time at which each occurred, the fact was substantiated
that the apparition presented itself to my mother almost
instantly after her brother had received the fatal
stroke."

HEREFORD.

The Rev. Dr. Bretton, towards the close of his career appointed rector of Ludgate, early in life held a living in Hereford. He had married a daughter of Dr. Santer, a lady well known for her piety and virtue, but who died and left an infant to her husband's care. The child was entrusted to the charge of an old servant of Mrs. Bretton, who had since married, and who nursed it in her own cottage, near the doctor's residence. The story, which has often been related in various collections and in different ways, according to the original account, states that one day when the woman was nursing the infant, the door of her cottage was opened, and a lady entered so exactly resembling the late Mrs. Bretton in dress and appearance, that she exclaimed, "If my mistress were not dead, I should think you were she!" Whereupon, the apparition told her she was so, and requested her to go with her, as she had business of importance to communicate. Alice objected, being very much frightened, and entreated her to address herself rather to Dr. Bretton; but Mrs. B. answered, *that she had endeavoured to do so, and had been several times in his room for that purpose, but he was still asleep, and she had no power to do more towards awakening him than once uncover his feet.* Alice then pleaded that she had nobody to leave with her child; but Mrs. B. promising that the child should sleep till her return, she at length obeyed the summons, and having accompanied the apparition into a large field, the latter bade her observe how much she measured off with her feet, and having taken a considerable compass, she made her go and tell her brother that all that portion had been wrongfully taken from the poor by their father, and that he must restore it to them, adding, that she was the more concerned about it, since her name had been used in the transaction. Alice then asking how she should satisfy the gentleman of the truth of her mission, Mrs. B. mentioned to her some circumstances known only to herself and this brother; she then entered into much discourse with the woman, and gave her a great deal of good advice, till, hearing the sound of horse-bells, she said, "Alice, I must be seen by none but yourself," and then disappeared.

When the apparition had gone away the servant proceeded to the residence of her master, and acquainted him with what had occurred. Dr. Bretton admitted that he had actually heard someone walking about in his room in a way that he could not account for, as no one was visible. He then mentioned the matter to his brother, who laughed heartily at it, until Alice communicated to him the secret which she was commissioned to reveal to him: upon hearing it he changed his tone, and declared himself ready to make the restitution required. Dr. Bretton, it may be remarked, never made any secret of the affair, but discussed it freely with many persons.

HENHOW COTTAGE.

An account of a haunted neighbourhood, as described in J. Sullivan's *Cumberland and Westmoreland*, illustrates either the long term of years apparitions are doomed to haunt the scenes of their former life, or the tenacity of tradition. Sullivan, referring to other previous cases of supernatural troubles it had been his lot to record, remarks, that if some incredulous individuals may consider the evidence already proffered unsatisfactory, they should investigate that of the Henhow spectre, "the truth of which they may ascertain by a little inquiry." This particular case, he remarks, happened about twenty-three years ago, and the man to whom the spectre appeared lived in Martindale, at a cottage called "Henhow." His wife had heard some unaccountable noises in or around the house, and informed her husband, but no further notice was taken. One morning he had to go to his work at an early hour, and, having several miles to walk, he started soon after midnight. He had not got above two hundred yards from the house, when the dog by which he was accompanied gave signs of alarm. He looked round—at the other side of the wall that bounded the road, appeared a woman, keeping pace with him, and carrying a child in her arms. There was no means of escape; he spoke to the figure, and asked her what "was troubling her." Then she told him her story. She had once lived at Henhow, and had been seduced.　Her seducer, to cloak his guilt and her frailty, met her by appointment at a certain market town, and gave her a medicine, the purpose of which is obvious.　It proved too potent, and killed both mother and child.　Her doom was to wander thus for a hundred years, forty of which were already expired. On his return home at night, the man told what he had seen and heard, and when the extraordinary story spread through the dale, the "old wives" were enabled to recall some almost forgotten incidents precisely identical with those related by the apparition.　The seducer was known to be a clergyman.　"The occurrence is believed to have made a lasting impression on the old man," says Sullivan, "who still lives, and was until very lately a shepherd on the fells.　There can be no moral doubt that he both saw and spoke with the apparition; but what share his imagination had therein, or how it had been excited, are mysteries, and so they are likely to remain."

HILTON CASTLE.

FORMERLY the homes of nearly every Scottish, and of many English, families of importance were haunted by domestic spirits known as "Brownies."　Hilton Castle, once one of the most magnificent dwellings in the north of England, but now hastening to decay, among other weird inhabitants was a long while, perchance still is,

frequented by a Brownie, popularly known as the " Cauld
Lad of Hilton." As a rule, these domestic spectres
appear to have taken up their abode in any suitable
dwelling, without the usual precedent of a crime, as is
the case with a ghost or apparition of the ordinary type,
and to have generally employed themselves for the
benefit of the household. The antiquary Surtees, in
his *History of Durham*, assumes the being that haunted
Hilton Castle to have been one of these somewhat
commonplace spirits, and although there are other more
eerie stories of the Cold Lad, it will be as well to give
the historian's account first.

The Cauld Lad, he says, was seldom seen, but was
heard nightly by the servants, who slept in the great
hall. If the kitchen were left in perfect order, they
heard him amusing himself by breaking plates and
dishes, hurling the pewter in all directions, and throwing everything into confusion. If, on the contrary, the
apartment had been left in disarray, a practice which
the servants found it most prudent to adopt, the inde-
fatigable goblin arranged everything with the greatest
precision. This poor spirit, whose pranks were never
of a dangerous or hurtful character, was at length
banished from his haunts by the usual and universally
known expedient of presenting him with a suit of
clothes. A green cloak and hood were laid before the
kitchen fire, and the domestics sat up watching at a
prudent distance. At twelve o'clock the sprite glided
gently in, stood by the glowing embers, and surveyed the
garments provided for him very attentively, tried them

on, and seemed delighted with his appearance in them, frisking about for some time and cutting several somersaults, till, on hearing the first cock-crow, he twitched his mantle about him and disappeared with the malediction usually adopted on such occasions :—

> "Here's a cloak, and here's a hood,
> The Cauld Lad o' Hilton will do no more good."

Although this spirit was thus summarily disposed of by the historian, the inhabitants of Hilton and its vicinity for many generations continued to believe in its frequent reappearance, and over the glowing embers told wonderful tales of its deeds. So strange were its doings at times, and so frequent its apparition, that it was difficult to retain the domestics in the castle. Among other stories told of the terror with which it contrived to imbue the minds of the servants, is one of a dairymaid who was too fond of helping herself to the richest cream the pantry afforded. One day, as this not over scrupulous young woman was taking her usual sips from the various pans, the Cauld Lad suddenly addressed her from some invisible vantage-ground, "Ye taste, and ye taste, and ye taste, but ye never gie the Cauld Lad a taste!". On hearing this appalling accusation, the affrighted maid dropped the spoon on the ground, rushed out of the place, and could never be induced to enter it again.

The local tradition of the "Cold Lad," more closely assimilates his nature to that of any ordinary ghost or apparition, and in no way to the Brownie of our forefathers. The popular idea is that a lad, a domestic of the house, was cruelly ill-treated and kept confined in a cupboard, and the cupboard is, or was quite recently, pointed out by the guide who shows visitors over the house, as "the place where they used to put the Cold Lad." He is supposed to have received the suggestively awesome name of the "Cold Lad," from his stiff and stark form having been discovered in the cupboard.

Surtees endeavours to explain the origin of this ancient legend by reference to a murder of Roger Skelton, apparently a servant, by his master, Robert Hilton, of Hilton, on the 3rd July 1609. Hilton was found guilty of having killed Skelton, but received a pardon some few months after his conviction. According to the old tale, the lord of Hilton one day, in a fit of wrath or intemperance, enraged at the delay in bringing his horse after he had ordered it, rushed to the stable, and finding the boy, whose duty it was to have brought the horse, loitering about, he seized a hay-fork, and struck him with it. Intentionally or not, he had given the lad a mortal blow. The tale proceeds to tell how the murderer covered his victim with straw until nighttime, when he took the body and flung it into the pond, where, indeed, the skeleton was discovered in the last Lord of Hilton's time.

With such ghastly and such ghostly traditions connected with it, it is no wonder that Hilton Castle is a haunted place.

HOLLAND HOUSE.

THE *History of Holland House* by the Princess
Marie Lichtenstein, the adopted daughter of the present
Lady Holland, is a well-known popular account of one
of the most interesting London residences extant. The
many highly-gifted men and beautiful women, who
have frequented Holland House for several generations
past, have endowed it with memories of a most attractive
nature; but the Princess Marie's work tells us that
reminiscences of a far less pleasing character hover
about the old house, and, indeed, that, like most respectable dwellings of any antiquity, Holland House is
haunted. At least two ghostly legends, according to
the fair authoress, are connected with it.

An ancient manor-house, belonging to Sir William
Cope, it is believed, formerly stood where Holland
House now stands, and, so it would seem, was incor-
porated in the present mansion. Sir William Cope's
daughter and heiress, Isabel, was married to Sir Henry
Rich, created Baron Kensington in 1622, and sent
to Spain by James the First, to assist in negociating
a marriage between Prince Charles and the Infanta.
In 1624 he was created Earl of Holland, and it was this
same nobleman, as the Princess tells us, "who added
to the building its wings and arcades, and more than
this, he employed the best artists of the time in
decorating the interior."

Clarendon describes the Earl as "a very handsome man, of a lovely and winning presence, and gentle conversation." He played, says the historian, a conspicuous part during the reign of Charles the First and the commencement of the struggle with the Parliament. After having stood in high favour with Queen Henrietta, he fell under suspicion of disloyalty, which was confirmed by his lending Holland House for a meeting between Fairfax and certain discontented members of Parliament. The year following, having rejoined the Royalists, he was taken in arms at St Neot's, and, having been imprisoned in Warwick Castle, he was condemned to death, and beheaded in March 1648-9 in Palace Yard. Warburton, in a note to Clarendon's History, says : "He lived like a knave, and died like a fool. He appeared on the scaffold dressed in a white satin waistcoat, and a white satin cap with silver lace. After some divine conference with a clergyman and an affectionate leave-taking with a friend, he turned to the executioner and said, 'Here, my friend, let my clothes and my body alone ; there is ten pounds for thee— that is better than my clothes, I am sure of it. And when you take up my head, do not take off my cap.'" He appears, however, even by Warburton's account, to have died with much firmness, and his head was severed by one blow from his body.

This Lord Holland, the first of his name, and the chief builder of Holland House, is, the Princess Lichtenstein tells us, believed to yet haunt one room of the splendid old mansion. "The gilt room is said to be tenanted by the solitary ghost of its first lord, who, according to tradition, issues forth at midnight from behind a secret door, and walks slowly through the scenes of former triumphs with his head in his hand. To add to this mystery, there is a tale of three spots of blood on one side of the recess whence he issues—three spots which can never be effaced."

In the grounds of Holland House is "the Green Lane," formerly called "Nightingale Lane," as long as nightingales frequented it. "It is," says the Princess, "a long avenue, like an immense gallery arched with trees and carpeted with grass, the distant light at the end softening down into that misty blue so peculiar to dear England." This avenue is the scene of a "spiritual experience," chronicled by Aubrey in his *Miscellanies*, and which is as follows :—

"The beautiful Lady Diana Rich, daughter to the Earl of Holland, as she was walking in her father's garden at Kensington, to take the air before dinner, about eleven o'clock, being then very well, met her own apparition, habit and everything, as in a looking-glass. About a month after she died of small-pox. And 'tis said that her sister, the Lady Isabella Thinne, saw the like of herself also before she died. This account I had from a person of honour."

"A third sister, Mary, was married to the Earl of Breadalbane," we are informed, and it has been recorded that she also, not long after her marriage, had some such warning of her approaching dissolution.

And so the old tradition has remained, and who would

wish it removed? Belonging to past times, it should be respected. But whether we respect tradition or not, it is a received fact that, whenever the mistress of Holland House meets herself, Death is hovering about her.

LAMBTON CASTLE.

AT Lambton Castle, in Durham, there is shown the figure of a man in armour, cut in stone, having something like razors set in his back-plate. He is represented in the act of thrusting his sword down the throat of a dragon or serpent. The tradition which is typified by this ancient figure, and which for centuries has been identified with the Lambton family, now represented by the Earl of Durham, is one of the most singular and notorious in England. Burke, in his *Vicissitudes of Families*, gives the tale at some length, but derives it chiefly from Surtees, the historian and antiquary, and from him, with some few additional particulars from other local authorities, we purpose giving it in a somewhat abridged form.

According to the old legend the Lambtons " were so brave that they feared neither man nor God," and, apparently, had no respect for the Sabbath. One Sunday, therefore, the reckless heir of the race, according to his profane custom, went to fish in the river Wear, and, after trying his piscatorial skill for a long time without

9

success, vented his disappointment in curses loud and deep, much to the distress of passers by on their road to church. At length his luck appeared as if about to change, for he felt something struggling at the end of his line. Pulling it carefully to land, in expectation of capturing a great fish, he was wofully disappointed and enraged to find it was a worm or snake, of repulsive appearance. He cleared it from his hook, and flung it into an adjacent well, remarking to a passer-by that he thought he had caught the devil, and requesting his opinion on the strange animal. The stranger, after looking into the well, remarked that he had never seen anything like it before, that it was like an eft, but that it had nine *holes* on each side of its mouth, and opined that it betokened no good. .

After a while, the heir of the Lambtons repented of his evil courses, and proceeded to a distant land, in order to wage war against the infidels. During the seven long years that he was absent from home, a most distressing and unexpected state of affairs had come to pass. The worm or serpent, which he had flung into the well on that desecrated Sabbath, had grown so large that it had to seek another and more capacious place of residence. The locality which it selected as its favourite abode was a small hill near the village of Fatfield, on the north side of the river Wear, about a mile and a half below Lambton Castle; and at last, so great was its length, and so great was its strength, that it could, and would, wind itself round this hill, which is upwards of three hundred yards in circumference, in a triple cord, in such a manner that traces of its folds have remained almost to within memory of the last generation. It became a terror to the whole country, committing all kinds of devastation on the flocks and herds, and poisoning the pasture with its reeking breath. In vain did the knights and gentlemen thereabouts endeavour to slay this monster, it was a match for the best of them, always leaving them minus life or limb; for although many of them had succeeded in cutting it asunder, the severed parts had reunited immediately, and the worm remained whole as before the conflict.

Finally, the heir of Lambton returned from the wars; he was naturally distressed to learn of the desolation of his ancestral lands, and still more so when he discovered that the cause of all the misery was really due to the monster he had drawn to land on the long bygone desecrated Sabbath. He determined, at all risks, to endeavour to destroy the monster; but as all previous adventurers had failed, he deemed it best, before undertaking the conflict, to consult a witch or wise woman as to the best method of proceeding. Accordingly, he applied to a witch, and, after having been reproached as the cause of all the misery brought upon the country, she advised him how to act. He was directed to provide himself with a coat of armour covered with razors, and, by means of that and his trusty sword, promised success, that is to say, conditionally upon his making a solemn vow to kill the first living thing which he should meet after slaying the worm. Lambton agreed to the conditions; but was informed that if he failed to keep his word, the

"Lords of Lambton for nine generations should not die in their beds," no very great hardship, it might be deemed, for that martial age.

According to his instructions, the knight had a suit of armour covered with razors made, and having donned this, he instructed his aged father that when he had destroyed the worm, he would blow three blasts upon his horn as a signal of his victory, whereupon his favourite greyhound was to be let loose, so that it might run to him, and therefore be the first thing that would meet him, and thus be slain in fulfilment of his agreement with the witch. The father promised and gave his blessing, and young Lambton, having made the vow enjoined, started on his dangerous expedition. As soon as he approached the hill round which the worm was coiled, it unwound itself and came down to the riverside to attack him. Nothing daunted by its hideous aspect, the knight struck at it with might and main, yet without appearing to make any impression upon it beyond increasing its rage. It now seized its opponent in its horrid folds and sought to strangle him; but the more tightly it grasped him, the more frightfully was it wounded, the razor blades cutting it through and through. But as often as the monster fell to the ground cut by the knight's terrible coat of mail, as often, says the legend, did the severed pieces re-unite, and the wounds heal up. Lambton, seeing that the worm was not to be destroyed in this way, stept into the river Wear, whither the monster followed him. The change of position proved fatal to the worm, for as fast as the pieces were cut off by the razors they were carried away by the stream, and the monster, being unable to re-unite itself was, after the desperate conflict, at last utterly destroyed.

As soon as Lambton had achieved the victory, he blew three blasts upon his horn ; but his father, in the excitement of the moment, forgot to have the greyhound unloosened, and in his impatience ran out of the castle to greet his son, and was the first living being that met his gaze. The knight embraced his father, and again blew his horn, upon which the hound was let loose, and, running towards Lambton, was slain. But this was too late to retrieve matters, his vow having enjoined the slaying of the *first* living creature that he should meet with, and his father had been the first to meet him. So the curse was on the house of Lambton, and for nine generations not one of its lords could die in his bed.

Sir Bernard Burke points out that popular tradition traces the curse back to Robert Lambton, who died without issue in 1442, leaving the estates to his brother Thomas, but bequeathing by his will to his "brother, John Lambton, knight of Rhodes, 100 marks." In an ancient pedigree this John Lambton, knight of Rhodes, is described as he "that slew the worm," and as "Lord of Lambton after the death of four brothers without male issue." His son Robert is said to have been drowned at Newbrig, near the chapel where the knight had registered his rash and unperformed vow, and tradition specifies a *bedless* death for each successive nine generations of the Lords of Lambton. After adverting to the various ways and places in which different heirs of Lambton met with death, our chief authority for this portion of the legend concludes :—

Great curiosity prevailed in the life-time of Henry to know if the curse would " hold good to the end." He died in his chariot, crossing the new bridge, in 1761, thus giving the last connecting link to the chain of circumstantial evidence connected with the history of the worm of Lambton. His succeeding brother, General Lambton, who lived to a great age, fearing that the prophecy might be possibly fulfilled by his servants, under the idea that he could not die in his bed, kept a horsewhip beside him in his last illness, and thus eluded the prediction. Although the spell put on this ancient family by the witch is said to have been broken by the death of Henry Lambton in 1761, yet neither of the two last lords have died at home, and this, to the knights of ancient times, says Burke, " would have been sorer punishment than dying in the battle-field, for they loved to sleep in their own country and with their fathers."

LITTLECOT HOUSE.

LITTLECOT HOUSE, or Hall as it is sometimes called, the ancient seat of the Darrells, is two miles from Hungerford in Berkshire. It stands in a low and lonely situation, and is thoroughly typical in appearance of a haunted dwelling.   On three sides it is surrounded by a park, which spreads over the adjacent hill, and on the fourth by meadows, through which runs the river Kennet.   A thick grove of lofty trees stands on one side of the gloomy building, which is of great antiquity, and would appear to have been erected towards the close of the age of feudal warfare, when defence came to be no longer the principal object in a country mansion.   The interior of the house, however, presents many objects appropriate to feudal times.   The hall is very spacious, paved by stones, and lighted by large transon windows. The walls are hung with coats-of-mail and helmets, and on every side are quantities of old-fashioned pistols and guns, and other suitable ornaments for an old baronial dwelling.   Below the cornice at the end of the hall, hangs a row of leathern jerkins, made in the form of shirts, and supposed to have been worn as armour by the retainers of the Darrell family, to whom the old Hall belonged.   An enormous oaken table, reaching nearly from one end of the chamber to the other, might have feasted the entire neighbourhood, and an appendage to one end of it made it answer at other times for the old game of shuffleboard.   The rest of the furniture is in a corresponding style, or was a few years ago; but the most noticeable article is an old chair of cumbrous workmanship, constructed of wood, curiously carved, with a high back and triangular seat; it is said to have been used by Judge Popham, in the days of Elizabeth.

The entrance into the hall of this ancient mansion is at one end by a low door, communicating with a passage

that leads from the outer door in the front of the house
to a quadrangle within ; at the other it opens upon a
gloomy stair-case, by which you ascend to the first floor,
and, passing the doors of some bed-chambers, enter a
narrow gallery which extends along the back front of the
house from one end to the other of it. This gallery is
hung with old family portraits, chiefly in Spanish costumes of the sixteenth century. In one of the bed-
chambers, which you pass in going towards the gallery,
is a bedstead with blue furniture, that time has now
made dingy and threadbare; and in the bottom of one
of the bed-curtains you are shown a place where a small
piece has been *cut out and sewn in again.* To account
for this curious circumstance, and for the apparitions
which tenant this haunted chamber, the following terrible
tale is told :—

" It was on a dark rainy night in the month of
November, that an old midwife sat musing by her cottage
fireside, when on a sudden she was startled by a loud
knocking at the door. On opening it she found a
horseman, who told her that her assistance was required
immediately by a person of rank, and that she should be
handsomely rewarded, but that there were reasons for
keeping the affair a strict secret, and therefore she
must submit to be blind-folded, and to be conducted in
that condition to the bed-chamber of the lady. With
some hesitation the midwife consented; the horseman
bound her eyes, and placed her on a pillion behind him.
After proceeding in silence for many miles, through
rough and dirty lanes, they stopped, and the midwife

was led into a house which, from the length of her walk through the apartments, as well as the sounds about her, she discovered to be the seat of wealth and power.

" When the bandage was removed from her eyes, she found herself in a bed-chamber, in which were the lady on whose account she had been sent for, and a man of a haughty and ferocious aspect. The lady was delivered of a fine boy. Immediately the man commanded the midwife to give him the child, and, catching it from her, he hurried across the room, and threw it on the back of the fire that was blazing in the chimney. The child, however, was strong, and by its struggles rolled itself off upon the hearth, when the ruffian again seized it with fury, and, in spite of the intercession of the midwife, and the more piteous entreaties of the mother, thrust it under the grate, and, raking the live coals upon it, soon put an end to its life.

" The midwife, after spending some time in affording all the relief in her power to the wretched mother, was told that she must be gone. Her former conductor appeared, who again bound her eyes, and conveyed her behind him to her own home; he then paid her handsomely and departed. The midwife was strongly agitated by the horrors of the preceding night, and she immediately made a deposition of the facts before a magistrate. Two circumstances afforded hopes of detecting the house in which the crime had been committed ; one was, that the midwife, as she sat by the bed-side, had, with a view to discover the place, *cut out a piece of the bed-curtain, and sewn it in again* ; the other was, that as she had

descended the staircase she had counted the steps.
Some suspicion fell upon one Darrell, at that time the
proprietor of Littlecot House and the domain around it.
The house was examined, and identified by the midwife,
and Darrell was tried at Salisbury for the murder. By
corrupting his judge, he escaped the sentence of the law,
but broke his neck by a fall from his horse in hunting,
a few months afterwards. The place where this happened is still known by the name of Darrell's Stile,—a
spot to be dreaded by the peasant whom the shades of
evening have overtaken on his way."

This is the fearsome legend connected with Littlecot
House, the circumstances related are declared to be true,
and to have happened in the reign of Elizabeth. With
such a tale attached to its guilty walls, no wonder that
the apparition of a woman with dishevelled hair, in
white garments, and bearing a babe in her arms, haunts
that gloomy chamber.

LONDON : ARGYLE ROOMS.

IN the well-known diary of Thomas Raikes, and under
date of December 26, 1832, is recounted a very singular
account of an apparition which appeared to a young
lady at the Argyle Rooms, a highly-fashionable establishment in those days, and, need it be stated, then noted
for a class of entertainment very different from that it
afterwards became known for. Mr. Raikes, who had

the anecdote from a member of the lady's family chiefly
concerned, tells the story in these words :—

"It is now about fifteen months ago that Miss
M——, a connection of my family, went with a party of
friends to a concert at the Argyle Rooms. She appeared
there to be suddenly seized with indisposition, and,
though she persisted for some time to struggle against
what seemed a violent nervous affection, it became at
last so oppressive that they were obliged to send for
their carriage and conduct her home. She was for a
long time unwilling to say what was the cause of her
indisposition ; but, on being more earnestly questioned,
she at length confessed that she had, immediately on
arriving in the concert-room, been terrified by a horrible
vision, which unceasingly presented itself to her sight.
It seemed to her as though a naked corpse was lying on
the floor at her feet ; the features of the face were
partly covered by a cloth mantle, but enough was
apparent to convince her that the body was that of Sir
J—— Y——. Every effort was made by her friends at
the time to tranquillize her mind by representing the
folly of allowing such delusions to prey upon her spirits,
and she thus retired to bed ; but on the following day
the family received the tidings of Sir J—— Y—— having
been drowned in Southampton river that very night by
the oversetting of his boat ; and the body was afterwards
found entangled in a *boat-cloak*. Here," remarks
Raikes, " is an authenticated case of second sight, and
of very recent date."

LONDON : BROAD STREET.

ONE of those stories of apparitions which are so
frequently alluded to, but of which the facts are apparently, chiefly or entirely unknown to most authors
of supernatural works, is that related by the Rev. Dr.
Scott, an eminent divine in his days. The narrative
of this most marvellous affair originally appeared in
The History and Reality of Apparitions, from which
curious little work we shall transcribe it. The editor
of that book, which was published in 1770, and who
was, apparently, de Foe, asserts that this story had never
appeared in print before, and adds of the Rev. Dr. Scott,
that he was not only a man whose learning and piety
were eminent, but one whose judgment was known
to be good, and who could not be easily imposed
upon.

According to the story, Dr. Scott was sitting alone
by his fireside in the library of his house in Broad
Street; he had shut himself in the room to study and,
so it is alleged, had locked the door. In the midst of
his reading happening to look up, he was much astounded
to see, sitting in an elbow-chair on the other side of the
fire-place, a grave, elderly gentleman, in a black velvet
gown and a long wig, looking at him with a pleased
countenance, and as if about to speak. Knowing that
he had locked the door, Dr. Scott was quite confounded
at seeing this uninvited visitor sitting in the elbow-

chair, and from the first appears to have suspected its supernatural character. Indeed, so disturbed was he at the sight of the apparition, for such it was, that he was unable to speak, as he himself acknowledged in telling the story. The spectre, however, began the discourse by telling the doctor not to be frightened, for it would do him no harm, but came to see him upon a matter of great importance to an injured family, which was in danger of being ruined. Although the doctor was a stranger to this family, the apparition stated that knowing him to be a man of integrity it had selected him to perform an act of great charity as well as justice.

At first Dr. Scott was not sufficiently composed to pay proper attention to what the apparition propounded; but was rather more inclined to escape from the room if he could, and made one or two futile attempts to knock for some of his household to come up; at which his visitor appeared to be somewhat displeased. But, as the doctor afterwards stated, he had no power to go out of the room, even if he had been next the door, nor to knock for help, even if any had been close at hand.

Then the apparition, seeing the doctor still so confused, again desired him to compose himself, assuring him that he would not do him the slightest injury, nor do anything to cause him the least uneasiness, but desired that he would permit him to deliver the business he came about, which, when he had heard, he said, he would probably see less cause to be surprised or apprehensive than he did now.

By this time Dr. Scott had somewhat recovered himself, and encouraged by the calm manner in which the apparition addressed him, contrived to falter out:

"In the name of God, what art thou?"

"I desire you will not be frightened," responded the apparition. "I am a stranger to you, and if I tell you my name you will not know it. But you may do the business without inquiring further." The doctor could not compose himself, but still remained very uneasy, and for some time said nothing. Again the apparition attempted to reassure him, but could only elicit from him a repetition of the ejaculation, "In the name of God, what art thou?"

Upon this, says the narration, the spectre appeared to be displeased, and expostulated with Dr. Scott, telling him that it could have terrified him into compliance, but that it chose to come quietly and calmly to him; and, indeed, made use of such civil and natural discourse that the doctor began to grow a little more familiar, and at last ventured to ask what it wanted of him. Upon this the apparition appeared to be very gratified, and began its story. It related that it had once owned a very good estate, which at that time was enjoyed by its grandson; two nephews, however, the sons of its younger brother, were then suing for possession of the property and, owing to certain family reasons which the doctor could not or would not specify, were likely to oust the young man from his property. A deed of settlement, being the conveyance of the inheritance, could not be found and without it the owner of the estate had every reason to fear he would be ejected.

"Well," said Dr. Scott, "what can I do in the case?"

"Go to my grandson," said the apparition, "and direct him where to find the missing deed, which is concealed in a place where I put it myself." And then it gave the doctor minute particulars of the chest wherein the needed document was hidden stowed away in an old lumber-room. When the apparition had impressed the matter thoroughly upon the doctor's mind, Dr. Scott not unnaturally asked his visitor why it could not direct the grandson himself to recover the missing deed. "Ask me not about that," said the apparition; "there are divers reasons, which you may know hereafter. I can depend upon your honesty in it in the meantime."

Still Dr. Scott did not like to take upon himself the strange mission, whereupon the apparition seemed to grow angry, and even begin to threaten him, so that he was at last compelled to promise compliance. The apparition then assumed a pleasant aspect, thanked him, and disappeared.

The strangest part of this strange story yet remains to be told. At the earliest opportunity Dr. Scott posted away to the address given him by the apparition, or dream as some persons deemed it. He asked for and was at once introduced to the gentleman the apparition had sent him to, and to his surprise was received most cordially by him. Dr. Scott's surprise was, indeed, quickened when the stranger entered most unreservedly into the particulars of his law-suit, telling him that he had had a dream the previous night, in which he had dreamed that a strange gentleman came to him, and assisted him to find the deed which was needed to confirm him in the possession of his estate.

This assured Dr. Scott that it was not a dream which he had had, and that he was really selected to discover the missing document. Making himself agreeable to his host, he eventually got him to take him all over his splendid old mansion. Finally, he beheld just such a lumber-room as the apparition had told him of, and on entering it, saw an exact *fac-simile* of the chest described to him by his supernatural visitant. There was an old rusty key in it that would neither turn round, nor come out of the lock, which was exactly what the apparition had forewarned him of! At the doctor's request a hammer and chisel were sent for, and the chest broken open, and, after some difficulty, a false drawer was found in it. This being split open, *there lay the missing parchment* spread out flat over the whole breadth of the bottom of the trunk !

The joy of the young heir, and of his family, may be imagined, whilst their surprise can have been no less. Whether Dr. Scott informed them of the means by which he was led to make the discovery is not stated; but it is alleged the production of the needed deed confirmed the owner in the possession of his estates. As this gentleman was still living, the narrator was not inclined to publish his name; and, now-a-days, the chances of discovering it are, doubtless, far less than they were in

his time of finding the missing document. Regard it
how we may, as a dream or a coincidence, certainly
Dr. Scott's adventure was a very marvellous one.

LONDON : JAMES STREET, W.C.

In his *Miscellanies*, Aubrey records in his very concise
manner, the account of an apparition that appeared to
a lady who lodged in James Street, Covent Garden.
This lady was beloved by Lord Mohun's son and heir,
" a gallant gentleman, valiant, and a great master of
fencing and horsemanship"; but, although she was
very handsome, she was of lowlier lineage than her lover.
Mr. Mohun, on account of some reason not stated, had
a quarrel with " Prince Griffin," and a challenge result-
ing therefrom, agreed to meet his antagonist in the
morning at Chelsea-fields, and there fight him on
horseback.

In the morning Mr. Mohun started off to keep his
appointment, but by Ebury Farm he was met by some
people who quarrelled with and shot him. These folk
were supposed to have been acting under " Prince
Griffin's " orders, as Mr. Mohun, being so much the
better horseman was, it is suggested, certain to have
proved victorious had he met his opponent in the
manner agreed upon.

Mr. Mohun was murdered about ten o'clock in the

morning; and at the identical time of his death, his mistress, being in bed at her lodgings in James Street, saw her lover come to her bed-side, draw the curtains, look upon her, and then go away. She called after him, but received no answer. She then knocked for her maid, and inquired for Mr. Mohun, but the maid said she had not seen him, and he could not have been in the room, as she had the key of it in her pocket.

This account the narrator had direct from the mouths of the lady and her maid.

LONDON: ST. JAMES'S PALACE.

In a small collection of more or less known accounts of apparitions, edited by T. M. Jarvis, and published in 1823, under the title of *Accredited Ghost Stories*, is one which describes the appearance of the Duchess of Mazarine, after her death, to Madame de Beauclair. The name of the authority for this story is not given, but Mr. Jarvis declares that he solemnly protested his conviction of the truth of it, and that several other persons of undoubted credit, alive when the narrative was published, were also satisfied as to its being a relation of fact.

The Duchess of Mazarine, need it be premised, was mistress to Charles the Second, whilst Madame de Beauclair held a similar position towards his brother and successor, James the Second. These two women are said to have been greatly attached to each other, a

somewhat singular circumstance when their positions
are taken into consideration.

After the burning of Whitehall these favourites of
royalty were removed to St. James's Palace, where they
were allotted very handsome suites of apartments, but,
says our author, " the face of public affairs being then
wholly changed, and a new set of courtiers as well as
rules of behaviour come into vogue, they conversed
almost wholly with each other." The truth would
appear to be that these women, being neglected on
account of new favourites, had a fellow-feeling for each
other, and, as is not unusual in such cases, began to
discuss matters of a graver nature than had been their
custom hitherto. In one of the more serious consulta-
tions which these *ci-devant* favourites held together on
the immortality of the soul, they discussed the doctrine
of apparitions, and made a solemn stipulation that
whichever one died first, she should return, if there was
a possibility of so doing, and give the other an accoun
of what position she was in in the next life.

This promise, says the account, was often repeated,
and the Duchess happening to fall sick, and her life
despaired of by all about her, Madame de Beauclair
reminded her of her solemn promise, to which Her Grace
responded that she might depend upon her performance
of it. These words passed between them not above an
hour before the dissolution of the Duchess, and were
spoken before several persons who were in the room,
although they did not comprehend the meaning of what
they heard.

"Some years after the Duchess's decease, happening," says our author, "in a visit I made to Madame de Beauclair, to fall on the topic of futurity, she expressed her disbelief of it with a great deal of warmth, which a little surprising me, as being of a quite contrary way of thinking myself, and had always, by the religion she professed, supposed her highly so." In answer to her interlocutor's arguments, the lady related her compact with her departed friend, and, in spite of all he could urge, deemed the non-appearance of her friend's apparition was a proof of the non-existence of a future state.

Some months after this conversation, its narrator states that he was visiting at an acquaintance of Madame de Beauclair. "We were just set down to cards, about nine o'clock in the evening, as near as I can remember," is his record, "when a servant came hastily into the room and acquainted the lady I was with that Madame de Beauclair had sent to entreat she would come that moment to her, adding that if she desired ever to see her more in this world she must not delay her visit."

The lady having a severe cold, and hearing that Madame de Beauclair was, apparently, in good health, declined to accede to this request, but on receiving a second, still more urgent message, accompanied by a *bequest* of a casket containing the watch, chain, necklace, and other trinkets of Madame de Beauclair, hastened to that lady's apartments, accompanied by our narrator. On arrival at Madame's, he sent up his name, and was requested to come up with his companion at once.

Upon entering the room where Madame de Beauclair

was, she informed him, after a few introductory words, that she would very soon pass from this world into that eternity which she once doubted, but was now assured of. She then proceeded to declare that she had seen the Duchess of Mazarine. "I perceived not how she entered," was her statement, "but, turning my eyes towards yonder corner of the room, I saw her stand in the same form and habit she was accustomed to appear in when living : fain would I have spoken, but had not the power of utterance. She took a little circuit round the chamber, seeming rather to swim than walk, then stopped by the side of that Indian chest, and, looking on me with her usual sweetness, said, ' Beauclair, between the hours of twelve and one this night you will be with me.' The surprise I was in at first being a little abated, I began to ask some questions concerning that future world I was so soon to visit ; but, on the opening of my lips for that purpose, she vanished from my sight."

It was now nearly twelve, and Madame de Beauclair not appearing to be suffering from any ailment, they endeavoured to revive her spirits ; but, says the narrator, " we scarce began to speak, when suddenly her countenance changed, and she cried out, ' O ! I am sick at heart.' Mrs. Wood applied some restoratives, but to no effect. She grew still worse, and in about half an hour expired, it being exactly the time the apparition had foretold."

LONDON : ST. JAMES STREET.

It is a curious circumstance that more buildings having a reputation for being haunted are discoverable in towns and cities than in sparsely populated places. The British metropolis, despite its gas-lamps and guardian police, contains many residences that even now are left to the mercies of those spectral tenants who alone inhabit them. It must be confessed, however, that instead of increasing, the number of these disturbed residences, for reasons obvious to all, is rapidly decreasing. It is not many years since a house in St. James Street, the number of which it is as well to omit, acquired considerable notoriety on account of the unpleasant noises which took place in it. It had stood empty for a long time, in consequence of the annoyances to which the various tenants who had tried it had been subjected. There was one apartment in particular which nobody was able to occupy without being disturbed.

On one occasion a youth who, having been abroad for a considerable time, had not any knowledge of the evil reputation this chamber had acquired, was put there to sleep on his arrival, as it was hoped his rest might not be disturbed. In the morning, however, he complained sadly of the terrible time he had had in the night, with people looking in at him between the curtains of his bed, and he avowed his determination to terminate his visit at once, as he could not possibly sleep there any more.

After this period the house was again vacant for a considerable time, but was at length taken and workmen were sent in to put it in habitable repair. One day, when the men were away at their dinner, says our informant, " the master builder took the key with him and went to inspect progress, and having examined the lower rooms, he was ascending the stairs, when he heard a man's foot behind him. He looked round, but there was nobody there, and he moved on again ; still there was somebody following, and he stopped and looked over the rails, but there was no one to be seen. So, though feeling rather queer, he advanced into the drawing-room, where a fire had been lighted, and wishing to combat the uncomfortable sensation that was creeping over him, he took hold of a chair, and drawing it resolutely along the floor, he slammed it down upon the hearth with some force, and seated himself in it ; when, to his amazement, the action, in all its particulars of sound, was immediately repeated by his unseen companion, who seemed to seat himself beside him on a chair as invisible as himself. Horror-stricken, the worthy builder started up and rushed out of the house."

LONDON : THE TOWER.

THERE is no place in the kingdom one would deem more likely to be haunted than that strange conglomeration of rooms, castles, and dungeons, known as the Tower of London. For many centuries it has been the scene of numberless deaths by violence, some by public execution and others by private murder, until it is scarcely metaphorical language to declare that its walls have been built out of human bones and cemented by human blood. That ghosts and spectres have haunted its weird precincts no believer in the supernatural can doubt; and, if we may credit all that has been told of it of late years, its apparitions are not yet quite beings of the past. In *Notes and Queries* for 1860, the late Edmund Lenthal Swifte, Keeper of the Crown Jewels, published a remarkable account of a spectral illusion witnessed by himself in the time-honoured fortress ; and his account, together with such additions and explanations as a subsequent correspondence invoked, shall now be presented to the reader :—

"I have often purposed to leave behind me a faithful record of all that I personally know of this strange story," writes Mr. Swifte, in response to an inquiry as to particulars of the ghost in the Tower of London. "Forty-three years have passed, and its impression is as vividly before me as on the moment of its occurrence . . . but there are yet survivors who can testify that I have not at any time either amplified or abridged my ghostly experiences.

"In 1814 I was appointed Keeper of the Crown Jewels in the Tower, where I resided with my family till my retirement in 1852. One Saturday night in October, 1817, about ' the witching hour,' I was at supper with my wife, her sister, and our little boy, in the sitting-room of the Jewel House, which—then comparatively modernised—is said to have been the ' doleful prison ' of Anne Boleyn, and of the ten bishops whom Oliver Cromwell piously accommodated therein. . . .

"The room was—as it still is—irregularly shaped, having three doors and two windows, which last are cut nearly nine feet deep into the outer wall ; between these is a chimney-piece, projecting far into the room, and (then) surmounted with a large oil-painting. On the night in question the doors were all closed, heavy and dark cloth curtains were let down over the windows, and the only light in the room was that of two candles on the table ; I sate at the foot of the table, my son on my right hand, his mother fronting the chimney-piece, and her sister on the opposite side. I had offered a glass of wine and water to my wife, when, on putting it to her lips, she paused, and exclaimed, ' Good God ! what is that ? ' I looked up, and saw a cylindrical figure, like a glass-tube, seemingly about the thickness of my arm, and hovering between the ceiling and the table ; its contents appeared to be a dense fluid, white and pale azure, like to the gathering of a summer-cloud, and incessantly mingling within the cylinder　This lasted

about two minutes, when it began slowly to move
before my sister-in-law ; then, following the oblong-
shape of the table, *before* my son and myself ; passing
behind my wife, it paused for a moment over her right
shoulder [observe, there was no mirror opposite to her in
which she could there behold it]. Instantly she crouched
down, and with both hands covering her shoulder, she
shrieked out, 'O Christ ! It has seized me !' Even
now, while writing, I feel the fresh horror of that
moment. I caught up my chair, struck at the wainscot
behind her, rushed up-stairs to the other children's
room, and told the terrified nurse what I had seen.
Meanwhile, the other domestics had hurried into the
parlour, where their mistress recounted to them the
scene, even as I was detailing it above stairs.

"The marvel," adds Mr. Swifte, "of all this is
enhanced by the fact that *neither my sister-in-law nor
my son beheld this 'appearance.'* When I the next
morning related the night's horror to our chaplain,
after the service in the Tower church, he asked me,
might not *one* person have his natural senses deceived ? And if *one*, why might not *two* ? My
answer was, if *two*, why not two thousand ? an argu-
ment which would reduce history, secular or sacred, to
a fable."

" Our chaplain," remarked Mr. Swifte in a subsequent
communication to *Notes and Queries*, " suggested the
possibilities of some foolery having been *intromitted* at
my windows, and proposed the visit of a scientific
friend, who minutely inspected the parlour, and made

the closest investigation, but could not in any way solve the mystery."

In reply to further communications later on, the Jewel-Keeper stated that his wife did not perceive any form in the cylindrical tube, but only the cloud or vapour which both of them at once described. Her health was not affected, nor was her life terminated, as had been suggested, by the apparition which both had seen; nor could it have been, as Mr. Swifte pertinently pointed out, a fog or vapour that seized his wife by the shoulder. Finally, replying to the suggestion of " phantasmagoric agency," Mr. Swifte not only made it clear that no optical action from outside could have produced any manifestation within, through the thick curtains, but also, that the most skilful operator could not produce an appearance visible to only half the persons present, and that could bodily lay hold of one individual among them. The mystery remains unsolved.

A more tragical incident, following hard on the visitation to his own habitation, is thus alluded to by Mr. Swifte ; and although the tale has been told by many, and in many different ways, as he was so closely connected with it, it is but just that the Keeper's version should be the one accepted.

" One of the night-sentries at the Jewel Office," records our authority, " was alarmed by a figure like a huge bear issuing from underneath the jewel-room door," —as ghostly a door as ever was opened to or closed on a doomed man. " He thrust at it with his bayonet, which stuck in the door, even as my chair dinted the wainscot; he dropped in a fit, and was carried senseless to the guard-room.

"When on the morrow I saw the unfortunate soldier in the main guard-room," continues Mr. Swifte, "his fellow-sentinel was also there, and testified to having seen him on his post just before the alarm, awake and alert, and even spoken to him. Moreover, I then heard the poor man tell his own story. . . . I saw him once again on the following day, but changed beyond my recognition; in another day or two the brave and steady soldier, who would have mounted a breach or led a forlorn hope with unshaken nerves, *died* at the presence of a shadow."

Mr. George Offor, referring to this tragedy, speaks of strange noises having also been heard when the figure resembling a bear was seen by the doomed soldier.

LOWTHER HALL.

ACCORDING to Mr. J. Sullivan, in his *Cumberland and Westmoreland*, the latter county never produced a more famous spectre, or "bogie," to give the local term, than Jemmy Lowther, well known for want of a more appropriate name, as the "bad Lord Lonsdale"; infamous as a man, he was famous as a ghost. This notorious character, who is described as a modern impersonation of the worst and coarsest feudal baron ever imported into England by the Conqueror, became a still greater terror to the neighbourhood after death than he had ever been during his life. So strongly had superstitious dread of the deceased nobleman impregnated the popular mind, that it was asserted as an absolute fact, that his body was buried with difficulty, and that whilst the clergyman was praying over it it very nearly knocked him from his desk.

When placed in his grave, Lord Lonsdale's power of creating alarm was not interred with his bones. There were continual disturbances in the hall and noises in the stables; and, according to popular belief, neither men nor animals were suffered to rest. His Lordship's phantom "coach and six" is still remembered and spoken of, and still believed in by some to be heard dashing across the country. Nothing is said of the "bad lord's" shape or appearance, and it is doubtful whether the spectre has ever appeared to sight, but it has frequently made itself audible. The hall became almost uninhabitable on account of the dead man's pranks, and out of doors was, for a long time, almost equally dreaded, as even there there was constant danger of encountering the miscreant ghost. Of late years this eccentric spirit appears to have relinquished its mortal haunts, and by the peasantry is believed to have been *laid* for ever under a large rock called Wallow Crag.

LUMLEY.

MANY judicial decisions have been based upon, or influenced by, the presumed testimony of apparitions. These pages contain more than one historical record of such cases, but none more singular than that of Anne Walker, which may be found fully detailed in the works of the famous Dr. Henry More, the Platonist.

In 1680, according to Dr. More, there lived at Lumley, a village near Chester-le-Street, in the county of Durham, a widower named Walker, who was a man in good circumstances. Anne Walker, a young relation of his, kept his house, to the great scandal of the neighbourhood, and, as it proved, with but too good cause. A few weeks before this young woman expected to become a mother, Walker placed her with her aunt, one Dame Cave, in Chester-le-Street, and promised to provide both for her and her future child. One evening towards the end of November, this man, in company with Mark Sharp, an acquaintance of his, came to Dame Cave's door, and told her they had made arrangements for removing her niece to a place where she could remain in safety till her confinement was over. They would not say where it was, but as Walker bore in most respects an excellent character, he was allowed to take the young woman away with him, and he professed to have sent her away with his acquaintance Sharp into Lancashire.

"Fourteen days after," runs the story, one Graeme, a fuller who lived about six miles from Lumley, had been engaged till past midnight in his mill; and on coming down-stairs to go home, in the middle of the ground floor he saw a woman, with dishevelled hair, covered with blood, and having five large wounds on her head. Graeme, on recovering a little from his first terror, demanded what the spectre wanted; "I," said the apparition, "am the spirit of Anne Walker," and then proceeded to tell Graeme the particulars which have already been related as to her removal from her aunt's abode. "When I was sent away with Mark Sharp," it proceeded, "he slew me on such a moor," naming one that Graeme knew, "with a collier's pick, threw my body into a coal pit, and hid the pick under the bank; and his shoes and stockings, which were covered with blood, he left in a stream." The apparition proceeded to tell Graeme that he must give information of this to the nearest Justice of the Peace, and that till this was done he must look to be continually haunted.

Graeme went home very sad; he dared not bring such a charge against a man of so unimpeachable a character as Walker, and yet he as little dared to incur the anger of the spirit that had appeared to him. So, as all weak minds will do, he went on procrastinating, only he took care to leave his mill early, and while in it never to be alone. Notwithstanding this caution on his part, one night, just as it began to be dark, the apparition met him again, in a more terrible shape, and with every circumstance of indignation. Yet he did not even then

fulfil its injunction, till, on St. Thomas's Eve, as he
was walking in his garden, just after sunset, it
threatened him so effectually that in the morning he
went to a magistrate, and revealed the whole thing.

" The place was examined, the body and the pickaxe
found, and a warrant was granted against Walker and
Sharp. They were, however, admitted to bail, but in
August, 1681, their trial came on before Judge Davenport, at Durham. Meanwhile the whole circumstances
were known all over the north of England, and the
greatest interest was excited by the case. Against
Sharp the fact was strong that his shoes and stockings,
covered with blood, were found in the place where the
murder had been committed; but against Walker,
except the accounts received from the ghost, there seemed
not a shadow of evidence. Nevertheless, the judge
summed up strongly against the prisoners, the jury
found them guilty, and the judge pronounced sentence
upon them that night, a thing which was unknown in
Durham, either before or after. The prisoners were
executed, and both died professing their innocence
to the last. Judge Davenport was much agitated
during the trial, and it was believed," says the historian,
" that the spirit had also appeared to him, as if to
supply in his mind the want of legal evidence."

MANNINGTON HALL.

WHETHER Lord Orford's Norfolk residence has the general reputation of being haunted, or whether the occasion of the much-talked-of spectral illusion to Dr. Augustus Jessop is the only known instance of an apparition having appeared there, we are not in a position to state. The remarkable story, as communicated by Dr. Jessop, the well-known antiquary, to the *Athenæum* of January 1880, is as follows.

On the 10th of October 1879, Dr. Jessop drove to Lord Orford's from Norwich. It was his intention to spend some time at the Hall in examining and making extracts from various scarce works, which he had long been seeking for, and which he now learnt were in Lord Orford's library.

He arrived at Mannington at four in the afternoon, and, after some agreeable conversation, dressed for dinner. Dinner took place at seven, and was partaken of by six persons, including Dr. Jessop and his host. The conversation is declared to have been of a pleasant character, to have been chiefly concerned with artistic questions, and the experiences of men of the world, and to have never trenched upon supernatural subjects. After dinner cards were introduced, and at half-past ten, two of the guests having to leave, the party broke up. Dr. Jessop now desired to be permitted to sit up for some hours, in order to make extracts from the works already referred to. Lord Orford wished to leave a valet with his guest, but the doctor deeming that this might embarrass him, and cause him to go to bed earlier than he wished, requested to be left to his own devices. This was agreed to, the servants were dismissed, and the host and his other guests retired to their rooms, so that by eleven o'clock Dr. Jessop was the only person down-stairs.

The apartment in which he was preparing to set to work for a few hours is a large one, with a huge fire-place and a great old-fashioned chimney, and is furnished with every luxury. The library, whence Dr. Jessop had to bring such volumes as he needed, opens into this room, and in order to obtain the works he wanted he had not only to go into it, but when there to mount a chair to get down the books he required. In his very circumstantial account of the affair, the anti-quary relates that he had altogether six small volumes, which he took down from their shelves and placed in a little pile on the table, at his right hand. In a little while he was busily at work, sometimes reading, sometimes writing, and thoroughly absorbed in his occupation. As he finished with a book he placed it in front of him, and then proceeded with the next, and so on until he had only one volume of his little pile of tomes left to deal with. The antiquary being, as he states, of a chilly temperament, sat himself at a corner of the table with the fire at his left. Occasionally he rose, knocked the fire together, and stood up to warm his feet. In this manner he went on until nearly one o'clock, when he appears to have congratulated himself upon the rapid progress he had made with his task, and that after all he should get to bed by two. He got up, and wound up his watch, opened a bottle of seltzer-water, and then, reseating himself at the table, upon which were four silver candlesticks containing lighted candles, he set to work upon the last little book of the heap. What now happened must be told in Dr. Jessop's own words:—

"I had been engaged upon it about half an hour," said he, referring to the little volume, "and was just beginning to think that my work was drawing to a close, when, *as I was actually writing*, I saw a large white hand within a foot of my elbow. Turning my head, there sat a figure of a somewhat large man, with his back to the fire, bending slightly over the table, and apparently examining the pile of books that I had been at work upon. The man's face was turned away from me, but I saw his closely-cut reddish-brown hair, his ear, and shaved cheek, the eye-brow, the corner of the right eye, the side of the forehead, and the large high cheek-bone. He was dressed in what I can only describe as a kind of ecclesiastical habit of thick-corded silk, or some such material, close up to the throat, and a narrow rim or edging, of about an inch broad, of satin or velvet, serving as a stand-up collar, and fitting close to the chin. The right hand, which had first attracted my attention, was clasping, without any great pressure, the left hand; both hands were in perfect repose, and the large blue veins of the right hand were conspicuous. I remember thinking that the hand was like the hand of Velasquez's magnificent 'Dead Knight,' in the National

11 *

Gallery. I looked at my visitor for some seconds, and
was perfectly sure that he was not a reality. A thousand thoughts came crowding upon me, but not the
least feeling of alarm, or even uneasiness; curiosity
and a strong interest were uppermost. For an instant I
felt eager to make a sketch of my friend, and I looked
at a tray on my right for a pencil; then I thought,
' Up-stairs I have a sketch-book—shall I fetch it? '
There he sat, and I was fascinated; afraid not of his
staying, *but lest he should go.*

" Stopping in my writing, I lifted my left hand from
the paper, stretched it out to the pile of books, and
moved the top one. I cannot explain why I did this—
my arm passed in front of the figure, and it vanished.
I was simply disappointed and nothing more. I went
on with my writing as if nothing had happened, perhaps
for another five minutes, and had actually got to the
last few words of what I had determined to extract, when
the figure appeared again, exactly in the same place and
attitude as before. I saw the hands close to my own ; I
turned my head again to examine him more closely, and
I was framing a sentence to address him when I discovered that I did not dare to speak. *I was afraid of
the sound of my own voice.* There he sat, and there
sat I. I turned my head again to my work, and finished
writing the two or three words I still had to write. The
paper and my notes are at this moment before me, and
exhibit not the slightest tremor or nervousness. I could
point out the words I was writing when the phantom
came, and when he disappeared. Having finished my

task, I shut the book, and threw it on the table; it made a slight noise as it fell—the figure vanished.

"Throwing myself back in my chair, I sat for some seconds looking at the fire with a curious mixture of feeling, and I remember wondering whether my friend would come again, and if he did whether he would hide the fire from me. Then first there stole upon me a dread and a suspicion that I was beginning to lose my nerve. I remember yawning; then I rose, lit my bed-room candle, took my books into the inner library, mounted the chair as before, and replaced five of the volumes; the sixth I brought back and laid upon the table where I had been writing when the phantom did me the honour to appear to me. By this time I had lost all sense of uneasiness. I blew out the four candles and marched off to bed, where I slept the sleep of the just or the guilty—I know not which—but I slept very soundly."

And that is the conclusion of the story, so far as Dr. Jessop's published account goes. Numerous elucidations have been attempted by the wise, and the—otherwise; but whether hallucination, spectral illusion, or trickery, no one has been enabled to prove, and as the hero of the tale declines to proffer "explanation, theory, or inference," the affair continues to be a mystery.

MILFORD HAVEN.

IN July 1858, Mr. John Pavin Phillips, a well-known contributor to *Notes and Queries*, furnished that valuable publication with some instances of " Second Sight and Supernatural Warnings," which had occurred either to himself, or to his most immediate relatives. The whole country of Pembroke, Mr. Pavin Phillips states, is rife with tales of this class, and, indeed, he might have added, every county of the three kingdoms as well, so universal and deeply-defined is the belief in them. From the stories, for the authenticity of which this gentleman vouches, may be cited the following.

"Many years ago, seven or eight members of the family of my paternal grandfather, were seated at the door of his house on a fine summer evening, between the hours of eight and nine o'clock. The parish church and its yard are only separated from the spot by a brook and a couple of meadows. The family happened to be looking in the direction of the churchyard, when they were amazed by witnessing the advent of a funeral procession. They saw the crowd, and the coffin borne on men's shoulders come down the pathway towards the church, but the distance was too great to enable them to recognise the faces of any of the actors in the scene. As the funeral *cortége* neared the church porch, they distinctly saw the clergyman, with whom they were personally acquainted, come out in his surplice to meet the mourners, and saw him precede them into the church. In a short time they came out, and my relatives saw them go to a particular part of the yard, where they remained for a time long enough to allow the remainder of the supposed funeral rites to be performed. Greatly amazed at what he beheld, my grandfather sent over to the church to inquire who had been buried at that unusual hour. The messenger returned with the intelligence that no person had been buried during that day, nor for several days before. A short time after this a neighbour died, and was buried in the precise spot where the phantom interment was seen."

The whole of Mr. Pavin Phillips's family would appear to have possessed the faculty of ghost-seeing, or rather to have been endowed with the capability, so well known among the Scotch, of Second Sight. In another instance of this power of foreseeing events his mother was the medium. Her father, says our authority, " lived on the banks of one of the many creeks or *pills* with which the beautiful harbour of Milford Haven is indented. In front of the house is a large court, built on a quay wall to protect it from the rising tide. In this court my mother was walking one fine evening, rather more than sixty years ago " (this was written in 1858), " enjoying the moonlight and the balmy summer breeze. *The tide was out,* so that the creek was empty. Suddenly my mother's attention was aroused by hearing the sound of a boat coming up the pill; the measured dip of the oars in the water, and the noise of their revolution in the rowlocks, were distinctly audible. Presently she heard the keel of the boat grate on the gravelly beach by the side of the quay wall. Greatly alarmed, as nothing was visible, she ran into the house, and related what she had heard. A few days afterwards, the mate of an East Indiaman, which had put into Milford Haven for the purpose of undergoing repair, died on board, and his coffined corpse was brought up the pill, and landed at the very spot where my mother heard the phantom boat touch the ground."

In the next incident of supernatural foresight related by Mr. Pavin Phillips, it is in a servant of the family that the power is manifested, so that it would appear as if the locality, rather than the dwellers in it, were haunted. He relates that in the year 1838 he was on a visit to his parents, "who, at that time, resided on the spot on which my mother was born, and where she passed the latter years of her life. Within a short distance of the house stood a large walled garden, which was approached through a gate leading into a stable-yard. From underneath the garden wall bubbled a well of delicious spring water, whence the domestic offices were supplied. It was a custom of the family, in the summer time, that the water for the use of the house should be brought in late in the evening, in order that it might be cool, and it was the duty of a servant to go out with a yoke and a couple of pails to fetch the water just before the time of closing up the house for the night. One evening the girl had gone out for this purpose; the night was beautifully fine, the moon shining so brightly that the smallest object was distinctly visible. The servant had not been absent many minutes when she ran into the house without her burden, and throwing herself into a chair in a state of extreme terror, fainted away. Restoratives having been used, she recovered a little and, upon being questioned as to the cause of her alarm, she told us that as she was stooping over the well, about to fill one of her pails, she suddenly found herself in the midst of a crowd of people who were carrying a coffin, which they had set down at the gate of the stable-yard. As she had received no intimation of the approach of the con-course by any sound of footsteps, she was greatly alarmed, and as the object borne by the throng did not tend to tranquillise her nerves, she took to her heels, leaving her pails behind her. As no persuasion could induce her to return to the well, I offered to do so for her, and to ascertain the cause of her terror. When I arrived at the stable-yard, there was neither coffin nor crowd to be seen, and upon asking a neighbour, whose cottage commanded a view of the well, whether she had seen a funeral go by, she put a stop to any further inquiry by asking me 'who had ever heard of a funeral at ten o'clock at night?' To which pertinent query I could only reply by stating what the servant professed to have seen. So the matter rested for a few weeks, when there occurred an unusually high tide in Milford Haven. The water rose above the level of the ordinary springs, filling the creek, and flowing into the court in front of the house. It only ebbed when it had reached the door. The roadway at the end of the pill was impassable. A person having died on the opposite side of the inlet a few days before this, the funeral took place on the morning of the high tide; and as it was impossible to take the corpse to the parish church by the usual route, the bearers crossed the pill in a boat with the coffin and having laid it down at the gate of our stable-yard, remained there until the boat could bring over the remainder of the funeral concourse."

The last instance of this insight into the future which we shall cite from Mr. Pavin Phillips's highly suggestive and interesting communication, is the record of an incident of the character referred to which occurred to him himself, in the year 1848, upon his return home after several years' absence. "A few days after my arrival," he states, "I took a walk one morning in the yard of one of our parish churches, through which there is a right of way for pedestrians. My object was a twofold one: firstly to enjoy the magnificent prospect visible from that elevated position; and secondly, to see whether any of my friends or acquaintances who had died during my absence were buried in the locality. After gazing around me for a short time, I sauntered on, looking at one tombstone and then at another, when my attention was arrested by an altar-tomb enclosed within an iron railing. I walked up to it, and read an inscription which informed me that it was in memory of Colonel ——. This gentleman had been the assistant Poor Law Commissioner for South Wales, and while on one of his periodical tours of inspection, he was seized with apoplexy in the workhouse of my native town, and died in a few hours. This was suggested to my mind as I read the inscription on the tomb, as the melancholy event occurred during the period of my absence, and I was only made cognisant of the fact through the medium of the local press. Not being acquainted with the late Colonel ——, and never having even seen him, the circumstances of his sudden demise had long passed from my memory, and were only revived by my thus viewing his tomb. I then passed on, and shortly afterwards returned home. On my arrival my father asked me in what direction I had been walking? I replied, ' In —— churchyard, looking at the tombs, and among others I have seen the tomb of Colonel ——, who died in the workhouse.' ' That,' replied my father, ' is impossible, as there is no tomb erected over Colonel ——'s grave.' At this remark I laughed. ' My dear father,' said I, ' you want to persuade me that I cannot read. I was not aware that Colonel —— was buried in the churchyard, and was only informed of the fact by reading the inscription on the tomb.' ' Whatever you may say to the contrary,' said my father, ' what I tell you is true, there is no tomb over Colonel ——'s grave.' Astounded by the reiteration of this statement, as soon as I had dined I returned to the churchyard, and again inspected all the tombs having railings round them, and found that my father was right. There was not only no tomb bearing the name of Colonel ——, but there was no tomb at all corresponding in appearance with the one I had seen. Unwilling to credit the evidence of my own senses, I went to the cottage of an old acquaintance of

my boyhood, who lived outside of the churchyard gate,
and asked her to show me the place where Colonel ——
lay buried.   She took me to the spot, which was a green
mound, undistinguished' in appearance from the sur-
rounding graves.   Nearly two years subsequent to this
occurrence, surviving relatives erected an altar-tomb,
with a railing round it, over the last resting-place of
Colonel ——, and it was, as nearly as I could remember, an exact reproduction of the memorial of my day-
dream."

Verily, " there are more things in heaven and earth
than are dreamt of in your philosophy."

NANNAU.

NANNAU, the ancient residence of the Vaughan family,
in Merionethshire, is said to stand upon the highest
ground of any gentleman's seat in Great Britain.   In
the days of the famous Owen Glendower, this roman-
tically-situated dwelling was occupied by Howel Sele, a
first cousin of the Welsh prince.   The cousins do not
appear to have lived on friendly terms, Howel Sele
siding with the Lancastrians, whilst Glendower, it need
scarcely be remarked, was a fierce Yorkist.   Ultimately
their antagonism came to a fatal termination.   There

are several versions of the legend, but it is better to
adopt that related by Pennant because, although it does
not accord with some of the ballads on the subject, it
appears to have a historic basis. The historian states
that Glendower and Sele having long been at variance,
the Abbot of Kymmer brought them together in hopes
of reconciling them, and had, apparently, succeeded in
effecting this charitable purpose. Whilst the two cousins
were out hunting together, after their apparent reconciliation, Owen observed a doe feeding, and remarked to
Howel, who was considered the best archer of the day,
that there was a fine mark for him. Howel bent his
bow and, pretending to take aim at the doe, suddenly
turned and discharged his arrow full at Glendower's
breast :—

> Then cursed Howel's cruel shaft,
> His royal brother's blood had quaffed,
>   Alas! for Cambria's weal!
> But the false arrow glanced aside,
> For 'neath the robe of royal pride,
>   Lay plate of Milan steel.*

Fortunately for him the Welsh chieftain, as described
by the poet, had armour beneath his clothes, and therefore received no hurt. But, enraged at his kinsman's
treachery, he turned upon him fiercely, and although
Howel was fully armed, after a short conflict, slew him!
The next thing was how to dispose of the body; and
according to the ballad of the *Spirit's Blasted Tree*, by
the Rev. George Warrington, it was Madog, Glen-

* *The Demon Oak*, by Walter Thornbury.

dower's companion, who suggested for the place of
sepulture—

> A broad and blasted oak,
>   Scorched by the lightning's vivid glare,
> Hollow its stem from branch to root,
>   And all its shrivelled arms were bare.
>
> Be this, I cried, the proper grave
>   (The thought in me was deadly sin):
> Aloft we raised the hapless chief,
>   And dropped his bleeding corpse within.

After this dire catastrophe Glendower returned in
haste to his stronghold, without, of course, giving any
information to the Lord of Nannau's people. Howel
was sought for in every direction, but was nowhere to
be found. His alarmed retainers hunted through all the
recesses of the neighbouring forest, the while his sorrow-
ing wife shut herself up from all comfort in the solitude
of her gloomy castle. The years passed by, and no
tidings reached Nannau of the missing lord :—

> Yet Fancy, in a thousand shapes,
>   Bore to his home the chief once more;
> Some saw him on High Moel's top,
>   Some saw him on the winding shore.
>
> With wonder fraught, the tale went round
>   Amazement chained the hearer's tongue
> Each peasant felt his own sad loss,
>   Yet fondly o'er the story hung.
>
> Oft by the moon's pale shadowy light,
>   His aged nurse, and steward gray,
> Would lean to catch the storied sounds,
>   Or mark the flitting spirit stray.

> Pale lights on Cader's rocks were seen,
> And midnight voices heard to moan;
> 'Twas even said the Blasted Oak,
> Convulsive, heaved a hollow groan.

But still the fate of Howel Sele remained unknown to everyone save Glendower and his companion Madog. At last, after ten years of silence, Glendower died, and the partaker of the chieftain's secret was at liberty to reveal the mystery; his lord's last words being :—

> To Sele's sad widow bear the tale,
> Nor let our horrid secret rest:
> Give but his corse to sacred earth,
> Then may my parting soul be blest.

Madog hastened to obey his prince's last behest, and, as soon as events allowed, betook himself to Nannau's saddened home, and told the horrified and long-hoping wife that she was a widow indeed. The revelation was rapidly noised abroad among the retainers, and confirmation of it demanded; Madog led them to the blasted oak, which was hastily rent open, and the bleaching skeleton exposed to view :—

> Back they recoiled—the right hand still,
> Contracted, grasped the rusty sword;
> Which erst in many a battle gleamed,
> And proudly decked their slaughtered lord.
>
> They bore the corse to Vanner's shrine,
> With holy rites and prayers address'd;
> Nine white-robed monks the last dirge sang,
> And gave the angry spirit rest.

But notwithstanding the burial rites were read, and

many masses said for their dead lord, his spirit was not believed to be at rest, and almost down to the present day the fearsome peasant has dreaded to pass at night by the blasted oak, "the hollow oak of the demons." Until its fall and destruction on the 13th of July 1813, the haunted tree was an object of nocturnal dread, and the poet could truly say :—

> And to this day the peasant still
> With fear avoids the ground;
> In each wild branch a spectre sees,
> And trembles at each rising sound.

NEWSTEAD ABBEY.

LIKE so many old baronial residences, Newstead has the reputation of being haunted, and that by more than one spectre. But the name and fame of the last of the Byrons of Newstead has over-clouded and obscured all previous tenants, mortal or otherwise, and flung a pall of poetic melancholy over the whole domain that no spiritual apparitions can survive. The legends connected with Newstead are many, and descend from that mysterious maid of Saracen birth or residence, whose form and features are so frequently repeated in the ancient panel-work of the Abbey's interior, down to Lord Byron's immediate predecessor in the title and estates. "Devil Byron," as this man was called, among other wild tales connected with his name, was said to be haunted by the spirit of a sister, whom he refused to speak to for years preceding her death, in consequence of a family scandal, notwithstanding her heart-rending appeals of "Speak to mo, my lord! Do speak to me!" Ebenezer Elliott, in a ballad he wrote on this legend, introduces the apparitions of both "Devil Byron" and his sister as riding forth together in foul weather, the lady still making passionate appeals to the immovable brother to speak to her :—

Well sleep the dead : in holy ground
    Well sleeps the heart of iron;
The worm that pares his sister's cheek,
    What cares it for Byron?

Yet when her night of death comes round,
    They ride and drive together ;
And ever, when they ride and drive,
    Wilful is the weather.

On mighty winds, in spectre coach,
    Fast speeds the heart of iron ;
On spectre-steed, the spectre-dame—
    Side by side with Byron.

    .   .   .   .

Oh, Night doth love her! Oh, the clouds
    They do her form environ!
The lightning weeps—it hears her sob—
    "Speak to me, Lord Byron!"

On winds, on clouds, they ride, they drive,—
    Oh, hark, thou heart of iron!
The thunder whispers mournfully,
    "Speak to her, Lord Byron!"

Another family apparition which is said to have

haunted the old Abbey, was that of "Sir John Byron the Little, with the Great Beard." An ancient portrait of this mysterious ancestor, some few years since, was still hanging over the door of the great saloon, and was said to sometimes descend at midnight from its sombre frame, and promenade the state apartments. Indeed, this ancient worthy's visitations were not confined to night only; one young lady, on a visit to the Abbey some years ago, positively asserting that in broad daylight, the room of his chamber being open, she saw Sir John the Little sitting by the fire-place, and reading out of an old-fashioned book.

Many other apparitions have been seen about this ancient time-honoured building, and Washington Irving mentions that a young lady, Lord Byron's cousin, when she was staying at the Abbey, slept in the room next the clock, and that one night, when she was in bed, she saw a lady in white come out of the wall on one side of the room and go into the wall on the other side. Many curious noises and strange sights have been heard and seen by residents and visitors at Newstead; but the best known and most noted spectre connected with the place, and immortalised by Byron's verse, is the "Goblin Friar." The particular chamber that this spectre is supposed to especially frequent, and which is known *par excellence*, as "the Haunted Chamber," adjoins Byron's bed-room. During the poet's residence this dismal-looking room was occupied by his page, a beautiful boy, whom the scandal-loving female servants would have was a girl.

Lord Byron, and many others, not only believed in the existence of the Black Friar, but asserted that they had really seen it. It did not confine its visitations, however, to the "haunted chamber," but at night walked the cloisters and other portions of the Abbey:

> A monk arrayed
> In cowl, and beads, and dusky garb, appeared,
> Now in the moonlight, and now lapsed in shade,
> With steps that trod as heavy, yet unheard.

This apparition is the evil genius of the Byrons, and its appearance portends misfortune of some kind to the member of the family to whom it appears. Lord Byron fully believed that he beheld this apparition a short time before the greatest misfortune of his life, his ill-starred union with Miss Millbanke. Alluding to his faith in these things, he said :—

> I merely mean to say what Johnson said,
> That in the course of some six thousand years,
> All nations have believed that from the dead
> A visitant at intervals appears ;
> And what is strangest upon this strange head,
> Is that whatever bar the reason rears
> 'Gainst such belief, there's something stronger still
> In its behalf, let those deny who will.

And he thus introduces the presumed duties, as it were, of the Black Friar :—

> By the marriage-bed of their lords, 'tis said,
> He flits on the bridal eve ;
> And 'tis held as faith, to their bed of death
> He comes—but not to grieve.

12 *

When an heir is born, he is heard to mourn,
     And when aught is to befall
That ancient line, in the pale moonshine,
     He walks from hall to hall.

His form you may trace, but not his face,
     'Tis shadowed by his cowl;
But his eyes may be seen from the folds between,
     And they seem of a parted soul.

Among the numerous people who have asserted that
they saw the Black Friar was a Miss Kitty Parkins, a
relative of the poet; and she is even said to have made
a sketch of the apparition from memory.

NORTH SHIELDS : STEVENSON STREET.

THE following account, certainly one of the most
remarkable in our collection, is related upon the authority of Mrs. Crowe, who introduces it in her *Night Side
of Nature*, as having been furnished to her by the Mrs.
L. of the story, herself a lady, remarks Mrs. Crowe,
" with whose family I am acquainted."

A few years since, Mrs. L. took a furnished house
in Stevenson Street, North Shields, and she had been in
it a very few hours before she was perplexed by hearing
feet in the passage, though whenever she opened the
door she could see nobody. She went to the kitchen,

and asked the servant if she had not heard the same sound; she said she had not, but there seemed to be strange noises in the house. When Mrs. L. went to bed, she could not go to sleep for the noise of a child's rattle, which seemed to be inside her curtains. It rattled round her head, first on one side then on the other; then there were sounds of feet and of a child crying, and a woman sobbing; and, in short, so many strange noises, that the servant became frightened, and went away. The next girl Mrs. L. engaged came from Leith, and was a stranger to the place; but she had only passed a night in the house, when she said to her mistress, "This is a troubled house you've got into ma'am," and she described, amongst the rest, that she had repeatedly heard her own name called by a voice near her, though she could see nobody.

One night Mrs. L. heard a voice, like nothing human, close to her, cry, "Weep! Weep! Weep!" Then there was a sound like someone struggling for breath, and again, "Weep! Weep! Weep!" Then the gasping, and a third time, "Weep! Weep! Weep!" She stood still, and looked steadfastly on the spot whence the voice proceeded, but could see nothing; and her little boy, who held her hand, kept saying, "What is that, Mamma? What is that?" She describes the sound as most frightful. All the noises seemed to suggest the idea of childhood, and of a woman in trouble. One night, when it was crying round her bed, Mrs. L. took courage and adjured it; upon which the noise ceased for that time, but there was no answer. Mr. L. was at sea when she took the house, and when he came home, he laughed at the story at first, but soon became so convinced the account she gave was correct, that he wanted to have the boards taken up, because, from the noises seeming to hover much about one·spot, he thought perhaps some explanation of the mystery might be found. But Mrs. L. objected that if anything of a painful nature were discovered she should not be able to continue in the house; and, as she must pay the year's rent, she wished, if possible, to continue for the whole period.

She never saw anything but twice; once, the appearance of a child seemed to fall from the ceiling close to her, and then disappear; and another time she saw a child run into a closet in a room at the top of the house; and it was most remarkable that a small door in that room which was used for going out on the roof, always stood open. However often they shut it, it was opened again immediately by an unseen hand, even before they got out of the room, and this continued the whole time they were in the house; whilst night and day, someone in creaking shoes was heard pacing backwards and forwards in the room over Mr. and Mrs. L.'s heads

At length the year expired, and, to their great relief, they quitted the house; but five or six years afterwards, a person who had bought it having taken up the floor of that upper room to repair it, there was found, close to the small door above alluded to, the skeleton of a child. It was then remembered that, some years before, a gentleman of somewhat dissolute habits had resided there, and that he was supposed to have been on very intimate terms with a young woman servant who lived with him; but there had been no suspicion of anything more criminal.

OTTERY.

THE famous Dr. Abercrombie, in his *Inquiries concerning the Intellectual Powers*, adduces, as an undoubted fact, one of the most singular and inexplicable stories on record. The marvel of this story does not merely consist in the wonderful coincidence of the two concurring and synchronous dreams, but also in the persistent way with which the mother held that she had not dreamed her son appeared to her, but that he had really, if not in body then in spirit, been to her bedside and spoken to her. The account of this extraordinary affair was written by one of the persons concerned; that is to say, the Rev. Joseph Wilkins, who at the time it occurred, in 1754, he being then twenty-three years of age, was usher in a school at St. Mary Ottery, Devonshire, celebrated as the birth-place of Coleridge. Wilkins subsequently became a well-known dissenting minister.

"One night," runs his narrative, "soon after I was in bed, I fell asleep, and dreamed I was going to Lon

don. I thought it would not be much out of my way
to go through Gloucestershire, and call upon my friends
there. Accordingly, I set out, but remembered nothing
that happened by the way till I came to my father's
house; when I went to the front door and tried to open
it, but found it fast. Then I went to the back door,
which I opened and went in; but finding all the
family were in bed, I crossed the rooms only, went up-
stairs, and entered the chamber where my father and
mother were in bed. As I went by the side of the bed
on which my father lay, I found him asleep, or thought
he was so; then I went to the other side, and having just
turned the foot of the bed, I found my mother awake,
to whom I said these words: "Mother, I am going a
long journey, and am come to bid you good-bye.'
Upon which she answered in a fright, 'Oh, dear son,
thou art dead!' With this I awoke, and took no
notice of it more than a common dream, except that it
appeared to me very perfect.

"In a few days after, as soon as a letter could reach
me, I received one by post from my father; upon the
receipt of which I was a little surprised, and concluded
something extraordinary must have happened, as it was
but a short time before I had a letter from my friends,
and all were well. Upon opening it I was more surprised still, for my father addressed me as though I
were dead, desiring me, if alive, or whose ever hands the
letter might fall into, to write immediately; but if the
letter should find me living, they concluded I should
not live long, and gave this as the reason of their fears:

That on a certain night, naming it, after they were in bed, my father asleep and *my mother awake,* she heard somebody try to open the front door; but finding it fast, he went to the back door, which he opened, came in, and came directly through the rooms upstairs, and she perfectly knew it to be my step; but I came to her bedside, and spoke to her these words: 'Mother, I am going a long journey, and have come to bid you good-bye.' Upon which she answered me in a fright, 'Oh, dear son, thou art dead!'—which were the circumstances and words of my dream. But she heard nothing more, and saw nothing more; neither did I in my dream. Much alarmed she woke my father, and told him what had occurred; but he endeavoured to appease her, persuading her it was only a dream. She insisted it was no dream, for that she was as perfectly awake as ever she was, and had not the least inclination to sleep since she was in bed.

"From these circumstances I am inclined to think it was at the very same instant when my dream happened, though the distance between us was about one hundred miles; but of this I cannot speak positively. This occurred while I was at the academy at Ottery, Devon, in the year 1754, and at this moment every circumstance is fresh upon my mind. I have, since, had frequent opportunities of talking over the affair with my mother, and the whole was as fresh upon her mind as it was upon mine. I have often thought that her sensations as to this matter were stronger than mine. What may appear strange is, that I cannot remember anything remarkable happening hereupon. This is only a plain, simple narrative of a matter of fact."

As the Rev. Joseph Wilkins points out, at the conclusion of this marvellous story, nothing remarkable followed it; his own death, which his mother had so much feared was portended, did not take place until November 22, 1800, when he was in the seventieth year of his age. The *Gentleman's Magazine*, in its obituary of Wilkins, remarked that, "for liberality of sentiment, generosity of disposition, and uniform integrity, he had few equals and hardly any superiors."

OULTON HIGH HOUSE.

OULTON High House, in Suffolk, now a school, was long known as "the Haunted House." It was built in 1550 by one of the Hobarts, and still retains a fine old mantelpiece, and other curious carved work, as ancient as the house itself. It is popularly believed to have acquired its ill-omened title on account of some deed of darkness committed within its precincts. At midnight, according to tradition, a wild huntsman and his hounds, together with a white lady carrying a poisoned cup, are supposed to issue forth and go their feverish rounds.

The origin of one member of this spectral group is traced back to the reign of George II., and the story is that the owner at that period of the High House, a roystering squire, returning home from the chase unexpectedly, discovered his wife with an officer, his guest, in too familiar a friendship. High words followed, and the injured husband striking his wife's lover, the man drew his sword and drove it through his assailant's heart. The assassin and his guilty love fled, carrying away with them all the jewels and gold they could obtain possession of.

After a lapse of several years the guilty woman's daughter, who had been forgotten in the hasty departure, having grown to womanhood, was affianced to a youthful farmer of the neighbourhood. A bleak November night, on the eve of the marriage, as the happy pair were sitting together in the old hall, a carriage, black and sombre as a hearse, with closely-drawn curtains, and attended by servants clad in sable liveries, drew up to the door. These men, who were masked, rushed into the hall, and seizing the young girl, carried her off in the carriage to her unnatural mother, after having stabbed her betrothed as he vainly endeavoured to rescue her. A grave is stated to be pointed out in the cemetery at Namur, as that in which was laid the corpse of the unhappy daughter, her mother having, so it is alleged, completed the catalogue of her crimes by poisoning the hapless girl. And after that, there is little wonder that the old residence was haunted by the spectre of the wretched woman, as wife and as mother equally criminal. As to what the weird huntsman and his ghostly hounds signify, tradition is silent.

OXFORD UNIVERSITY: QUEEN'S COLLEGE.

LIKE most of the older foundations of *Alma Mater*, Queen's College has had its ghost. The Rev. Mr. More of Leyton, Essex, formerly of Queen's, Oxford, a man of veracity and learning, who died in 1778, left this story of an apparition that favoured his own college with a visit.

Mr. John Bonnell was a commoner of Queen's College, Oxford. He was remarkable in his person and gait, and, from a peculiar manner he had of holding up his gown behind, might be recognised almost as readily by his back as by his face.

"On Sunday, November the 18th, 1750, at noon, Mr. Ballard, who was then of Magdalen College, and myself," says Mr. More, "were talking together at Parker's door. I was then waiting for the sound of the trumpet for dinner, and suddenly Mr. Ballard cried out, 'Dear me, who is that coming out of your college?' I looked, and saw, as I supposed, Mr. Bonnell, and replied, 'He is a gentleman of our house, and his name is Bonnell; he comes from Stanton Harcourt.' 'Why, bless me,' said Mr. Ballard, 'I never saw such a face in all my life.' I answered slightly, 'His face is much the same as it always is; I think it is a little more inflamed and swelled than it is sometimes, perhaps he has buckled his band too tight, but I should not have observed it if you had not spoken.' 'Well,' said Mr. Ballard again, 'I never shall forget him, as long as I live'; and appeared to be much disconcerted and frightened.

"This figure I saw without any emotion or suspicion," proceeds Mr. More; "it came down the quadrangle, came out at the gate, and walked up the High Street. We followed it with our eyes till it came to Catherine Street, where it was lost.

"The trumpet then sounded, and Mr. Ballard and I parted; and I went into the hall, and thought no more of Mr. Bonnell.

"In the evening the prayers of the chapel were desired for one who was in a very sick and dangerous condition. When I came out of the chapel, I inquired of one of the scholars, James Harrison, in the hearing of several others who were standing before the kitchen fire, who it was that was prayed for, and was answered, 'Mr. Bonnell, senior.' 'Bonnell senior!' said I, with astonishment; what is the matter with him? He was very well to-day, for I saw him go out to dinner.' 'You are very much mistaken,' answered Harrison, 'for he has not been out of his bed for some days.' I then asserted more positively that I had seen him, and that a gentleman was with me who saw him too.

"This came presently to the ears of Dr. Fothergill, who had been my tutor. After supper he took me aside, and questioned me about it, and said he was very sorry I had mentioned the matter so publicly, for Mr. Bonnell was dangerously ill. I replied I was very sorry too, but I had done it innocently. The next day Mr. Bonnell died."

Mr. More states that Mr. Ballard was applied to, and bore witness to the fact that the figure he had so particularly noticed was stated to be Mr. Bonnell, who was of Queen's, and came from Stanton Harcourt. It may, also, be added that when this curious story, found among the Rev. Mr. More's papers at his decease, was published in the *Gentleman's Magazine*, and other contemporary publications, the particulars were confirmed, in various ways, by persons referred to in the story. As the account of an apparition or wraith of a person on the point of death, seen by more than one individual, it is by no means unique in literary records.

PEELE CASTLE.

IN no portion of the British kingdom are legends more rife, and superstitions more tenacious, than in the Isle of Man. Of the various romantic ruins which bedeck the island, and around which tradition has flung its ivy-like tendrils, none are more picturesque or more closely connected with mediæval myths than Peele Castle. Among other marvellous stories told of the supernatural beings which haunt its precincts is the following, to be found in the pages of Waldron, whose account of the island is an inexhaustible mine of Manx legendary and folk lore.

"An apparition, which they call the Manthe Doog, in the shape of a shaggy spaniel, was stated to haunt the Castle in all parts, but particularly the guard-chamber, where the dog would constantly come and lie down by the fire at candle-light. The soldiers lost much of their terror by the frequency of the sight; yet, as they believed it to be an evil spirit, waiting for an opportunity to injure them, that belief kept them so far in order, that they refrained from swearing and discourse in its presence, and none chose to be left alone with such an insidious enemy. Now, as the Manthe Doog used to come out and return by the passage through the church, by which also somebody must go to deliver the keys every night to the Captain, they continued to go together, he whose turn it was to do that duty being accompanied by the next in rotation.

"But one of the soldiers, on a certain night, being much disguised in liquor, would go with the key alone, though it really was not his turn. His comrades in vain endeavoured to dissuade him; he said he wanted the Manthe Doog's company, and he would try whether he were dog or devil; and then, after much profane talk, he snatched up the keys and departed. Some time afterwards a great noise alarmed the soldiers, but none of them would venture to go and see what was the cause. When the adventurer returned, he was struck with horror and speechless, nor could he even make such signs as might give them to understand what had happened to him, but he died, with distorted features, in violent agony. After this none would go through the passage, which was soon closed up, and the apparition was never more seen in the castle."

"This accident happened about three-score years since," says Waldron, "and I heard it attested by several, but especially by an old soldier, who assured me he had seen it (*i.e.* the Manthe Doog), oftener than he had then hairs on his head."

PLYMOUTH.

AMONGST the innumerable multitude of buildings which have the reputation of being haunted, it will be noted that by far the larger number are haunted by strange noises and mysterious sounds only, but few of them really attaining to the dignity of being visited by visible beings. Some of the places, however, which have had the character of being disturbed by unusual and unaccountable noises are very interesting from the suggestiveness of these noises: in the following account, for instance, and indeed in many others, the ghostly but invisible visitants appear to be condemned to return to the occupations they followed before they shuffled off the mortal coil, and to resume, after their incorporeal fashion, the labours of their past life.

The mother of the famous premier, George Canning,

after the death of her first husband, became an actress, and married an actor. Becoming a widow for the second time, she married a third husband, named Hunn, and under his name appears to have acted in the provinces. Among other provincial towns Mrs. Hunn visited Plymouth, but previous to her arrival there she had requested Mr. Bernard, who was in some way connected with the theatre there, to procure lodgings for her in the town. When Mrs. Hunn arrived, she was met by Mr. Bernard with the intimation that if she were not afraid of a ghost, he could obtain very comfortable lodgings for her at a very low rate, " for there is," said he, " a house belonging to our carpenter that is reported to be haunted, and nobody will live in it. If you like to have it, you may, and for nothing, I believe, for he is so anxious to get a tenant; only you must not let it be known that you do not pay any rent for it."

Mrs. Hunn, alluding to theatrical apparitions, said it would not be the first time she had had to do with a ghost, and that she was very willing to encounter this one ; so she had her luggage taken into the house in question, and the bed prepared. At her usual hour, she sent her maid and her children to bed, and curious to see if there was any foundation for the rumour she had heard, she seated herself with a couple of candles and a book, to watch the event. Beneath the room she occupied was the carpenter's workshop, which had two doors ; the one which opened into the street was barred and bolted within; the other, a smaller one, opening into the passage, was only on the latch ; and the house was, of course, closed for the night. She had read somewhat more than half an hour, when she perceived a noise issuing from this lower apartment, which sounded very much like the sawing of wood ; presently, other such noises as usually proceed from a carpenter's workshop were added, till, by-and-bye, there was a regular concert of knocking and hammering, and sawing and planing, &c.; the whole sounding like half a dozen busy men in full employment. Being a woman of considerable courage, Mrs. Hunn resolved, if possible, to penetrate the mystery ; so, taking off her shoes, that her approach might not be heard, with her candle in her hand, she very softly opened her door and descended the stairs, the noise continuing as loud as ever, and evidently proceeding from the workshop, till she opened the door, when instantly all was silent—all was still—not a mouse was stirring ; and the tools and the wood, and everything else, lay as they had been left by the workmen when they went away. Having examined every part of the place, and satisfied herself that there was nobody there, and that nobody could get into it, Mrs. Hunn ascended to her room again, beginning almost to doubt her own senses, and question with herself whether she had really heard the noise or not, when it re-commenced, and continued, without intermission, for about half an hour. She however went to bed, and the next day told nobody what had occurred, having determined to watch another night before mentioning the affair to anyone. As, however, this strange scene was acted over again, without her being able to discover the cause of it, she now mentioned the circumstance to the owner of the house and to her friend Mr. Bernard; and the former, who would not believe it, agreed to watch with her, which he did. The noise began as before, and he was so horror-struck that, instead of entering the workshop as she wished him to do, he rushed into the street. Mrs. Hunn continued to inhabit the house the whole summer, and when referring afterwards to the adventure, she observed that use was second nature; and that she was sure, if any night these ghostly carpenters had not pursued their visionary labours, she should have been quite frightened lest they should pay her a visit up-stairs.

POWIS CASTLE.

ACCORDING to Camden this ancient stronghold was formerly called "Kasteth Koch," or Red Castle, on account of the colour of the stone with which it was built. It stands on a rocky elevation in the midst of a well-wooded park, and despite the restoration which it has undergone at the hands of Sir Robert Smirke is not considered "a thing of beauty." If the outside be irregular in style the interior is heavy and gloomy, and thoroughly appropriate for the localisation of ghostly legends. It possesses, among other interesting relics,

3 *

a state chamber, still maintained in the exact condition
it was in when prepared for the reception of Charles I.
Since the time of Queen Elizabeth, when the surround-
ing estate was purchased by the Heberts, Powis Castle
has been the seat of the Earls Powis. There are
naturally various legends connected with this time-
honoured dwelling, one being that the lake in the Castle
park, from which the adjacent town of Welshpool takes
its name, " shall sometime overflow and deluge the
town." But there is also a well-authenticated and most
circumstantial ghost story of Powis Castle, for the
record of which we are indebted to the Autobiography of
Thomas Wright, of Birkenshaw.

In 1780, it became known to the townsfolk of Welshpool, that there was living amongst them a certain poor
unmarried woman who had conversed with the Castle
ghost, and that it had confided a great secret to her.
The woman thus selected for this alleged trust was a
member of the Methodist Society, and "had become
serious under their ministry." Mr. John Hampson, a
well-known preacher amongst the Wesleyan Methodists,
being desirous of probing this strange story to the core,
sent for the woman, and earnestly besought her to tell
him the whole truth about the affair. She promised to
give him as exact an account as she possibly could, and
then proceeded with the following narration, to the
correctness of which many persons could bear witness.
She described herself as a poor woman who obtained a
livelihood by spinning hemp and line, and stated that it
was customary for the farmers and gentlemen of the

district to grow enough hemp or line in their fields for their own home-consumption, and as she was a good hand at spinning, she was accustomed to go from house to house to inquire for work. It was the custom at houses where she stayed, to provide her with meat and drink, and if necessary with lodging, whilst she was thus employed, and when she left to make her some little present.

One day she chanced to call at Earl Powis's country residence, Red Castle as it was called, to inquire for work, according to custom. The "quality," as she termed the family, were at this time in London, but had, as usual, left the steward and his wife, with certain other servants, to take charge of the place during their absence. The steward's wife set her to work, and in the evening told her that she must stay all night with them, as they had more work for her to do next day. When it was time to go to bed, three of the servants, each carrying a lighted candle in her hand, conducted her to the room she was to sleep in. It was an apartment on the ground floor, with a boarded floor and two sash windows, and was grandly furnished, with a handsome bedstead in one corner of it. They had made up a good fire for her, and had placed a chair and table before it, with a large lighted candle upon the table. They informed her that that was to be her bed-room, and that she might go to bed whenever she pleased. They then wished her a good night, and all withdrew together, pulling the door quickly after them, so as to hasp the spring-sneck in the brass lock that was upon it.

When the servants had thus hastily departed, the poor spinster gazed around at the grand furniture, and was in no slight astonishment that they should put such a person as she was in so fine a room and so comfortable a bed, with all the conveniences of fire, chair, table, and candle. After having made a survey of the place, she sat down, and took out of her pocket a small Welsh Bible which she always carried about with her, and in which she always read a chapter, chiefly in the New Testament, before she said her prayers and retired to rest.

Whilst the woman was reading she heard the door open, and turning her head, was astonished to see a gentleman enter the room; he wore a gold-laced hat and waistcoat, with coat and the rest of his attire to correspond. He walked down by the sash window to the corner of the room, and then returned. When he came, as he returned to the first window, the bottom of which was nearly breast high, he rested his elbow on the bottom of the window and the side of his face upon the palm of his hand, and stood in that leaning posture for some time, with his side partly towards her. She looked at him earnestly to see if she knew him, but although, from her frequent intercourse with them, she had a personal knowledge of all the family and its retainers, he appeared to be a perfect stranger to her. She supposed, afterwards, that he stood in this manner to encourage her to speak; but as she did not utter a word, after some little time he walked off, pulling the door to after him as the servants had done previously. She began now to be much alarmed, concluding it to be an apparition, and that they had put her in that grand room because it was haunted. And that was really the case.

For some long time past the room had been so disturbed that nobody could sleep in it peaceably, and as she passed for a very serious woman, the servants conceived the fine project of putting the poor Methodist and the spirit together, in order to see what the result would be.

Startled at the thought that it was an apparition she had seen, the woman rose from her chair, and kneeling down by the bedside, began saying her prayers. Whilst she was praying the apparition came in again, walked round the room, and came close behind her. She now endeavoured to speak, but when she attempted it she was so agitated that she could not utter a word. The apparition walked out of the room again, pulling the door after it as it had done before. She begged that God would strengthen her, and not suffer her to be tried beyond what she was able to bear; she now recovered her spirits somewhat, and thought she felt more confidence and resolution, and determined if it came in again she would speak to it if possible. Presently it came in again, walked round the room, and came behind her as before. She turned her head and said,—

" Pray, Sir, who are you, and what do you want? "

It lifted its finger, and said,—

"Take up the candle and follow me, and I will tell you."

She got up, took up the candle, and followed it out

of the room. It led her through a long boarded passage till they got to the door of another room, which it opened and went into. It was a very small room, or what might be called a large closet.

"As the room was small, and I believed him to be a spirit," said she, in her recital of the affair, "I stopped at the door; he turned and said,—

"'Walk in; I will not hurt you.'

"So I walked in. Then he said,—

"'Observe what I do.'

"I said, 'I will.'

"He stooped and tore up one of the boards of the floor, and there appeared under it a box with an iron handle in the lid. He said,—

"'Do you see that box?'

"I said, 'Yes, I do.'

"He then stepped to one side of the room, and showed me a crevice in the wall, where he said a key was hid that would open it. He said,—

"'This box and key must be taken out and sent to the Earl in London'; naming the Earl and his place of residence in the metropolis. He said,—

"'Will you see it done?'

"I said, 'I will do my best to get it done.'

"He said, 'Do, and I will trouble the house no more.'"

It then walked out of the room and left her. As soon as the woman saw that the apparition had departed, she went to the room-door and set up a loud shout. The steward and his wife, together with all the other servants, ran to her immediately; they were all clinging to one another and carrying lights. It seems that they had all been waiting to see the issue of the interview between the woman and the apparition. They asked her what was the matter. She then told them all that had taken place, and showed them the box. The steward dare not meddle with it, but his wife was of a more courageous temperament, and with the assistance of the other servants, tugged it out, and found the key in the place indicated by the apparition. The woman stated that, by the way in which they lifted it, it appeared to be pretty heavy, but that she did not see it opened, and, therefore, did not know what it contained; whether money or writings of importance to the family, or both. The servants took it away with them, and the woman averred that she then went to bed and slept peaceably till the morning.

It appeared, from what was subsequently learnt, that the box and its contents were sent to the Earl in London, together with an account of how it was discovered and by whom. The Earl immediately sent down orders to his steward to inform the poor woman, who had been the means of the discovery, that if she would come and reside in his family she should be comfortably provided for for the remainder of her days; or, if she did not care to reside constantly with them, if she would let him know when she wanted assistance, she should be liberally supplied at his lordship's expense as long as she lived.

And according to the account related by Mr. John

Hampson, it was a fact well known in the neighbourhood that the woman had been supplied from the Earl's
family ever since the time when the affair was said to
have happened.

RAINHAM.

RAINHAM, the seat of the Marquis Townshend, in Norfolk, has long been noted for its ghost known as "the
Brown Lady." Mrs. Crowe, and many other writers on
apparitions and kindred themes, have alluded to the
circumstance of this family residence being haunted by
a spectral woman, but their references are very slight
and the particulars they give exceedingly meagre. Mrs.
Crowe, indeed, mentions that many persons have seen
"the Brown Lady," and speaks of a guest who one day
inquired of his host, "Who was the lady in brown that
he had met frequently on the stairs?" But the most
circumstantial account of the appearance of this apparition would appear to be that given by Lucia C. Stone,
in *Rifts in the Veil*. This record she states she received from an eye-witness, and as a proof of its
authenticity draws attention to the fact that the names
of all parties concerned are given in full. The time of
the incidents, however, cannot be given any nearer than
between 1835 and 1849.

According to this narrative, a large party had assem-

bled at Rainham, in order to pass the Christmas there.
Lord and Lady Charles Townshend were the host and
hostess on this occasion, and among the assembled
guests were Colonel and Mrs. Loftus, and Miss Page, a
cousin of the latter. Colonel Loftus was a brother of
Lady Charles and cousin to Lord Charles, being a
Townshend on his mother's side.

There was a tradition in the Townshend family that
at certain intervals the apparition of a lady attired in
brown brocade had been seen flitting about the building; but nothing had occurred for some long time past,
and the old stories respecting the hauntings had been
well-nigh forgotten.

One night Colonel Loftus and a gentleman named
Hawkins sat up rather late over a game of chess; they
went up-stairs, and were bidding each other "good-
night," when Mr. Hawkins exclaimed, "Loftus, who is
that standing at your sister's door? How strangely
she is dressed." Colonel Loftus, who was near-sighted,
put up his glass and followed the figure, which went on
for some little distance, when he lost sight of it. A
second night she appeared to him, and this time, to
prevent her escape, he went up a staircase which would
bring him face to face with her. There, in a full light,
stood a stately lady in her rich brocade, a sort of coif
on her head, the features clearly defined; but where
there should have been eyes were nothing but dark
hollows.

"These were the two appearances he described to
me," says Lucia Stone, "and he sketched her after-

wards. I saw the sketch just after his return from
Rainham. The lady was seen by several others, and I
have heard the stories, but not from their own lips, so
I forbear to give them ; but perhaps I should mention
that the cousin of Mrs. Loftus, Miss Page, whom I
knew very intimately, asked Lord Charles if he too
believed in the apparition? He replied, ' I cannot but
believe, for she ushered me into my room last night.' "

The servants were frightened, and one after the other
gave warning. Lord Charles Townshend, thinking that,
perhaps, after all, it might be a trick on the part of
someone in the house, had various alterations made in
the way of bolts, locks, and so forth. This proving
useless, he engaged some of the London police force to
come down, and made them assume his livery ; but they
were unable to discover anything during their stay at
Rainham.

There does not seem to be any known legend connected with the appearance of the apparition of " the
Brown Lady."

RAMHURST MANOR-HOUSE.

WHEN the complicated developments of the tale connected with this Kentish Manor-house are known, it
must be acknowledged that the affair is one of the most
mysterious on record. Robert Dale Owen, from whose

singular work, *Footfalls on the Boundary of Another World*, this strange story is extracted, does not furnish the actual names of the ladies from whom he derived his information about the haunting of Ramhurst, but veils their identity under initials; and as we have no other authority for the account than his, it will be necessary, in this instance to follow his example.

Ramhurst Manor-house, it must be premised, is an ancient residence near Leigh, in Kent. In October 1857, and for several subsequent months, it was occupied by Mrs. R——, the wife of an English officer of high rank, and her servants. From the time this lady first occupied the place she, and every inmate, were disturbed by knockings, unaccountable voices, and the sounds of mysterious footsteps. The strange voices were generally, but not invariably, heard proceeding from an unoccupied room, and were sometimes as of someone talking in a loud tone, sometimes as if some person were reading aloud, and occasionally as if screaming. The servants were, as may be imagined, in a great state of terror, and although they did not see anything, the cook one day informed Mrs. R—— that in broad day she heard the rustle of a silk-dress close behind her, and which seemed to touch her; but on turning suddenly round, thinking it was her mistress, she could not see anyone, much to her surprise and horror. Mrs. R——'s brother, a young officer addicted to field sports, and quite incredulous on the subject of ghostly visitations, was much disturbed and annoyed by these strange voices, which he asserted must be those of his sister and a lady friend of hers sitting up chatting at night. Twice, when a voice which he considered to resemble his sister's rose to a scream, he rushed into her bed-room, between two and three o'clock in the morning, with a gun in his hand, but only to find her sleeping quietly.

"On the second Saturday in the above month of October," says our authority, "Mrs. R—— drove over to the railway station at Tunbridge, to meet her friend Miss S——, whom she had invited to spend some weeks with her. This young lady had been in the habit of seeing apparitions, at times, from early childhood.

"When, on their return, at about four o'clock in the afternoon, they drove up to the entrance of the Manorhouse, Miss S—— perceived on the threshold the appearance of two figures, apparently an elderly couple, habited in the costume of a former age. They appeared as if standing on the ground. She did not hear any voice, and not wishing to render her friend uneasy, she made at that time no remark to her in connection with this apparition.

"She saw the appearance of the same figures, in the same dress, several times within the next ten days, sometimes in one of the rooms of the house, sometimes in one of the passages—always by daylight. They appeared to her surrounded by an atmosphere nearly of the colour usually called 'neutral tint.' On the third occasion they spoke to her, and stated that they had been husband and wife, that in the former days they had possessed and occupied that Manor-house, and that their name was *Children*. They appeared sad and downcast, and, when Miss S—— inquired the cause of their melancholy, they replied that they had idolized this property of theirs; that their pride and pleasure had centred in its possession; that its improvement had engrossed their thoughts; and it troubled them to know that it had passed away from their family, and to see it now in the hands of careless strangers."

To Miss S——, the ghost-seer, the voices of the apparitions were not only perfectly audible, but also intelligible; but it does not appear certain, so far as our record goes, that others who heard the conversing were enabled to comprehend what was said by the spirits. Meanwhile, Mrs. R——, thinking that something unusual had occurred to her friend in connection with the household disturbances, questioned her on the subject, and was then informed by Miss S—— of what she had seen and heard from the apparitions. Hitherto Mrs. R——, though her rest had been disturbed by the frequent noises, had not seen anything, nor, indeed, had anyone save Miss S——; but about a month after the latter lady had had the interview with the spectres styling themselves Mr. and Mrs. Children, they made another optical manifestation.

One day, Mrs. R——, who had ceased to expect the appearance of the apparitions to herself, was hurriedly dressing for dinner, " her brother," to cite from Owen, " who had just returned from a day's shooting, having called to her in impatient tones that dinner was served and that he was quite famished. At the moment of completing her toilet, and as she hastily turned to leave her bed-chamber, not dreaming of anything spiritual, there in the doorway stood the same female figure Miss S—— had described, identical in appearance and in costume, even to the old point-lace on her brocaded silk dress, while beside her on the left, but less distinctly visible, was the figure of her husband. They uttered no sound; but above the figure of the lady, as if written in phosphoric light in the dusk atmosphere that surrounded her, were the words '*Dame Children,*' together with some other words, intimating that, having never aspired beyond the joys and sorrows of this world, she had remained 'earth-bound.'

"These last words Mrs. R—— scarcely paused to decipher; for a renewed appeal from her brother, as to whether they were to have any dinner that day, urged her forward. The figure, filling up the doorway, remained stationary. There was no time for hesitation, she closed her eyes, rushed through the apparition and into the dining-room, throwing up her hands and exclaiming to Miss S——, 'Oh! my dear, I've walked through Mrs. Children!'"

This was the only time Mrs. R—— saw anything of the apparitions during her residence in the old Manor-house, nor do they seem to have appeared again to anyone there, save Miss S——. Mrs. R—— had her bedroom not only lit up by a blazing fire, but also by candles, whilst a lighted lamp was kept burning in the corridor. Miss S——, however, appears to have

been honoured with subsequent interviews by the apparitions, and from her conversations with them learnt
that the husband's name was Richard, and that he had
died in 1753. She remarked that the costumes in
which they appeared "were of the period of Queen
Anne or one of the early Georges, she could not be
sure which, as the fashions in both were similar."

Deeply impressed with the mystery that appertained
to the old Manor-house, Mr. R—— endeavoured to
elucidate it by making inquiries among the servants
and in the neighbourhood, but without success. No one
knew that the house had ever been owned or inhabited
by persons of the name of " Uhildren," although a nurse
in the family, Sophy O——, had spent all her life in the
vicinity. About four months afterwards, and when her
mistress had given up all hopes of unravelling the
mystery, Sophy went home for a holiday to her father's
at Riverhead, near Sevenoaks. During her visit she
called on a sister-in-law, an old woman of seventy, who
fifty years previous had been housemaid in a family
residing in Ramhurst Manor-house. Sophy asked her
old sister-in-law if she had ever heard of a family
named Children living at the Manor, and was informed
that there was no such family there in her time, but
she recollected having been informed by an old man,
that in his boyhood he had assisted to keep the hounds
of the Childrens who were then residing at Ramhurst.
On her return Sophy communicated this information to
Mrs. R——, who thus learnt that a family named
Children had once really occupied the Manor-house,

14

but beyond that she was unable to learn anything about them.

In December 1858, Robert Dale Owen, being in the company of the two ladies referred to, Mrs. R—— and Miss S——, learnt all the particulars of the haunting and the apparitions already given. Having accepted an invitation to spend Christmas week with some friends living near Sevenoaks, he determined to prosecute further inquiries about the haunted Manor, and its former inhabitants in the neighbourhood. He sought out Sophy and questioned her closely about the disturbances at the Manor-house during Mrs. R——'s residence, but was enabled to elicit little more than confirmatory evidence of what the reader knows already. Nor did his inspection of the churches and graveyards of Leigh and Tunbridge afford him any fresh information about the Children family, save that a certain George Children left, in the year 1718, a weekly gift of bread to the poor, and that another George Children, his descendant, who had died about forty years previous, and who had not resided at Ramhurst, had a marble tablet in Tunbridge Church erected to his memory.

Thus far Mr. Owen had not obtained any further particulars of much value, but having been referred to a neighbouring clergyman, by him he was lent a document that contained the following extract from the *Hasted Papers*, which are preserved in the British Museum, and may be consulted there :—

" George Children . . . who was High Sheriff of

Kent in 1698, died without issue in 1718, and by will devised the bulk of his estate to *Richard* Children, eldest son of his late uncle, William Children, of Hedcorn, and his heirs.   This Richard Children, *who settled himself at Ramhurst*, in the Parish of Leigh, married Anne, daughter of John Saxby, in the parish of Leeds, by whom he had issue four sons and two daughters," &c.

Thus Mr. Owen had ascertained that the first of the Children family who had occupied Ramhurst as a residence was named Richard, and that he settled there in the early part of George I.'s reign, but he was still ignorant of the date of his death, which, it will have been noted, was given by the apparition as 1753. Being referred by an antiquarian friend to Hasted's *History of Kent*, published in 1778, he found the following paragraph :—

" In the eastern part of the parish of Lyghe (now Leigh), near the river Medway, stands an ancient mansion, called Ramhurst, once reputed a manor, and held of the honour of Gloucester. . . . It continued in the Culpepper family for several generations. . . . It passed by sale into that of Saxby, and Mr. William Saxby conveyed it by sale to Children.   Richard Children, Esq., resided here, *and died possessed of it in* 1753, aged eighty-three years.   He was succeeded in it by his eldest son, John Children, of Tunbridge, Esq.," &c.

" Thus I verified," remarks Robert Dale Owen, " the last remaining particular, the date of Richard Children s death.   It appears from the above, also, that Richard

14 *

Children was the *only* representative of the family who lived and died at Ramhurst; his son John being designated not as of Ramhurst, but as of Tunbridge. From the private memoir above referred to, I had previously ascertained that the family seat after Richard's time was Ferox Hall, near Tunbridge.

"It remains to be added that in 1816, in consequence of events reflecting no discredit on the family, they lost all their property, and were compelled to sell Ramhurst, which has since been occupied, though a somewhat spacious mansion, not as a family residence, but as a farm-house. I visited it, and the occupants assured me that nothing worse than rats or mice disturb it now."

ROCHESTER.

BAXTER's *Certainty of the World of Spirits* contains one of the most marvellous and, apparently, best authenticated stories of modern miracles extant. If it be accepted as fact it will be a difficult matter to doubt any supernatural incident merely on account of its inexplicability. The story was sent to Baxter by the Rev. Thomas Tilson, the minister of Aylesford, near Maidstone, in Kent, within five weeks of the event to which it referred happening; the narrator was on the spot, and therefore had every opportunity of disproving or confirming the statements made; whilst the names and residences of the witnesses are given, together with the exact time and place of the occurrences to which they testify. It would be difficult to adduce any historic event with, apparently, better testimony of its accuracy. Mr. Tilson's story, as written out for Baxter, is this :—

"Mary, the wife of John Goffe, of Rochester, being afflicted with a long illness, removed to her father's house at West Malling, which is about nine miles distant from her own. There she died June the 4th, this present year, 1691.

"The day before her departure she grew very impatiently desirous to see her two children, whom she had left at home to the care of a nurse. She prayed her husband to hire a horse, for she must go home and die with the children. When they persuaded her to the contrary, telling her she was not fit to be taken out of her bed, nor able to sit on horseback, she entreated them, however, to try. 'If I cannot sit,' said she, 'I will lie all along upon the horse; for I must go to see my poor babes.'

"A minister who lived in the town was with her at ten o'clock that night, to whom she expressed good hopes in the mercies of God, and a willingness to die. 'But,' said she, 'it is my misery that I cannot see my children.' Between one and two o'clock in the morning she fell into a trance. One, widow Turner, who watched with her that night, says that her eyes were open and fixed and her jaw fallen. She put her hand upon her mouth and nostrils, but could perceive no breath. She thought her to be in a fit, and doubted whether she were dead or alive.

"The next morning this dying woman told her mother that she had been at home with her children. 'That is impossible,' said the mother, 'for you have been in bed all the while.' 'Yes,' replied the other, 'but I was with them last night when I was asleep.'

"The nurse at Rochester, widow Alexander by name, affirms, and says she will take her oath on't before a magistrate, and take the sacrament upon it, that a little while before two o'clock that morning she saw the likeness of the said Mary Goffe come out of the next chamber (where the elder child lay in a bed by itself), the door being left open, and stood by her bedside for about a quarter of an hour; the younger child was there lying by her. Her eyes moved and her mouth went, but she said nothing. The nurse, moreover, says that she was perfectly awake; it was then daylight, being one of the longest days in the year. She sat up in her bed and looked steadfastly upon the apparition. In that time she heard the bridge clock strike two, and a while after said, 'In the name of the Father, who art thou.' Thereupon the appearance removed and went away. She slipped on her clothes and followed, but what became on't she cannot tell. Then, and not before, she began to be grievously affrighted, and went out of doors and walked upon the wharf (the house is just on the river-side) for some hours, only going in now and then to look to the children. At five o'clock she went to a neighbour's house and knocked at the door, but they would not rise. At six she went again; then they rose and let her in. She related to them all that had passed; they would persuade her she was mistaken or dreamt. But she confidently affirmed, 'If ever I saw her in all my life, I saw her this night.'

"One of those to whom she made the relation (Mary the wife of John Sweet), had a messenger come from Malling that forenoon, to let her know her neighbour Goffe was dying and desired to speak with her. She went over the same day, and found her just departing. The mother, among other discourse, related to her how much her daughter had longed to see the children, and said she had seen them. This brought to Mrs. Sweet's mind what the nurse had told her that morning; for till then she had not thought to mention it, but disguised it, rather, as the woman's disturbed imagination.

"The substance of this I had related to me," says Mr. Tilson, "by John Carpenter, the father of the deceased, the next day after her burial, July the 2nd. I fully discoursed the matter with the nurse and two neighbours, to whose house she went that morning. Two days after, I had it from the mother, the minister that was with her in the evening, and the woman who sat up with her that last night. They all agree in the same story, and everyone helps to strengthen the other's testimony. They appear to be sober, intelligent persons, far enough off from designing to impose a cheat upon the world, or to manage a lie; and what temptation they could lie under for so doing I cannot conceive."

And thus ends this incomprehensible affair.

RUSHEN CASTLE.

To mention many of the curious supernatural legends connected with the Castle of Rushen, in Castletown, Isle of Man, might only excite ridicule, and yet belief in the wildest of them still lingers in the vicinity. Among other terrifying apparitions which still, or until very recently did haunt this ancient stronghold is that of a woman who, some years ago, was executed for the murder of her child. The quantity and quality of the testimony adduced in corroboration of the appearance of this spectre is absolutely startling, many persons of good position and acknowledged veracity giving confirmatory evidence. Their united testimony is to the effect that an apparition of the executed woman frequently passes in and out of the castle gates when they are shut, in the presence of the sentinels and other spectators. Indeed, it is alleged that the sight of this phantom has become quite familiar to them; but no one has yet had the courage to speak to it, therefore it has not been enabled to unfold the object of its appearance.

In his quaint *Description* of the island, Waldron gives the following curious tradition as connected with the venerable Manx Castle, in which, he states, there is an apartment that has never been opened in the memory of man. The persons belonging to the castle are very cautious in giving any reason for it, it is alleged, but the natives unconnected with the castle aver that there is something supernatural in it, and tell you that formerly the place was inhabited by giants, who were dislodged by Merlin, and such as were not driven away are spell-bound beneath the castle. In proof of this they relate a very strange story which is told by Waldron in these terms :—

"They say there are a great many fine apartments under ground, exceeding in magnificence any of the upper rooms. Several men of more than ordinary courage have, in former times, ventured down to explore the secrets of this subterranean dwelling-place, but none of them ever returned to give an account of what they saw. It was, therefore, judged expedient that all the passages to it should be continually shut, that no more might suffer by their temerity. About some fifty or fifty-five years since a person possessed of uncommon boldness and resolution begged permission to visit these dark abodes. He at length obtained his request, went down, and returned by the help of a clue of pack-thread which he took with him, which no man before had ever done, and brought this amazing discovery :—That after he had passed through a great number of vaults, he came into a long narrow place, which, the further he penetrated, he perceived that he went more and more on a descent, till having travelled, as near as he could guess, for the space of a mile, he began to see a gleam of light which, though it seemed to come from a vast distance, was the most delightful object he ever beheld. Having at length arrived at the end of that lane of darkness, he perceived a large and magnificent house, illuminated with many candles, whence proceeded the light he had seen. Having, before he began the expedition, well fortified himself with brandy, he had courage enough to knock at the door, which, on the third knock, was opened by a servant, who asked him what he wanted. ' I would go as far as I can,' replied our adventurer; ' be so kind, therefore, as to direct me how to accomplish my design, for I see no passage but that dark cavern through which I came.' The servant told him he must go through that house, and accordingly led him through a long entry and out at a back door. He then walked a considerable way, till he beheld another house more magnificent than the first, and, all the windows being open, he discovered innumerable lamps burning in every room.

" Here also he designed to knock, but had the curiosity to step on a little bank which commanded a view of a low parlour, and looking in, he beheld a vast table in the middle of the room, and on it, extended at full length, a man, or rather monster, at least fourteen feet long, and ten or twelve round the body. This prodigious fabric lay as if sleeping, with his head upon a book, with a sword by him, answerable to the hand which he supposed made use of it. The sight was more terrifying to our traveller than all the dark and dreary mansions through which he had passed. He resolved, therefore, not to attempt an entrance into a place inhabited by persons of such monstrous stature, and made the best of his way back to the other house,

when the same servant who reconducted him informed
him that if he had knocked at the second door he would
have seen company enough, but could never have returned, on which he desired to know what place it was,
and by whom possessed. The other replied that these
things were not to be revealed. He then took his leave,
and by the same dark passage got into the vaults, and
soon afterwards once more ascended to the light of the
sun."

Such is the marvellous legend told by the historian
of Manxland, and he adds to it the statement that
" whoever seems to disbelieve it is looked on as a person
of weak faith," by the islanders, of course.

SARRATT, HERTFORDSHIRE.

IN that most curious collection of stories by Mrs.
Crowe, styled *The Night Side of Nature*, is recounted a
marvellous narrative, received from a professional gentleman resident in London ; his relation is to this
effect :—

" I was, some few years since, invited to pass a day
and night at the house of a friend in Hertfordshire, with
whom I was intimately acquainted. His name was
B——, and he had formerly been in business as a
saddler, in Oxford Street, where he had realised a hand-

some fortune, and had now retired to enjoy his *otium cum dignitate* in the rural and beautiful village of Sarratt.

"It was a gloomy Sunday, in the month of November, when I mounted my horse for the journey, and there was so much appearance of rain, that I should certainly have selected some other mode of conveyance had I not been desirous of leaving the animal in Mr. B——'s straw-yard for the winter. Before I got as far as St. John's Wood, the threatening clouds broke, and by the time I reached Watford I was completely soaked. However, I proceeded, and arrived at Sarratt before my friend and his wife had returned from church. The moment they did so, they furnished me with dry clothes, and I was informed that we were to dine at the house of Mr. D——, a very agreeable neighbour. I felt some little hesitation about presenting myself in such a costume, for I was decked out in a full suit of Mr. B——'s, who was a stout man, of six feet in height, whilst I am rather of the diminutive order; but my objections were over-ruled; we went, and my appearance added not a little to the hilarity of the party. At ten o'clock we separated, and I returned with Mr. and Mrs. B—— to their house, where I was shortly afterwards conducted to a very comfortable bed-room.

"Fatigued with my day's ride, I was soon in bed, and soon asleep; but I do not think I could have slept long before I was awakened by the violent barking of dogs. I found that the noise had disturbed others as well as myself, for I heard Mr. B——, who was lodged in the adjoining room, open his window and call to them to be quiet. They were obedient to his voice, and as soon as quietness ensued, I dropped asleep again; but I was again awakened by an extraordinary pressure upon my feet; *that I was perfectly awake I declare*; the light that stood in the chimney-corner shone strongly across the foot of the bed, and I saw the figure of a well-dressed man in the act of stooping, and supporting himself in so doing by the bed-clothes. He had on a blue coat, with bright gilt buttons, but I saw no head; the curtains at the foot of the bed, which were partly looped back, just hung so as to conceal that part of his person. At first, I thought it was my host, and as I had dropped my clothes, as is my habit, on the floor, at the foot of the bed, I supposed he was come to look after them, which rather surprised me; but just as I had raised myself upright in bed, and was about to inquire into the occasion of his visit, the figure passed on. I then recollected that I had locked the door; and becoming somewhat puzzled, I jumped out of bed; but I could see nobody; and on examining the room, I found no means of ingress but the door through which I had entered, and one other; both of which were locked on the inside. Amazed and puzzled, I got into bed again, and sat some time ruminating on the extraordinary circumstance, when it occurred to me that I had not looked under the bed. So I got out again, fully expecting to find my visitor, whoever he was, there; but I was disappointed. So after looking at my watch, and ascertaining that it was ten minutes past two, I stepped into bed again, hoping now to get some rest. But alas! sleep was banished for that night; and after turning from side to side, and making vain endeavours at forgetfulness, I gave up the point, and lay till the clock struck seven, perplexing my brain with the question of who my midnight visitor could be; and also how he had got in and how he had got out of my room. About eight o'clock, I met my host and his wife at the breakfast-table, when, in answer to their hospitable inquiries of how I had passed the night, I mentioned, first, that I had been awaked by the barking of some dogs, and that I had heard Mr. B—— open his window and call to them. He answered that two strange dogs had got into the yard and had disturbed the others. I then mentioned. my midnight visitor, expecting that they would either explain the circumstance, or else laugh at me and declare I must have dreamt it. But, to my surprise, my story was listened to with grave attention; and they related to me the tradition with which this spectre, for such I found they deemed it to be, was supposed to be connected. This was to the effect, that many years ago a gentleman so attired, had been murdered there, under some frightful circumstances; and that his head had been cut off. On perceiving that I was very unwilling to accept this explanation of the mystery—for I had always been an entire disbeliever in supernatural appearances—they begged me to prolong my visit for a day or two, when they would introduce me to the rector of the parish, who could furnish me with such evidence with regard to circumstances of a similar nature, as would leave no doubt on my mind as to the possibility of their occurrence. But I had made an engagement to dine at Watford, on my way back; and I confess, moreover, that after what I had heard, I did not feel disposed to encounter the chance of another visit from the mysterious stranger; so I declined the proffered hospitality, and took my leave.

"Some time after this, I happened to be dining in C—— Street, in company with some ladies resident in the same county, when, chancing to allude to my visit to Sarratt, I added that I had met with a very extraordinary adventure there, which I had never been able to account for; when one of these ladies immediately said, that she hoped I had not had a visit from the headless gentleman, in a blue coat and gilt buttons, who was said to have been seen by many people in that house.

"Such is the conclusion of this marvellous tale as regards myself; and I can only assure you that I have related facts as they occurred; and that I had never heard a word about this apparition in my life, till Mr. B—— related to me the tradition above alluded to. Still, as I am no believer in supernatural appearances, I am constrained to suppose that the whole affair was the product of my imagination."

SCORRIER HOUSE.

It seems impossible to explain away the well vouched-
for facts of the following marvellous historic incident
by any theory of coincidence. The points of identity
between the tragedy enacted afar off and the dreams in
Cornwall are so many, that the Calculus of Probabilities
would scarcely include their agreement within the rules
of the Possible. And if not by coincidence, by what
law can the mystery be analysed? It is not our task,
however, to attempt to solve the problem, but to tell
the story, basing our narrative upon the account which
was given in the *Times* newspaper of August 16th, 1868.

It was on the night of the 11th of May 1812, according to the version of the story told by the *Times* during
the life-time of Mr. Williams, that that gentleman, then
residing at Scorrier House, near Redruth, in Cornwall,
awoke his wife, and in great agitation informed her that
he had dreamed he was in the lobby of the House of
Commons, and had seen a man shoot with a pistol a
gentleman who had just entered the lobby, and who
was said to be the Chancellor. Mrs. Williams very
naturally replied that it was only a dream and endeavoured to calm her husband by recommending him to
go to sleep again. He did fall asleep again, but shortly
afterwards awoke his wife and told her that he had had
the same dream a second time. Upon this, Mrs. Williams suggested that he had been so disturbed by his

former dream that it had probably dwelt on his mind, and, therefore, begged him to try and compose himself and go to sleep, which he did. Once more, for the third time, the vision was repeated; whereupon, notwithstanding his wife's entreaties that he would be quiet and try to forget the affair, Mr. Williams arose and dressed himself, it then being between one and two o'clock in the morning.

At breakfast Mr. Williams's sole subject of conversation was the vivid dreams by which his night's rest had been disturbed. In the afternoon he had occasion to go to Falmouth, where he gave every acquaintance he met particulars of his strange visions.

The following day Mr. Tucker, of Trematon Castle, accompanied by his wife, a daughter of Mr. Williams, visited at Scorrier House. No sooner were the family greetings over than Mr. Williams related his wonderful dream to the new arrivals; as Mrs. Williams laughingly remarked to her daughter, her father would not even allow Mr. Tucker to be seated before he told him of his nocturnal visitation. Upon hearing his father-in-law's statement, Mr. Tucker observed that it might do very well in a dream to have the Chancellor in the lobby of the House of Commons, but that he would never be found there in reality.

Subsequently, Mr. Tucker inquired what sort of a man the person shot appeared to be; and when Mr. Williams described him with great minuteness, he remarked, "Your description is not at all that of the Chancellor, but is certainly exactly that of Mr. Perceval, the Chancellor of the Exchequer ; and, although he has been to me the greatest enemy I ever met with, for a supposed cause which had no foundation in truth " (or words to that effect), " I should be exceedingly sorry, indeed, to hear of his being assassinated, or of any injury of the kind happening to him." Mr. Tucker then asked Mr. Williams if he had ever seen Mr. Perceval, and was told that he never had seen him, nor had ever even written to him, either on public or private matters ; in short, that he had never had anything to do with him, nor had he ever been in the lobby of the House of Commons in his life.

In the midst of this conversation, and whilst the two gentlemen were still standing, they heard a horse gallop up to the door of the house, and immediately afterwards Mr. Michael Williams, of Treviner, son of Mr. Williams, of Scorrier, entered the room, and said that he had galloped out from Truro, a distance of seven miles, having seen a gentleman there who had come by that evening's mail from London, who said that he was in the lobby of the House of Commons on the evening of the 11th, when a man called Bellingham had shot Mr. Perceval, the Chancellor of the Exchequer ; and that, as it might occasion some great ministerial changes, and might affect Mr. Tucker's political friends, he had come out as fast as he could to make him acquainted with it, having heard at Truro that he had passed through that place in the afternoon on his way to Scorrier House.

After the astonishment which this unexpected fulfilment of the dream caused had a little subsided, Mr. Williams most particularly described the appearance and dress of the man whom he beheld in his dreams fire the pistol, as he had previously described Mr. Perceval.

Some six weeks after the fatal affair, Mr. Williams, having business in London, availed himself of the opportunity to go, accompanied by a friend, to the House of Commons, where, as has already been stated, he had never been before. As soon as he came to the steps at the entrance of the lobby, he stopped and said, "This place is as distinctly within my recollection in my dream as any room in my house "; and he repeated the observation when he entered the lobby. He then pointed out the exact spot where Bellingham stood when he fired, and which Mr. Perceval had reached when he was struck by the ball, and where and how he fell. The dress and appearance of both Mr. Perceval and his assassin, Bellingham, are declared to have agreed exactly, even to the most minute particular, with the descriptions given by Mr. Williams.

The *Times*, when furnishing its readers with this wonderful story, drew attention to the fact that Mr. Williams was still alive, and would, therefore, have denied any inaccuracy in their account, whilst many of the witnesses to whom he had made known the particulars of his dreams directly after he had had them were also living. Moreover, added the editor, he had received the whole statement from a correspondent of unquestionable veracity.

SETTLE.

In April, 1876, the following very curious account of an apparition that was seen by three children at once was communicated to the Psychological Society by Mr. Hensleigh Wedgwood. The documentary story, written by Mrs. S. H. Fox, of Falmouth, had been handed to Mr. Wedgwood by Mrs. Backhouse, wife of the Member of Parliament for Darlington. It is to this effect :—

In the early part of the last century a member of the Society of Friends, living at Settle, in Craven, had to take a journey to the borders of Scotland. This lady left her family, consisting of a little boy and two little girls, in charge of a relative, who, in lieu of sending frequent letters (in those days a slow and costly mode of communication between places widely remote), engaged to keep a journal, to be transmitted to the mother at any convenient opportunity, of all that concerned the little ones, who were aged respectively seven, six, and four.

After an absence of about three weeks, and when on her homeward journey, the Quakeress was seized with illness and died at Cockermouth, even before her husband at Settle could hear by post that she had been taken ill. The season was winter, when in the mountainous borderland between the counties the conveyance of letters by postmen on foot was an especially lengthened and difficult process. The friends at whose house the event occurred, seeing the hopeless nature of the attack, made notes of every circumstance attending the last hours of the dying wife and mother, for the satisfaction of her family, so that the accuracy of the several statements as to time as well as facts was beyond the doubtfulness of mere memory, or of even any unconscious attempt to bring them into agreement with each other. One morning, between seven and eight o'clock, on the relation at Settle going into the sleeping room of the three children, she found them all sitting up in their beds in great excitement and delight, crying out, "Mamma has been here! Mamma has been here!" And the little one said, "She called, 'Come, Esther!'" Nothing could make them doubt the fact, intensely visible as it was to each of them, and it was carefully noted down to entertain the mother on her speedily expected return to her home.

That same morning, as she lay dying on her bed at Cockermouth, to those who were watching her tenderly and listening for her latest breath, she said, "I should be ready to go if I could but see my children." She then closed her eyes, they thought to re-open them no more; but after ten minutes of perfect stillness she looked up brightly and said, "I am ready now; I have been with my children," and then at once peacefully passed away. When the notes taken at the two places were compared, the day, hour, and minute were the same.

"One of the three children," says Mrs. Fox, "was my grandmother, Sarah Birkbeck (daughter of William

Birkbeck, banker, of Settle), afterwards wife of Dr. Fell, of Ulverton, from whom I had the above account almost literally as I have repeated it. The elder was Morris Birkbeck, afterwards of Guildford. Both these lived to old age, and retained to the last so solemn and reverential a remembrance of the circumstance that they rarely would speak of it, or permit any allusion to it, lest it should be treated with doubt or levity. Esther, the youngest of the three, died soon after. Her brother and sister only heard the child say that her mother called her, but could not speak with any certainty of having themselves heard the words, nor did they seem sensible of any communication from her but simply of her standing there and looking at them. My grandmother and her brother," is the testimony of Mrs. Fox, " were both persons remarkable for strong matter-of-fact, rather than imaginative, minds, and to whom it was especially difficult to accept anything on faith, or merely hearsay evidence, and who by nature would be disposed to reject whatever seemed beyond the region of reason or of common experience."

SOULDERN RECTORY.

In the register of Brisly Church, Norfolk, against the 12th of December 1706, stands the following words, which may serve as introduction to the extraordinary

story we have to tell in connection with Souldern
Rectory :—

"I, Robert Withers, M.A., vicar of Gately, do insert
here a story which I had from undoubted hands; for I
have all the moral certainty of the truth of it possible."

The narrative referred to by Mr. Withers is as given
in the following sentences, but not in the precise words
of that gentleman, as they only furnish a very abridged
account of the mysterious affair, besides deviating
slightly from the more circumstantial and exact particulars given in the private correspondence, subsequently published in the *Gentleman's Magazine*, which
passed between the Rev. John Hughes, of Jesus College,
Cambridge (the learned editor of *St. Chrysostom on the
Priesthood*), and the Rev. Mr. Bonwicke, very shortly
after the events referred to took place. Mr. Hughes,
who derived his information from Mr. Grove, public
registrar of the Cambridge University, and the intimate
friend of Mr. Shaw, writes thus :—

"The Rev. Mr. Shaw, formerly fellow of St. John's
College, Cambridge, and subsequently rector of
Souldern, a college living within twelve miles of
Oxford, on the night of the 21st of July 1706, was
sitting by himself smoking a pipe and reading, when
he observed somebody open the door, and turning round
was astounded to see the appearance of Mr. Naylor,
formerly his fellow collegian at St. John's, and his
intimate friend, but who had been dead fully five years.
The apparition came into the room, garbed apparently
in exactly the same clothes, and in exactly the same

manner, as Mr. Naylor had been accustomed to at the
University. Mr. Shaw was, of course, intensely amazed,
but asserted that he "was not much affrighted," and,
after a little while recollecting himself, desired his
visitor to sit down; this the apparition of Mr. Naylor
did, drawing the chair up to his old friend and sitting
by him. They then had a conference of upwards of an
hour and a half, during which the visitor informed Mr.
Shaw that he had been sent to give his old friend
warning of his death, which would be very soon and
very sudden. The apparition also mentioned several
others of St. John's, particularly the famous Orchard,
whose deaths were at hand. Mr. Shaw asked him if he
could not give him another visit; but he said " No," as
his (the apparition's) alloted time was but three days,
and that he had others to visit who were at great
distances apart. Mr. Shaw had an intense desire to
inquire about the apparition's present condition, but was
afraid to mention it, not knowing how it would be
taken. At last he expressed himself in this manner :—

" Mr. Naylor, how is it with you in the other world ? "

He, the apparition, answered with a brisk and cheerful countenance, " Very well."

Mr. Shaw proceeded to ask, " Are there any of our
old friends with you ? "

" Not one," responded he; "but Orchard will be with
me soon, and you not long after."

After this discourse the apparition took its leave and
went out. Mr. Shaw offered to accompany it out of
the room, but it beckoned with its hand that he should

stay where he was, and seeming to turn into the next room, disappeared.

The next day Mr. Shaw made his will, and not very long after, being seized with an apoplectic fit while he was reading service in church, he fell out of the desk, and died almost immediately.

"He was ever looked upon as a pious man and a good scholar," says Mr. Hughes, who had the story of the apparition from Mr. Grove, a particular friend of Mr. Shaw, and who, being on a visit to Souldern soon after the event, had the whole particulars from the minister's own lips. Mr. Grove returned to Cambridge soon afterwards, and meeting with one of his college, was told that Mr. Arthur Orchard was dead.

On the 21st of January 1707, the Rev. M. Turner, writing to the Rev. Mr. Bonwicke, with reference to this story, says, "There's a circumstance relating to the apparition which adds a great confirmation to it, which, I suppose, Mr. Hughes did not tell you. There is one, Mr. Cartwright, a Member of Parliament,* a man of good credit and integrity, an intimate friend of Mr. Shaw, who told the same story with Dr. Grove (which he had from Mr. Shaw), at the Archbishop of Canterbury's table; but he says further, that Mr. Shaw told him of some great revolutions in states, which he won't discover, being either obliged to silence by Mr. Shaw, or concealing them upon some prudent and polite reason."

Mr. Shaw, it may be added, had been a noted enemy

* *I.e.* for Northamptonshire.—*Editor*

to a belief in apparitions, and in company was accustomed to inveigh against any credence being placed in them, but after his presumed interview with the apparition of his old friend, spoke of that in such a way, with his more intimate acquaintances, as quite convinced them of his belief in its spirituality; one of whom, the Rev. Richard Chambre, vicar of Soppington, Shropshire, wrote out an account, still extant, of the affair as related to him by Mr. Shaw.

SPEDLIN'S TOWER.

THIS ancient fortress bore the reputation, for a long number of years, of being haunted by the spirit of a certain man, known in the flesh as Porteous. The story of this haunting has been frequently told by Grose, the antiquary, and other well-known writers, and the truth of the events about to be recorded has been most emphatically asserted by persons of respectability and credit; indeed, many a ghost story passes current that has not had such corroborative evidence as this tale of antique lore.

Spedlin's Tower, which stands on the south-west bank of the Annan, in the time of Charles the Second was in the possession of Sir Alexander Jardine, of Applegarth. At one time this baronet had confined in the dungeon of his tower a miller, named Porteous, who was suspected, truthfully or not cannot be known, of having set fire wilfully to his own premises; the alleged object tradition does not condescend to inform us. Sir Alexander Jardine, soon after this man's incarceration, was suddenly called away to Edinburgh, and carrying the keys of the dungeons with him, forgot or disregarded his prisoner, until he was passing through the West Port, when, it has been suggested, perhaps the sight of the warder's keys brought to his mind his own. He sent back immediately a courier to liberate the unfortunate man, but Porteous had, in the meantime, perished of hunger.

No sooner was he dead than his ghost began to torment the household, and no rest was to be had within Spedlin's Tower by day or by night. In this dilemma Sir Alexander, according to old use and wont, summoned a whole legion of ministers to his aid; and by their strenuous efforts, Porteous was at length confined to the scene of his mortal agonies where, however, he continued to scream occasionally at night, "Let me out, let me out, for I'm deein' o' hunger!" He also used to flutter against the door of the vault, and was always sure to remove the bark from any twig that was sportively thrust through the key-hole.

The spell which thus compelled the spirit to remain in bondage was attached to a large black-lettered Bible, used by the exorcists, and afterwards deposited in a stone-niche, which still remains in the wall of the staircase; and it is certain that after the lapse of many years, when the family repaired to a newer mansion (Jardine Hall), built on the other side of the river, the

Bible was left behind, to keep the restless spirit in order. On one occasion, indeed, the volume requiring to be re-bound was sent to Edinburgh; but the ghost, getting out of the dungeon, and crossing the river, made such a disturbance in the new house, hauling the baronet and his lady out of bed, and committing other annoyances, that the Bible was recalled before it reached Edinburgh, and replaced in its former situation.

The good woman who told Grose this story in 1788, declared that should the Bible again be taken off the premises, no consideration whatever should induce her to remain there a single night. But the charm seems to be now broken, or the ghost must have become either quiet or disregarded; for the old Bible has been removed, and is now kept at Jardine Hall.

STRACHUR MANSE.

ALTHOUGH the name of the person chiefly concerned in the following narrative is concealed under the initial "S," the reference to the house where he had his remarkable vision, and the fact that it was then occupied by a relative of the gallant Captain, will afford sufficient means of identification to the curious. Premising this, it will now suffice to say that some few years ago Captain S—— was spending a single night in the Manse of Strachur, in Argyleshire. This residence was then in the occupation of some relations of the Captain, and, so far as is known, had not at that time the reputation of being haunted.

Soon after the weary guest had retired to rest, the curtains of the bed were opened and somebody looked in upon him. Supposing it to be some inmate of the house who was not aware that the bed was occupied, the Captain took no notice of the circumstance till, it being two or three times repeated, he at length said, "What do you want? Why do you disturb me in this manner?"

"I come," replied a voice, "to tell you that this day twelvemonth you will be with your father."

After this Captain S—— was no more disturbed. In the morning he related the circumstance to his host, but, being an entire disbeliever in all spiritual phenomena, without attaching any importance to the warning.

In the natural course of events, and quite irrespective of this visitation, on that day twelvemonth he was again at the Manse of Strachur, on his way to the north, for which purpose it was necessary that he should cross the ferry of Craigie. The day was, however, so exceedingly stormy, that his friend begged him not to go; but he pleaded his business, adding that he was determined not to be withheld from his intention by the ghost, and although the minister delayed his departure by engaging him in a game of backgammon, he at length started up, declaring he could stay no longer. They therefore proceeded to the water, but found the boat was moored to the side of the lake, and the boatman assured them that it would be impossible to cross. Captain S——, however, insisted, and as the old man was firm in his refusal, he became somewhat irritated, and laid his cane lightly across his shoulders.

"It ill becomes you, Sir," said the ferryman, "to strike an old man like me; but since you will have your way, you must. I cannot go with you, but my son will; but you will never reach the other side, he will be drowned, and you too."

The boat was then set afloat, and Captain S——, together with his horse and servant, and the ferryman's son, embarked in it.

The distance was not great, but the storm was tremendous; and having, with great difficulty, got half way across the lake, it was found impossible to proceed. The danger of tacking was of course considerable; but, since they could not advance, there was no alternative but to turn back, and it was resolved to attempt it. The manœuvre, however, failed, the boat capsized, and they were all precipitated into the water.

"You keep hold of the horse, I can swim," said Captain S—— to his servant, when he saw what was about to happen.

Being an excellent swimmer, and the distance from the shore inconsiderable, he hoped to save himself, but he had on a heavy topcoat, with boots and spurs. The coat he contrived to take off in the water, and then struck out with confidence; but, alas! the coat had got entangled with one of the spurs, and as he swam it clung to him, getting heavier and heavier as it became saturated with water, even dragging him beneath the stream. He, however, reached the shore, where his anxious friend still stood watching the event, and as the latter bent over him, he was just able to make a gesture with his hand, which seemed to say, " You see, it was to be ! " and then expired.

The boatman was also drowned, but, by the aid of the horse, the servant escaped.

TAUNTON.

STORIES of haunted houses and ghostly tales are very prevalent in the western counties. Somersetshire is especially rich in these things, and one of the most suggestive accounts, of the many which have appeared in the pages of *Notes and Queries*, relates to this county. Mr. T. Westwood, who furnished the following narrative to the above publication, gave it as a faithful report, so far as he was concerned, and we reproduce it in the words of our authority :—

In the year 1840 I was detained for several months in the sleepy old town of Taunton. My chief associate during that time was a fox-hunting squire—a bluff, hearty, genial type of his order, with just sufficient intellectuality to temper his animal exuberance. Many were our merry rides among the thorpes and hamlets of pleasant Somersetshire ; and it was in one of these excursions, while the evening sky was like molten copper, and a fiery March wind coursed like a race-horse over the open downs, that he related to me the story of what he called his Luminous Chamber.

" Coming back from the hunt, after dark, he said he had frequently observed a central window, in an old hall not far from the roadside, illuminated. All the other windows were dark, but from this one a wan, dreary light was visible ; and as the owners had deserted the place, and he knew it had no occupant, the lighted window became a puzzle to him.

" On one occasion, having a brother squire with him, and both carrying good store of port wine under their girdles, they declared they would solve the mystery of the Luminous Chamber then and there. The lodge was still tenanted by an aged porter ; him they roused up, and after some delay, having obtained a lantern, and the keys of the hall, they proceeded to make their entry. Before opening the great door, however, my squire averred he had made careful inspection of the front of the house from the lawn. Sure enough, the central window *was* illuminated—an eerie, forlorn-looking light, made it stand out in contrast to the rest —a dismal light, that seemed to have nothing in common with the world, or the life that is. The two squires visited all the other rooms, leaving the luminous room till the last. There was nothing noticeable in any of them ; they were totally obscure. But on enter-ing the luminous room a marked change was percep-tible. The light in it was not full, but sufficiently so beneath them to distinguish its various articles of furniture, which were common and scanty enough. What struck them most was the uniform diffusion of the light; it was as strong *under* the table as *on* the table, so that no single object projected any shadow on the floor, nor did they themselves project any shadow. Looking into a great mirror over the mantel-piece, nothing could be weirder, the squire declared, than the reflection in it of the dim, wan-lighted chamber, and of the two awe-stricken faces that glared on them from the midst—his own and his companion's. He told me, too, that he had not been many seconds in the room before a sick faintness stole over him, a feeling—such was his expression, I remember—as if his life *were being sucked out of him.* His friend owned afterwards to a similar sensation. The upshot of it was that both squires decamped crestfallen, and made no further attempt at solving the mystery.

"It had always been the same, the old porter grumbled; the family had never occupied the room, but there were no ghosts—*the room had a light of its own.*

"A less sceptical spirit might have opined that the room was *full* of ghosts—an awful conclave—viewless, inscrutable, but from whom emanated that deathly and deadly luminousness.

"My squires must have gone the way of all squires ere this. After 'life's fitful fever,' do they 'sleep well'? Or have they both been 'sucked' into the luminous medium, as a penalty for their intrusion?"

TEDWORTH.

JOSEPH GLANVIL, whose unjustly neglected *Essays* contain some of the most magnificent germ thoughts of his age, wrote a curious work on witchcraft entitled *Saddu-cismus Triumphatus*. This work contains what its author styles " a choice collection of modern relations," referring to more or less known cases of apparitions, and similar supernatural phenomena. The chief of these relations is an account of the haunting of a house at Tedworth, Wiltshire, belonging to a Mr. John Mompesson, and considering the length of time the disturbances endured, the position of the people who investigated the case, and the unfathomable mystery in which it still remains, it may be considered one of the most remarkable instances of its kind on record. Following the particulars furnished by Glanvil, who personally investigated the whole affair, the extraordinary story may be thus detailed :—

In March, 1661, Mr. Mompesson, who was a man of good family and well endowed with worldly possessions, in his magisterial capacity caused to be arrested and sent to Gloucester Jail as a rogue and vagabond a wandering beggar, who had been going about the country annoying people by his vehement solicitations for alms, and disturbing their quiet by the noisy beating of a large drum. Mr. Mompesson committed him to prison and had the drum consigned to the custody of the bailiff, and to this circumstance was attributed all the disturbances to which the unfortunate magistrate and his household were subsequently subjected.

In the month following the vagrant's arrest Mr. Mompesson had occasion to visit London, but just before his departure the bailiff, for reasons not stated, took an opportunity of sending the man's drum to the magistrate's house. When he returned from his journey to the metropolis, Mr. Mompesson was informed by his wife that they had been much frightened during his absence by thieves, and that the house had been nearly broken into. He had not been home above three nights when noises similar to those that had terrified his family in his absence were again heard. It was a great knocking at the doors and outside of the house. "Hereupon he got up," to follow Glanvil's account, "and went about the house with a brace of pistols in his hands. He opened the door where the great knocking was, and then he heard the noise at another door. He opened that also, and went out round his house, but could discover nothing, only he still heard a strange noise and hollow sound. When he got back to bed there was a thumping and drumming on the top of his house, which continued a good space, and then by degrees went off into the air.

"After this," according to Glanvil, "the noise of thumping and drumming was very frequent, usually five nights together, and then it would intermit three. It was on the outside of the house, which was most of it of board. It constantly came as they were going to

16 *

sleep, whether early or late. After a month's disturbance without, it came into the room where the drum
lay, four or five nights in seven, within half an hour
after they were in bed, continuing almost two. The
sign of it, just before it came, was a hurling in the air
over the house; and at its going off, the beating of a
drum, like that at the breaking up of a guard. It
continued in this room for the space of two months,
which time Mr. Mompesson himself lay there to
observe it."

Mrs. Mompesson's confinement now taking place, the
distressing noises politely refrained from manifesting
themselves; but "after this civil cessation," as Glanvil
phrases it, of about three weeks, the disturbances returned "in a ruder manner than before, and followed
and vexed the youngest children, beating their bedsteads
with that violence that all present expected that they
would fall to pieces. In laying hands on them one
could feel no blows, but might perceive them to shake
exceedingly. For an hour together it would beat" the
"Tattoo," and "several other points of war, as well
as any drummer. After this they would hear a scratching under the children's bed, as if by something that
had iron talons. It would lift the children up in their
beds, follow them from one room to another, and for a
while haunted none particularly but them."

"On the 5th of November," says Glanvil, "it made
a mighty noise; and a servant observing two boards
in the children's room seeming to move, he bid *it* give
him one of them. Upon which the board came (nothing

moving it that he saw) within a yard of him. The man added, 'Nay, let me have it in my hand'; upon which the spirit, devil, or drummer pushed it towards him so close that he might touch it. This," continues Glanvil, " was in the day-time, and seen by a whole roomful of people. That morning it left a sulphureous smell behind it which was very offensive.

"At night the minister, one Mr. Cragg, and several of the neighbours came to the house on a visit. Mr. Cragg went to prayers with them, kneeling at the children's bedside, where it then became very troublesome and loud. During prayer-time the spirit withdrew into tho cock-loft, but roturnod as soon as prayors woro done; and then, in sight of the company, the chairs walked about the room of themselves, the children's shoes were hurled over their heads, and every loose thing moved above the chamber. At the same time a bed-staff was thrown against the minister, which hit him on the leg, but so favourably that a lock of wool could not have fallen more softly."

As Mr. Mompesson found his youngest children were suffering so much from these persecutions, he had them removed, and lodged them at the house of a neighbour. His eldest daughter, who was about ten years of age, was taken into her father's own room, where there had not been any disturbance for a month or so. " As soon as she was in bed," continues the narration, " the disturbance began there again, continuing three weeks, drumming and making other noises; and it was observed that it would answer exactly, in drumming, anything that was beaten or called for," just in the same way as with the modern spirit-rappings, it has been suggested.

Among the many things noted or reported of this house-haunting was, " that when the noise was loudest, and came with the most sudden and surprising violence, no dog about the house would move, though the knocking was oft so boisterous and rude that it hath been heard at a considerable distance in the fields, and awakened the neighbours in the village," none of whom lived very near Mr. Mompesson's bewitched abode.

On one occasion when the village blacksmith, a fellow who feared neither man nor devil, slept with John, the footman, so that he might hear the supernatural noises and be cured of his incredulity, " there came a noise in the room as if one had been shoeing a horse, and somewhat came, as it were, with a pair of pincers," snipping away at the sceptical blacksmith the chief part of the night. Next day the invisible being came panting like a dog out of breath, and a woman who was present taking up a staff to knock at it, the weapon "was caught suddenly out of her hand and thrown away; and company coming up, the room was presently filled with a bloomy noisome smell, and was very hot, though without fire, in a very sharp and severe winter. It continued in the bed, panting and scratching for an hour and a half, and then went into the next room, when it knocked a little, and seemed to rattle a chain."

For two whole years, with some occasional intermissions, these disturbances continued, creating such intense excitement, not only in the vicinity of Tedworth, but all over the country, that at last the King sent a Commission to specially investigate the circumstances, and to draw up and furnish him with a report of the whole affair. Whatever, however, may have been the cause, during the visit of the Royal Commission the disturbances ceased, and no manifestations took place. "As to the quiet of the house when the courtiers were there," says Glanvil, "the intermission may have been accidental, or, perhaps, the demon was not willing to give so public a testimony of those transactions which might possibly convince those whom he had rather should continue in unbelief of his existence."

However, no sooner were the Royal Commissioners gone than the mysterious annoyance recommenced, and was manifested in many unpleasant fashions; sometimes it purred like a cat, or beat the children's legs black and blue; once it put a long spike into Mr. Mompesson's bed, and a knife into his mother's; filled the porringers with ashes, hid a Bible in the grate, and turned the money in people's pockets black. On one occasion a servant of Mr. Mompesson's averred that he had not only heard but seen this pertinacious demon, which came and stood at the foot of his bed. "The exact shape and proportion of it he could not discover; but he saw a great body, with two red and glaring eyes, which, for some time, were fixed steadily on him, and at length disappeared."

In the meanwhile, Mr. Mompesson believed, and several of his friends appear to have had a similar opinion, that all the noises and troubles were occasioned by the imprisoned drummer who was still in jail at Gloucester. In confirmation, as it were, of this idea, the following evidence is given:

"During the time of the knocking," says Glanvil, "when many were present, a gentleman of the company said, 'Satan, if the drummer set thee to work, give three knocks, and no more,' which it did very distinctly, and stopt. Then the gentleman knockt to see if it would answer him as it was wont; but it did not. For farther trial, he bid it, for confirmation, if it were the drummer, to give five knocks and no more that night, which it did, and let the house quiet all the night after. This was done in the presence of Sir Thomas Chamberlain, of Oxford, and divers others."

In the meantime, the drummer being visited one day in jail by a person from the neighbourhood of Tedworth, he asked what was the news in Wiltshire, and, so it is alleged, whether people did not talk a great deal about a drumming in a gentleman's house there? The visitor replied that he had heard of nothing; to which the drummer responded: "I have done it; I have thus plagued him; and he shall never be quiet until he hath made me satisfaction for taking away my drum."

Mr. Mompesson had the drummer taken up again, and this time for felony, for the supposed witchcraft about his house. The grand jury found a true bill against the man, but he was acquitted, his connection with the disturbances not being proved.

What subsequently became of the drummer is rather uncertain, but that he was eventually tried and convicted of witchcraft at Salisbury appears to be a fact, as also that he was sentenced to transportation for the crime. The leniency of the sentence is said to have excited no little surprise at that time, the offence of which he was found guilty generally being punished by death.

Hitherto the history of the haunting at Tedworth is only a recapitulation of what Glanvil took down from the mouths of other people, but his own personal experiences should not be ignored in any account of this extraordinary affair. In January 1662 he visited the scene of the disturbance himself, and furnishes the following record of what he observed :—

"About this time I went to the house on purpose to inquire the truth of those passages, of which there was so loud a report. It had ceased from its drumming and ruder noises before I came thither; but most of the more remarkable circumstances before related were confirmed to me there, by several of the neighbours together, who had been present at them. At this time it used to haunt the children, and that as soon as they were laid in bed. They went to bed that night I was there, about eight of the clock, when a maid-servant, coming down from them, told us it was come. The neighbours that were there, and two ministers who had seen and heard divers times, went away; but Mr. Mompesson and I, and a gentleman that came with me, went up. I heard a strange scratching as we went up the stairs, and when we came into the room, I perceived it was just behind the bolster of the children's bed, and seemed to be against the tick. It was loud scratching, as one with long nails could make upon a bolster. There were two little modest girls in the bed, between seven and eleven years old, as I guessed. I saw their hands out of the clothes, and they could not contribute to the noise that was behind their heads. They had been used to it, and had still somebody or other in the chamber with them, and therefore seemed not to be much affrighted. I, standing at the bed's head, thrust my hand behind the bolster, directing it to the place whence the noise seemed to come. Whereupon the noise ceased there, and was heard in another part of the bed. But when I had taken out my hand it returned, and was heard in the same place as before. I had been told that it would imitate noises, and made trial by scratching several times upon the sheet, as five, and seven, and ten, which it followed, and still stopped at my number. I searched under and behind the bed, turned up the clothes to the bed-cords, graspt the bolster, sounded the wall behind, and made all the search that possibly I could, to find if there were any trick, contrivance, or common cause of it. The like did my friend; but we could discover nothing. So that I was then verily persuaded, and am so still, that the noise was made by some demon or spirit. After it had scratched about half an hour or more, it went into the midst of the bed, under the children, and then seemed to pant, like a dog out of breath, very loudly. I put my hand upon the place, and felt the bed bearing up against it, as if something within had thrust it up. I grasped the feathers to feel if any living thing were in it. I looked under, and everywhere about, to see if there were any dog, or cat, or any such creature, in the room, and so we all did, but found nothing. The motion it caused by this panting was so strong, that it shook the rooms and windows very sensibly. It continued more than half an hour, while my friend and I stayed in the room, and as long after, as we were told.

"It will, I know, be said by some, that my friend and I were under some affright, and so fancied noises and sights that were not. This is the eternal evasion. But if it be possible to know how a man is affected when in fear, and when unaffected, I certainly know, for mine own part, that during the whole time of my being in the room, and in the house, I was under no more affrightment than I am while I write this relation. And if I know that I am now awake, and that I see the objects that are before me, I know that I heard and saw the particulars that I have told."

Thus ends the Rev. Joseph Glanvil's account of this extraordinary affair, from which Mr. Mompesson, as he remarks, " suffered by it in his name, in his estate, in all his affairs, and in the general peace of his family," because, as the same authority points out, " the un-believers, in the matter of spirits and witches, took him for an impostor, many others judged the permission of such an extraordinary evil to be the judgment of God upon him for some notorious wickedness or impiety. Thus his name was continually exposed to censure, and his estate suffered by the concourse of people from all parts to his house; by the diversion it gave him from his affairs; by the discouragement of servants, by reason of which he could hardly get any to live with him; to which I add the continual hurry that his family was in, the affrights, and the watchings and disturbance of his whole house (in which himself must needs be the most concerned). I say if these things are considered, there will be little reason to think he would have any interest to put a cheat upon the world, in which he would most of all have injured and abused himself."

Mr. Mompesson, writing on the 8th of November 1672, or ten years after the events recorded had taken place, besides pointing out that no discovery had been made of any cheat, declared most solemnly that he knew of none, as he had, indeed, testified at the assizes. "If the world will not believe it," he concluded, "it shall be indifferent to me, praying God to keep me from the same or the like affliction."

TRURO.

PROBABLY the last person one would imagine selected for a supernatural warning was Samuel Foote, the mimic and buffoon. And yet the so-called "English Aristophenes" not only dwelt in a haunted house, or at least believed so, but was closely connected with the chief characters of one of the most unnatural tragedies our judicial records have preserved. Foote's maternal uncles were Sir John Goodere and Captain Goodere, a naval officer. In 1740 the two brothers dined at a friend's house near Bristol; for a long time they had been on bad terms owing to certain money transactions, but at the dinner table a reconciliation was, to all appearance, arrived at between them. On his return home, however, Sir John was waylaid by some men from his brother's vessel, acting by his brother's authority, carried on board, and deliberately strangled; Captain Goodere not only unconcernedly looking on, but actually furnishing the rope with which the crime was committed. For this atrocity the fratricidal officer and his confederates were tried at the Bristol assizes, found guilty, and executed.

But, say the biographers of Foote, the strangest part of this terrible tale remains to be told. On the night the murder was perpetrated Foote arrived at his father's house at Truro; he describes himself as having been kept awake for some time by the softest and sweetest strains of music he had ever heard. At first he tried to fancy it was a serenade got up by some of the family to welcome him home; but not being able to discover any trace of the musicians, he was compelled to come to the conclusion that the sounds were the mere offspring of his imagination.

Some short time afterwards Foote learnt the particulars of his uncle's terrible fate, and remarking that the murder had been consummated at the same hour of the same night that he had been haunted by the mysterious sounds, he arrived at the conclusion that it was a supernatural warning, and this impression he is said to have retained to the last moments of his existence.

WALTHAM, ESSEX.

IN his *Treatise on Spirits,* John Beaumont recites a very singular account of an apparition seen by the daughter of Sir Charles Lee, and related to the Bishop of Gloucester by the lady's father himself. It is considered one of the best authenticated cases on record.

Sir Charles Lee had one only daughter by his first wife, who died at the child's birth. At her own desire, Lady Everard, sister of the deceased lady, had the child with her to educate it, and kept it under her care until she was of marriageable age. Ultimately, Miss Lee was engaged to Sir William Perkins, and the marriage was agreed upon, when it was prevented in an extraordinary manner. "Upon a Thursday night," to quote the Bishop's own words, Miss Lee, "thinking she saw a light in her chamber after she was in bed, knocked for her maid, who presently came to her; and she asked her why she left a candle burning in her chamber. The maid said she left none, and there was none but what she brought with her at that time. Then she said it was the fire; but that, her maid told her, was quite out, and said she believed it was only a dream, whereupon she said it might be so, and composed herself again to sleep. But about two of the clock she was awakened again, and saw the apparition of a little woman between her curtain and her pillow, who told her she was her mother, that she was happy, and that by twelve o'clock that day she should be with her. Whereupon she knocked again for her maid, called for her clothes, and when she was dressed went into her closet, and came not out again till nine, and then brought out with her a letter, sealed, to her father, brought it to her aunt, the Lady Everard, told her what had happened, and desired that as soon as she was dead it might be sent to him. But the lady thought she was suddenly fallen mad, and thereupon sent presently away to Chelmsford for a physician and surgeon, who both came immediately; but the physician could discern no indication of what the lady imagined, or of any indisposition of her body. Notwithstanding the lady would needs have her let blood, which was done accordingly. And when the young woman had patiently let them do what they would with her, she desired that the chaplain might be called to read prayers; and when the prayers were ended she took her guitar and psalm-book, and sate down upon a chair without arms, and played and sung so melodiously and admirably, that her music-master, who was there, admired at it. And near the stroke of twelve she rose, and sat herself down in a great chair with arms, and presently, fetching a strong breathing or two, immediately expired; and was so suddenly cold as was much wondered at by the physician and surgeon. She died at Waltham, in Essex, three miles from Chelmsford; and the letter was sent to Sir Charles, at his house in Warwickshire; but he was so afflicted with the death of his daughter, that he came not till she was buried. But when he came he caused her body to be taken up and to be buried by her mother at Edmonton, as she desired in her letter."

This event occurred in 1662, and there is no record, so far as we are aware, that any later, or, indeed, any previous, supernatural manifestations took place at Lady Everard's place.

WARBLINGTON PARSONAGE.

The following account of the hauntings at Warblington Parsonage, Hampshire, furnishes particulars of a story often referred to by writers on the supernatural, but which, apparently, they have never read, and only speak of by repute. The original version, as now repeated, was given in a letter written by Caswell, the mathematician, to the learned Dr. Bentley, whilst the latter was living at the house of Stillingfleet, the celebrated Bishop of Worcester. The name of the deceased person who was supposed to have appeared was suppressed at the time, for obvious reasons, but it has since been discovered to have been the Rev. Sebastian Pitfield, who was incumbent in 1677. An extract from Caswell's letter to Bentley will serve to introduce the narrative itself; he writes :—

"I have sent you enclosed a relation of an apparition. The story I had from two persons, who each had it from the author, and yet their accounts somewhat varied, and passing through more mouths has varied much more; therefore I got a friend to bring me the author, at a chamber, where I wrote it down from the author's mouth, and which, when I read it to him, and gave him another copy, he said he could swear to the truth of it as far as he was concerned. He is the curate of Warblington, Bachelor of Arts in Trinity College, Oxford, about six years standing in the University. I hear no ill report of his behaviour here. He is now gone to his curacy. He has promised to send up the hands of the tenant and his man, and the farmer's men, as far as they are concerned. Mr. Brereton, the rector, would have him say nothing of the story, for that he can get no tenant, though he has offered the house for ten pounds a year less. Mr. P., the former incumbent, whom the apparition represented, was a man of a very ill report, supposed to have got children of his maid, and to have murdered them; but I advised the curate to say nothing himself of this last part of P., but to leave that to the parishioners who knew him."

The narrative enclosed by Caswell, of the apparition, as written out by the curate, the Rev. Thomas Wilkins, on the 15th of December 1695, is as follows :—

"At Warblington, near Havant, Hampshire, within six miles of Portsmouth, in the parsonage-house, dwelt

17

Thomas Perce, the tenant, with his wife and child, a man-servant Thomas, and a maid-servant. About the beginning of August 1695, on a Monday, about nine or ten at night, all being gone to bed except the maid with the child, she being in the kitchen, and having raked up the fire, took a candle in one hand, and the child in the other arm, and turning about, saw someone in a black gown walking through the room, and thence out of the door into the orchard. Upon this the maid, hasting up-stairs, having recovered but two steps, cried out; on which the master and mistress ran down, found the candle in her hand, she grasping the child about its neck with the other arm. She told them the reason of her crying out; she would not that night tarry in the house, but removed to another belonging to one Henry Salter, farmer, where she cried out all the night from the terror she was in, and she could not be persuaded to go to the house upon any terms.

" On the morrow, Tuesday, the tenant's wife came to me, lodging then at Havant, to desire my advice, and have consultation with some friends about it. I told her I thought it was a flam, and that they had a mind to abuse Mr. Brereton, the rector, whose house it was. She desired me to come up. I told her I would come up and sit up, or lie there, as she pleased; for then, as to all stories of ghosts, or apparitions, I was an infidel. I went thither and sat up the Tuesday night with the tenant and his man-servant. About twelve or one o'clock I searched all the rooms in the house, to see if anybody were hid there to impose upon me. At last we came

into a lumber-room; there I smiling told the tenant
that was with me, that I would call for the apparition,
if there was any, and oblige him to come. The tenant
then seemed to be afraid, but I told him I would defend
him from harm, and then I repeated *Barbara celarent
Darii*, &c. jestingly; on this the tenant's countenance
changed, so that he was ready to drop down with fear.
Then I told him I perceived he was afraid, and I would
prevent its coming, and repeated *Baralipton*, &c., and
then he recovered his spirits pretty well, and we left
the room and went down into the kitchen, where we
were before, and sate up there the remaining part of the
night, and had no manner of disturbance.

"Thursday night the tenant and I lay together in
one room, and he saw something walk along in a black
gown and place itself against a window, and there stood
for some time, and then walked off. Friday morning,
the man relating this, I asked him why he did not call
me, and I told him I thought that it was a trick or flam;
he told me the reason why he did not call me was
that he was not able to speak or move. Friday night
we lay as before, and Saturday night, and had no disturbance either of the nights.

"Sunday I lay by myself in one room (not that
where the man saw the apparition), and the tenant, and
his man in one bed in another room, and betwixt
twelve and two the man heard something walk in their
room at the bed's foot, and whistling very well, and at
last it came to the bed's side, drew the curtain, and
looked on them. After some time it moved off; then the

man called to me, desired me to come, for that there was something in the room went about whistling. I asked him whether he had any light, or could strike one; he told me no. Then I leapt out of bed, and not staying to put on my clothes, went out of my room, and along a gallery to the door, which I found locked or bolted. I desired him to unlock the door, for that I could not get in; then he got out of bed and opened the door, which was near, and went immediately to bed again. I went in three or four steps, and it being a moonlight light, I saw the apparition move from the bedside, and stop up against the wall that divided their room and mine. I went and stood directly against it, within my arm's length of it, and asked it, in the name of God, what it was that made it come disturbing of us? I stood some time expecting an answer and receiving none, and thinking it might be some fellow hid in the room to fright me, *I put out my arm to feel it, and my hand seemingly went through the body of it, and felt no manner of substance till it came to the wall*; *then I drew back my hand, and still it was in the same place.*

"Till now," declares Mr. Wilkins, "I had not the least fear, and even now had very little; then I adjured it to tell me what it was. When I had said those words it, keeping its back against the wall, moved gently along towards the door. I followed it, and it, going out at the door, turned its back towards me. It went a little along the gallery, I followed it a little into the gallery, and it disappeared, where there was no

corner for it to turn, and before it came to the end of
the gallery, where were the stairs. Then I found myself
very cold from my feet as high as my middle, though I
was not in great fear. I went into the bed betwixt
the tenant and his man, and they complained of my
being exceedingly cold. The tenant's man leaned over
his master in the bed, and saw me stretch out my hand
towards the apparition, and heard me speak the words;
the tenant also heard the words. The apparition
seemed to have a morning gown of a darkish colour, no
hat nor cap, short black hair, a thin, meagre visage of a
pale swarthy colour, seemed to be of about forty-
five or fifty years old, the eyes half shut, the arms
hanging down, the hands visible beneath the sleeves, of a
middle stature. I related this description to Mr. John
Lardner, rector of Havant, and to Major Battin of
Langstone, in Havant parish; they both said the
description agreed very well to Mr. P(itfield), a former
rector of the place, who has been dead above twenty
years. Upon this the tenant and his wife left the house,
which has remained void since.

"The Monday after last Michaelmas," resumes Mr.
Wilkins, "a man of Chodson, in Warwickshire, having
been at Havant fair, passed by the foresaid parsonage
house about nine or ten at night, and saw a light in
most of the rooms of the house. His pathway being
close by the house, he, wondering at the light, looked
into the kitchen window, and saw only a light; but
turning himself to go away, he saw the appearance of a
man in a long gown. He made haste away; the appa-

rition followed him over a piece of glebe-land of several acres to a lane, which he crossed, and over a little meadow, and then over another lane to some pales which belong to farmer Henry Salter, my landlord, near a barn, in which were some of the farmer's men and some others. This man went into the barn, told them how he was frighted and followed from the parsonage-house by an apparition, which they might see standing against the pales if they went out. They went out, and saw it scratch against the pales, and make a hideous noise. It stood there some time, and then disappeared. Their description agreed with what I saw. This last account I had from the man himself whom it followed, and also from the farmer's men."

In conclusion may be appended to this very circumstantial document of the Rev. Thomas Wilkins, the statement that it was subsequently alleged that the Rev. Sebastian Pitfield, whom the apparition was presumed to personify, had murdered his own illegitimate children.

WESTMINSTER.

AMONG the many extremely curious stories of apparitions which correspondence on them and kindred subjects has elicited, is the following, which was furnished by Mr. T. J. Allman to the columns of *Notes and Queries*. It was communicated to that gentleman, the well-known publisher (it is believed), by the Rev. Mr. L——, a clergyman of the Church of England; but as it was published without Mr. L——'s consent having been first obtained, his name was not given. Unfortunately, no more definite address than Westminster can be given, that being the locality, however, where the apparition appeared to Captain L——. The clergyman's narrative is this:—

"One evening, some two years since, my brother, an officer in the army, residing at Westminster, surprised me with a late visit at my house in Holloway, just as we were retiring to rest. 'Brother!' exclaimed he, in an excited manner, 'mother is dead!' 'When and how did you hear?' I replied, as she was living some considerable distance from town, and was, as far as we both knew, although aged, in good health. 'I have seen her pass me twice this evening in my room, with her head bandaged up, and I could not rest till I saw you,' was his answer.

"In consequence of his conviction and entreaties, it was determined to take the first train in the morning to the locality where our mother resided, and, upon our arrival, sure enough we found, to *my* surprise, that our mother had died suddenly the previous evening at the exact hour my brother had witnessed the apparition."

For the truth of this story Mr. Allman stated he would vouch.

WESTMINSTER : KING STREET.

In his *Miscellanies*, Aubrey cites the singular narrative of Captain Henry Bell, originally given in the Preface to the translation of Luther's *Table Talk*. Captain Bell begins by declaring that whilst employed beyond the seas in various State affairs for King Charles II. and his successor, James II., he had heard much lamentation made over the great destruction, by burning and otherwise, of Martin Luther's *Discourses*. This work, which was supposed to have largely promoted the reformation, was condemned by Pope Gregory XIII., and placed under the ban of the Empire by Rudolph III. This latter monarch ordered that all printed copies of the work should be burned, and that any person retaining a copy would be liable to the punishment of death. In consequence of this rigorous edict, and the stringency with which it was enforced, in a little while no copies were obtainable.

A certain Caspar von Sparr, however, according to Captain Bell's account, accidentally discovered a copy, in 1626, which had escaped the wholesale destruction the work had suffered. As the prosecution of Protestantism still continued, this gentleman was afraid to retain possession of the interdicted book, and yet, unwilling to destroy it, thought of Captain Bell. Knowing that he was thoroughly acquainted with German, he forwarded him the wonderfully preserved work, earnestly impressing upon him the utility of translating it into English.

Captain Bell did not appear to be in any great haste to comply with this request, but, nevertheless, took the work in hand, "and many times began to translate the same," as he remarks, "but always I was hindered therein, being called upon about other business, insomuch that by no possible means I could remain by that work." About six weeks after he had received the book from Germany, "it fell out," to cite his own words, "that being in bed with my wife, one night between twelve and one o'clock, she being asleep, but myself yet awake, there appeared unto me an ancient man, standing at my bedside, arrayed in white, having a long and broad white beard hanging down to his girdle, who, taking me by the right ear, spake these words following unto me : 'Sirrah, will not you take time to translate that book which is sent unto you out of Germany? I will provide for you both place and time to do it'; and then he vanished out of my sight.

"Whereupon, being much affrighted," Captain Bell continues, "I fell into an extreme sweat, insomuch that, my wife awaking, she asked me what I ailed. I told her what I had seen and heard ; but I never did heed or regard visions nor dreams, and so the same fell soon out of my mind.

"Then about a fortnight after I had seen the vision, on a Sunday, I went to Whitehall to hear the sermon, after which ended, I returned to my lodging, which was then in King Street, Westminster, and sitting down to dinner with my wife, two messengers were sent from the Council Board to carry me to the keeper of the gate-house at Westminster, there to be safely kept, until further orders from the Lords of the Council."

This was done, avers Bell, without any cause being shown; but his real offence, according to Aubrey, was that he had much importuned the Lord Treasurer for considerable arrears which were due to him, and which that official not being willing to discharge, "clapt him up into prison." Be the cause what it may, Bell was detained in close confinement for ten years, five of which, he states, he spent in translating the work of Luther above referred to. As he quaintly remarks, "I found the words very true which the old man in the aforesaid vision said unto me, '*I will shortly provide you both place and time to translate it.*'"

WILLINGTON MILL.

WILLINGTON is a hamlet, lying in a deep valley between Newcastle-on-Tyne and North Shields. Thirty years ago it consisted of a parsonage, some few cottages, a mill, and the miller's house. The mill is, or was thirty years ago, a large steam flour-mill, like a factory, and near it, but completely detached, was the miller's house.

Messrs. Unthank and Proctor were the proprietors and workers of the mill, and Mr. Joseph Procter, one of the partners, resided in the house adjoining it. Mr. Procter, a respectable member of the Society of Friends, a man in the prime of life, was married to a lady belonging to the same religious fraternity, and was the father of several young children.

The house in which Mr. Procter resided was built about the beginning of the present century, and as described by Mr. Howitt in 1847, had nothing spectral in its appearance, although located in a somewhat wild-looking region, just off the river Tyne. The railway runs close by it, and engines connected with coal mines are constantly at work in its vicinity. When rumours as to the miller's residence being haunted began to spread, Mr. Procter, it is alleged, although evidently much troubled by the disturbances in his dwelling, was unwilling to give publicity to his troubles. Apparently this unwillingness wore off eventually, as in course of time Mr. Procter frequently communicated with the Press on matters connected with the singular events at Willington.

The chief published authority for an account of the haunted house at Willington, would appear to be a pamphlet reprinted in *The Local Historian's Table Book*, whence Mr. Howitt and Mrs. Crowe derived their particulars, and whence the following statement is chiefly taken.

"We have visited the house in question," says the writer of the pamphlet referred to, "and it may not be irrelevant to mention that it is quite detached from the mill, or any other premises, and has no cellaring under it. The proprietor of the house, who lives in it, declines to make public the particulars of the disturbance to which he has been subjected, and it must be understood that the account of the visit we are about to lay before our readers is derived from a friend to whom Mr. Drury presented a copy of his correspondence on the subject, with power to make such use of it as he thought proper. We learned that the house had been reputed, at least one room in it, to have been haunted forty years ago, and had afterwards been undisturbed for a long period, during some years of which quietude the present occupant lived in it unmolested. We are also informed that, about the time that the premises were building there were reports of some deeds of darkness having been committed by someone employed about them."

The writer of this account, after alluding to the strange things seen and heard, or said to have been seen and heard, by various persons in the neighbourhood, proceeds to quote the following correspondence which, he remarks, " passed between individuals of undoubted veracity." The copy of the first letter on the subject, written by Mr. Edward Drury, of Sunderland, to Mr. Procter, reads thus:—

" 17th June 1840.

" SIR,—Having heard from indisputable authority, viz. that of my excellent friend, Mr. Davison, of Low Willington, farmer, that you and your family are disturbed by most unaccountable noises at night, I beg leave to tell you that I have read attentively Wesley's account of such things, but with, I must confess, no great belief; but on account of this report coming from one of your sect, which I admire for candour and simplicity, my curiosity is excited to a high pitch, which I would fain satisfy. My desire is to remain alone in the house all night, with no companion but my own watch-dog, in which, as far as courage and fidelity are concerned, I place much more reliance than upon any three young gentlemen I know of. And it is, also, my hope that if I have a fair trial I shall be able to unravel this mystery. Mr. Davison will give you every satisfaction if you take the trouble to inquire of him concerning me. I am, &c."

In response to this application, Mr. Procter sent the following note :—

"Joseph Procter's respects to Edward Drury, whose note he received a few days ago, expressing a wish to pass a night in his house at Willington. As the family is going from home on the 23rd instant, and one of Unthank and Procter's men will sleep in the house, if E. D. feels inclined to come, on or after the 24th, to spend a night (*sic*) in it, he is at liberty so to do, with or without his faithful dog, which, by-the-bye, can be of no possible use, except as company. At the same time, J. P. thinks it best to inform him that particular disturbances are far from frequent at present, being only occasional, and quite uncertain ; and, therefore, the satisfaction of E. D.'s curiosity must be considered as problematical. The best chance will be afforded by his sitting up alone in the third story till it be fairly daylight, say 2 or 3 A.M.

"Willington, 6th mo. 21st, 1840.

"J. P. will leave word with T. Maun, foreman, to admit E.D."

The Procters left home on the 23rd of June, leaving the house in charge of an old servant, who, being out of place on account of ill-health, was induced to undertake the duty during their absence. On the 3rd of July, Mr. Procter returned home, having been recalled by business matters, and on the evening of the same day Mr. Drury and a companion arrived unexpectedly. After the house had been locked up for the night, every corner of it underwent minute examination on the part of the visitors. The room out of which the apparition was accustomed to issue was found to be too shallow to contain any person. Mr. Drury and his companion were well provided with lights, and satisfied themselves that there was no one in the house besides Mr. Procter, his servant, and themselves.

Some correspondence which subsequently took place between Mr. Drury and Mr. Proctor, with respect to the ill effects of what he did see had had upon the former, and the request of the latter for a detailed account of his visitor's experience, need not be given, as the following letter, copied *verbatim*, will fully describe what Mr. Drury says he really saw and heard :—

                    " Sunderland, July 13th, 1840.

" Dear Sir,

        " I hereby, according to promise in my last letter, forward you a true account of what I heard and saw at your house, in which I was led to pass the night from various rumours circulated by most respectable parties, particularly from an account by my esteemed friend, Mr. Davison, whose name I mentioned to you in a former letter. Having received your sanction to visit your mysterious dwelling, I went, on the 3rd of July, accompanied by a friend of mine, T. Hudson. This was not according to promise, nor in accordance with my first intent, as I wrote you I would come alone; but I felt gratified at your kindness in not alluding to the liberty I had taken, as it ultimately proved for the best. I must here mention that, not expecting you at home, I had in my pocket a brace of pistols, determining in my mind to let one of them drop before the miller, as if by accident, for fear he should presume to play tricks upon me; but after my interview with you, I felt there was no occasion for weapons, and did not load them, after you had allowed us to inspect as minutely as we pleased every portion of the house. I sat down on the third-story landing, fully expecting to account for any noises that I might hear in a philosophical manner. This was about eleven o'clock P.M. About ten minutes to twelve we both heard a noise, as if a number of people were pattering with their bare feet upon the floor, and yet, so singular was the noise, that I could not minutely determine from whence it proceeded. A few minutes afterwards we heard a noise, as if someone was knocking with his knuckles among our feet; this was followed by a hollow cough from the very room from which the apparition proceeded. The only noise after this, was as if a person was rustling against the wall in coming up-stairs. At a quarter to one, I told my friend that, feeling a little cold, I would like to go to bed, as we might hear the noise equally well there ; he replied, that he would not go to bed till daylight. I took up a note which I had accidentally dropped, and began to read it, after which I took out my watch to ascertain the time, and found that it wanted ten minutes to one. In taking my eyes from the watch they became riveted upon a closet door, which I distinctly saw open, and saw also the figure of a female, attired in greyish garments, with the head inclining downwards and one hand pressed upon the chest as if in pain, and the other, viz. the right hand, extended towards the floor with the index finger pointing downwards. It advanced with an apparently cautious step across the floor towards me; immediately as it approached my friend, who was slumbering, its right hand was extended towards him. I then rushed at it, giving, as Mr. Procter states, a most awful yell ; but, instead of grasping it, I fell upon my friend, and I recollect nothing distinctly for nearly three hours afterwards. I have since learnt that

I was carried down-stairs in an agony of fear and terror.

"I hereby certify that the above account is strictly true and correct in every respect.

"EDWARD DRURY."

The appearance in print of Mr. Drury's letter naturally created a great sensation. Mr. Procter received a large number of letters in consequence of the publication, many of them, it is alleged, being from individuals in various positions of society, informing him that their residences were, and had long been, subjected to similar disturbances to those alleged to trouble his.

Other instances of the way in which Mr. Procter's house was haunted are recorded by Mr. Howitt. On one occasion another apparition was seen by four witnesses, who were enabled to watch its proceedings for the space of ten minutes. They were on the outside of the building, when they beheld the apparition of a bare-headed man, in a flowing robe like a surplice, gliding backwards and forwards about three feet from the floor, or level with the bottom of the second-story window, seeming to enter the wall on each side, thus presenting the spectators with a side view in passing. "It then stood still in the window, and a part of the figure came through both the blind, which was close down, and the window, as its luminous body intercepted the view of the framework of the window. It was semi-transparent, and as bright as a star, diffusing a radiance all around.

As it grew more dim, it assumed a blue tinge, and gradually faded away from the head downwards." The foreman, one of the spectators, passed close to the house under the window, and also went up to inform the family, but found the house locked up. "There was no moonlight," says the account, "nor a ray of light visible anywhere about, and no person near."

"One of Mrs. Procter's brothers, a gentleman in middle life and of a peculiarly sensible, sedate, and candid disposition," says Mr. Howitt, "assured me that he had himself, on a visit there, been disturbed by the strangest noises. That he had resolved, before going, that if any noises occurred he would speak, and demand of the invisible actor who he was, and why he came thither. But the occasion came, and he found himself unable to fulfil his intention. As he lay in bed one night, he heard a heavy step ascend the stairs towards his room, and someone striking, as it were, with a thick stick on the bannisters as he went along. It came to his door, and he essayed to call, but his voice died in his throat. He then sprang from his bed, and, opening the door, found no one there, but now heard the same heavy steps deliberately descending, though perfectly invisible, the steps before his face, and accompanying the descent with the same loud blows on the bannisters." A thorough search was at once made of the premises, in the company of Mr. Procter, but nothing was discovered that would account for the mysterious noises.

From two young ladies who, whilst on a visit to Mr.

Procter's, were annoyed by the apparition, Mr. Howitt received this terrifying account of their experiences :— " The first night, as they were sleeping in the same bed, they felt the bed lifted up beneath them. Of course they were much alarmed. They feared lost someone had concealed himself there for the purpose of robbery. They gave an alarm, search was made, but nothing was found. On another night their bed was violently shaken, and the curtains suddenly hoisted up all round to the very tester, as if pulled by chords, and as rapidly let down again, several times. Search again produced no evidence of the cause. The next day they had the curtains totally removed from the bed, resolving to sleep without them, as they felt as though evil eyes were. lurking behind them. The consequences of this, however, were still more striking and terrific. The following night, as they happened to awake, and the chamber was light enough—for it was summer—to see everything in it, they both saw a female figure, of a misty substance and bluish-grey hue, come out of the wall at the bed's head, and through the head-board, in a horizontal position, and lean over them. They saw it most distinctly. They saw it, as a female figure, come out of, and again pass into, the wall. Their terror became intense, and one of the sisters, from that night, refused to sleep any more in the house, but took refuge in the house of the foreman during her stay, the other shifting her quarters to another part of the house."

Among the various forms in which these disturbances were manifested at Mr. Procter's house were, according to the statements made by different persons to Mr. Howitt a noise like that of a pavior with his hammer thumping on the floor; at other times similar noises are heard coming down the stairs; frequently are heard coughs, sighs and groans, as of a person in distress, and sometimes there is the sound of a number of little feet pattering on the floor of the upper chamber when the female apparition has more particularly exhibited itself, and which, for that reason, is solely used as a lumberroom. "Here these little footsteps," says the narrative, "may be often heard, as if careering a child's carriage about, which in bad weather is kept up there." Sometimes, again, it utters the most blood-curdling laughter, whilst it does not even confine itself to making "night hideous," but appears in broad daylight. "On one occasion, a young lady assured me," says Mr. Howitt, "she opened the door in answer to a knock, the housemaid being absent, and a lady in a fawn-coloured silk entered and proceeded up-stairs. As the young lady, of course, supposed it to be a neighbour come to make a morning call on Mrs. Procter, she followed her up to the drawing-room, where, however, to her astonishment, she did not find her, nor was anything more seen of her."

Two apparitions appear to have haunted the house, one in the likeness of a man, as already described, which is luminous, and passes through the walls as if they offered no solid obstacle to it, and which is well known to the neighbours by the name of "Old Jeffrey." The other is the figure of a female in greyish garments, as described by Mr. Drury. She is said to be sometimes seen sitting wrapped in a sort of mantle. with her head depressed and her hands crossed on her lap. "The most terrible fact is that she is without eyes."

After enduring these terrible annoyances for some years, Mr. Procter, apprehensive of the ill effect they might have upon his children, says Mr. Howitt, quitted Willington and removed to North Shields, and subsequently to Tynemouth. At neither of these new abodes was he troubled by any similar manifestations. Mr. Procter states that a strange lady, strange to the district, being thrown into a clairvoyant state, and asked to go to the Mill, she described the priest and the grey lady, the two apparitions which haunted it. She also added that the priest had refused to allow the female ghost to confess a deadly crime committed at that spot many years ago, and that this was the troubling cause of the poor woman's apparition.

WINDSOR CASTLE.

WINDSOR, like most of our old castles, whether the residences of royalty, nobility, or commonalty, has had its apparitions. It is well known that previous to the assassination of George Villiers, Duke of Buckingham by Felton, an apparition of the Duke's father, Sir George Villiers, had appeared to, and sent him warning of his approaching fate by, a certain person ; but it has created endless controversy that the accounts of this apparition, as recorded by Aubrey, Lord Clarendon, and others, are so various and varied. It never appears to have occurred to anyone to remark that it is just as probable that the apparition may have appeared to three or more persons, at different times and places, as to one, and that, looking at the different stories from this point of view, all the alleged discrepancies disappear, and, in fact, the various records of the marvellous story, instead of contradicting, serve to corroborate one another.

In *Notes and Queries* for July, 1860, Mr. Hargrave Jennings published a very curious and circumstantial account of the appearance, on three separate occasions, of an apparition of Sir George Villiers to one Parker, formerly a servant of Sir George, and at that time in the employment of his son, the Duke. This letter, originally published some few years after the Duke's death, is of considerable interest; but as it, in many respects, parallels other and less accessible accounts, it may be passed over in favour of the story as told by Lord Clarendon and Aubrey. According to the account furnished by the former in his *History of the Rebellion*, the apparition of Sir George Villiers appeared to an officer in the King's Wardrobe, in Windsor Castle. This man, says Clarendon, was of a good reputation for honesty and discretion, and at the time referred to was about fifty years of age.

" He had in his youth been bred in a school in the parish where Sir George Villiers, the father of the Duke, lived, and had been much cherished and obliged, in that season of his age, by the said Sir George, whom afterwards he never saw.

"About six months before the miserable end of the Duke of Buckingham, about midnight, this man being in his bed at Windsor, where his office was, and in good health, there appeared to him, at the side of his bed, a man of a very venerable aspect, who drew the curtains of his bed, and, fixing his eyes upon him, asked him if he knew him.

"The poor man, half dead with fright and apprehension, being asked the second time whether he remembered him, and having in that time called to his memory the presence of Sir George Villiers, and the very clothes he used to wear, in which at that time he seemed to be habited, he answered him that he thought him to be that person. He replied he was in the right, he was the same, and that he expected a service from him, which was, that he should go from him to his son, the Duke of Buckingham, and tell him if he did not somewhat to ingratiate himself with the people, or at least to abate the extreme malice which they had against him, he would be suffered to live but a short time.

"After this discourse he disappeared, and the poor man (if he had been at all waking), slept very well till morning, when he believed all this to be a dream, and considered it no otherwise.

"The next night, or shortly after, the same person appeared to him again, in the same place, and about the same time of the night, with an aspect a little more severe than before, and asked him whether he had done as he required of him; and perceiving he had not, gave him very severe reprehensions, told him he expected more compliance from him, and that, if he did not perform his commands, he should enjoy no more peace of mind, but should always be pursued by him, upon which he promised him to obey.

"But the next morning, waking out of a good sleep, though he was exceedingly perplexed with the lively representation of all particulars to his memory, he was willing still to persuade himself that he had only dreamed, and considered that he was a person at such a distance from the Duke, that he knew not how to gain admission to his presence, much less had any hope of being believed in what he should say; so he spent some time in thinking what he should do, and in the end he resolved to do nothing in the matter.

"The same person appeared to him the third time, with a terrible countenance, and bitterly reproached him for not performing what he had promised to do. The poor man had by this time recovered the courage to tell him that, in truth, he had deferred the execution of his commands, upon considering how difficult a thing it would be for him to get any access to the Duke, having acquaintance with no person about him; and if he should obtain admission to him, he should never be able to persuade him that he was sent in such a manner; that he should at least be thought to be mad, or to be set on and employed by his own, or the malice of other men, to abuse the Duke, and so he should be sure to be undone.

"The apparition replied, as he had done before, that

he should never find rest till he had performed what he
required, and therefore he were better to despatch it;
that the access to his son was known to be very easy, and
that few men waited long for him. As for his gaining
credit, he would tell him two or three particulars, which
he charged him never to mention to any person living
but to the Duke himself, and he should no sooner hear
them but he should believe all the rest he said ; and so,
repeating his threats, he left him.

"In the morning the poor man, more confirmed by
the last appearance, made his journey to London, where
the Court then was. He was very well known to Sir
Ralph Freeman, one of the Masters of Requests, who
married a lady that was nearly allied to the Duke,
and was himself well received by him. To him this
man went, and though he did not acquaint him with all
the particulars, he said enough to let him know there
was something extraordinary in it, and the knowledge
he had of the sobriety and discretion of the man made
the more impression on him. He desired that, by his
means, he might be brought to the Duke, in such a
place and in such a manner as should be thought fit,
affirming that he had much to say to him, and of such
a nature as would require much privacy, and some time
and patience in the hearing.

"Sir Ralph promised that he would first speak to
the Duke of him, and then he should understand his
pleasure. Accordingly, the first opportunity, he did
inform him of the reputation and honesty of the man, and
then what he desired, and of all he knew of the matter,

"The Duke, according to his usual openness and condescension, told him that he was the next day early to hunt with the King, that his horses should attend him at Lambeth bridge, where he should land by five o'clock in the morning, and, if the man attended him there at that hour, he would walk and speak with him as long as should be necessary.

"Sir Ralph carried the man with him the next morning, and presented him to the Duke at his landing, who received him courteously, and walked aside in conference near an hour; none but his own servants being at that hour in that place, and they and Sir Ralph at such a distance that they could not hear a word, though the Duke sometimes spoke loud, and with great commotion, which Sir Ralph the more easily perceived, because he kept his eyes always fixed upon the Duke, having procured the conference upon somewhat he knew there was of extraordinary.

"The man told him, in his return over the water, that when he mentioned those particulars which were to gain him credit (the substance whereof, he said, he durst not impart to him), the Duke's colour changed, and he swore he could come at that knowledge only by the Devil, for that those particulars were only known to himself, and to one person more, who he was sure would never speak of it.

"The Duke pursued his purpose of hunting, but was observed to ride all the morning with great pensiveness, and in deep thoughts, without any delight in the exercise he was upon; and before the morning was spent, he left

the field and alighted at his mother's lodgings in Whitehall, with whom he was shut up for the space of two or
three hours, the noise of their discourse frequently
reaching the ears of those who attended in the next
rooms. And when the Duke left her, his countenance
appeared full of trouble, with a mixture of anger—a
countenance that was never before observed in him in
any conversation with her, towards whom he had a
profound reverence; and the Countess herself (for
though she was married to a private gentleman, Sir
Thomas Compton, she had been created Countess of
Buckingham shortly after her son had first assumed
that title) was, at the Duke's leaving, found overwhelmed
in tears, and in the highest agony imaginable.

"Whatever there was in all this," says Clarendon,
"it is a notorious truth, that when the news of the
Duke's murder (which happened within a few months
after), was brought to his mother, she seemed not in the
least degree surprised, but received it as if she had
foreseen it; nor did afterwards express such a degree of
sorrow as was expected from such a mother, for the loss
of such a son."

This is the story as repeated by the grave historian of
the so-called "Rebellion," with the assurance that it is
"upon a better foundation of credit than usually such
discourses are founded upon." Other versions of the
mysterious affair were published some few years after
the Duke of Buckingham's murder; and although the
discrepancies in them have never been explained, still
there has been a sufficient similarity in the leading

features of the narratives to cause most people to imagine that they were all derived from one source. But this does not necessarily follow. If the apparition appeared to different people and at different times—and it does not seem more wonderful that it should have manifested itself to two or more individuals than to one —the variations in the tales told of its appearance are readily explicable. Lilly, the astrologer, notoriously published a false version of the story; and it was for that reason only that Sir Edmund Wyndham, who was fully acquainted with the facts of the case, gave the narrative that ultimately passed into the hands of Aubrey, the antiquary, and by him is thus told :—

"To one, Mr. Towes, who had been school-fellow with Sir George Villiers, the father of the first Duke of Buckingham (and was his friend and neighbour), as he lay in his bed awake (and it was daylight), came into his chamber the phantom of his dear friend, Sir George Villiers. Said Mr. Towes to him, 'Why, you are dead, what make you here?' Said the knight, 'I am dead, but cannot rest in peace for the wickedness and abomination of my son George, at Court. I do appear to you, to tell him of it, and to advise and dehort him from his evil ways.' Said Mr. Towes, 'The Duke will not believe me, but will say that I am mad, or dote.' Said Sir George, 'Go to him from me, and tell him by such a token (a mole) that he had in some secret place, which none but himself knew of.' According, Mr. Towes went to the Duke, who laughed at his message. At his return home, the phantom appeared again, and told him that the Duke would be stabbed a quarter of a year after; 'and the warning which you will have of your death, will be, that your nose will fall a bleeding.' All which accordingly fell out so.

"This account I have had in the main," says Aubrey, "from two or three; but Sir William Dugdale affirms what I have here taken from him to be true, and that the apparition told him of several things to come, which proved true, e.g. of a prisoner in the Tower that shall be honourably delivered. This Mr. Towes had so often the ghost of his old friend appear to him, that it was not at all terrible to him. He was Surveyor of the Works at Windsor, by the favour of the Duke. Being then (i.e. at that time) sitting in the hall, he cried out, 'The Duke of Buckingham is stabbed!' He was stabbed that very moment."

"This relation Sir William Dugdale had from Mr. Pine, neighbour to Mr. Towes; they were sworn brothers." Sir Edmund Wyndham married the daughter of Mr. Pine, and possessed a large roll of manuscript wherein Mr. Towes had recorded the particulars of his conferences with the apparition.

WOODHOUSELEE.

MANY of our haunted houses are indebted to ancient feuds, in which their owners suffered or inflicted murder, for their present troubles. Scotland especially has

reaped a crop of ghostly legends and terrifying traditions from the homicidal tendencies of its former
notables. The apparition of Lady Hamilton, of Bothwellhaugh, is an enduring monument of the bloodthirsty spirit of the age in which she lived. Her
husband, Hamilton of Bothwellhaugh, exists in history
as the barbarous murderer of the Regent Murray, whom
he shot as he passed through Linlithgow on the 23rd
of January 1569 ; but if any man can be excused for
such a crime as assassination, it must be pleaded that
Bothwellhaugh is he. Whilst Hamilton was from
home, a favourite of the Regent seized his house and,
in a cold night, turned out his wife, Lady Bothwell,
naked into the open fields, where before next morning
she became furiously mad. Her infant, it would seem,
also perished either by cold, neglect, or, more probably,
murder. The ruins of the mansion of Woodhouslee,
whence Lady Bothwell was expelled in the brutal
manner which occasioned her insanity and death, are
still to be seen, or were some few years since, in a
hollow glen beside the river Esk. Popular report
tenants these ruins with the unfortunate lady's ghost ;
and so tenacious is this spectre of its rights, that, a part
of the stones of the ancient edifice having been employed
in building or repairing the present mansion, the
apparition has deemed it one of her privileges to haunt
that house also. But a very few years since this
apparition of Lady Bothwell, who always appears in
white, and with her child in her arms, excited no slight
disturbance and terror among the domestics at the new

Woodhouselee, which is situated on the slope of the Pentland Hills, distant at least four miles from the ancient dwelling. Whether this apparition still haunts either old or new mansion we have been unable to learn.

YORKSHIRE : —— HALL.

In March, 1880, a communication was handed to the editor of *Notes and Queries* by a well-known contributor of that invaluable publication. The narrative it contained was headed, " Ghost or Nightmare ? " clearly an incorrect title, if any credence is to be given to its author. The young lady who indited the communication is described as intelligent, whilst " her hereditary acumen" is declared to be such as "precludes altogether the possibility of any self-deceit in regard to her own personal experiences, as narrated by herself. Moreover, as it is pointed out, hers is not the only evidence on the subject, as the reader will notice. The contributor to *Notes and Queries* remarks that it is " in the conviction that this statement contains matter of unquestionable interest to every sort of thinker," that it is submitted to the consideration of his readers. Evidently acquainted, not only with the fair communicator of the narrative, but also with the locality to which his friend refers, H.C.C. states that " the scene of the occurrences is an old mansion in the north of

Yorkshire; cosy and cheerful, though large, and lonely in point of site."

The young lady's experiences in this haunted dwelling are thus graphically described:—

"What I am going to relate happened to myself while staying with some north-country cousins, last July, at their house in Yorkshire. I had spent a few days there in the summer of the previous year, but without then hearing or seeing anything out of the common. On my second visit, arriving early in the afternoon, I went out boating with some of the family, spent a very jolly evening, and finally went to bed, a little tired, perhaps, with the day's work, but not the least nervous. I slept soundly until between three and four, just when the day was beginning to break. I had been awake for a short time when suddenly the door of my bed-room opened, and shut again rather quickly. I fancied it might be one of the servants, and called out, 'Come in!' After a short time the door opened again, but no one came in—at least, no one that I could see. Almost at the same time that the door opened for the second time, I was a little startled by the rustling of some curtains belonging to a hanging wardrobe, which stood by the side of the bed; the rustling continued, and I was seized with a most uncomfortable feeling, not exactly of fright, but a strange, unearthly sensation *that I was not alone.* I had had that feeling for some minutes, when I saw at the foot of the bed a child, about seven or nine years old. The child seemed as if it were on the bed, and came gliding towards me as I lay. It was the figure of a little girl in her night-dress—a little girl with dark hair and a very white face. I tried to speak to her, but could not. She came slowly on up to the top of the bed, and I then saw her face clearly. She seemed in great trouble; her hands were clasped and her eyes were turned up with a look of entreaty, an almost agonized look. Then, slowly unclasping her hands, she touched me on the shoulder. The hand felt icy cold, and while I strove to speak she was gone. I felt more frightened after the child was gone than before, and began to be very anxious for the time when the servant would make her appearance. Whether I slept again or not, I hardly know. But by the time the servant did come, I had almost persuaded myself that the whole affair was nothing but a very vivid nightmare. However, when I came down to breakfast, there were many remarks made about my not looking well—it was observed that I was pale. In answer I told my cousins that I had had a most vivid nightmare, and I remarked if I was a believer in ghosts I should imagine I had seen one. Nothing more was said at the time upon this subject, except that my host, who was a doctor, observed that I had better not sleep in the room again, at any rate not alone.

"So the following night one of my cousins slept in the same room with me. Neither of us saw or heard anything out of the way during that night or the early morning. That being the case, I persuaded myself that what I had seen had been only imagination, and much against everybody's expressed wish, I insisted the next night on sleeping in the room again, and alone. Accordingly, having retired again to the same room, I was kneeling down at the bed-side to say my prayers, when exactly the same dread as before came over me. The curtains of the wardrobe swayed about, and I had the same sensation as previously, that I was not alone. I felt too frightened to stir, when, luckily for me, one of my cousins came in for something which she had left On looking at me she exclaimed, 'Have you seen anything?' I said 'No,' but told her how I felt, and without much persuasion being necessary, I left the room with her, and never returned to it. When my hostess learnt what had happened (as she did immediately) she told me I must not sleep in that room again, as the nightmare had made such an impression on me; I should imagine (she said) all sorts of things and make myself quite ill. I went to another room, and during the rest of my visit (a week), I was not troubled by any reappearance of the little girl.

"On leaving, my cousin, the eldest daughter of the doctor, went on a visit with me to the house of an uncle of mine in the same county. We stayed there for about a fortnight, and during that time the 'little girl' was alluded to only as my 'nightmare.'

"In this I afterwards found there was a little reticence, for, just before leaving my uncle's, my cousin said to me, 'I must tell you something I have been longing to tell you ever since I left home. But my father desired me not to tell you, as, not being very strong, you might be too frightened. Your nightmare was not a nightmare at all, but the apparition of a little girl! She then went on to tell me that this 'little girl' had been seen three times before, by three different members of the family; but as this was some nine or ten years since, they had almost ceased to think anything about it until I related my experiences on the morning after the first night of my second visit.

"My cousin further went on to tell me that her younger sister whilst in bed had one morning, about day-break, to her great surprise, seen a little girl with dark hair, standing with her back to her, looking out of the window. She took this figure for her little sister, and spoke to it. The child not replying, or moving from her position, she called out to it, 'It's no use standing like that; I know you. You can't play tricks with me.' On looking round, however, she saw that her little sister, the one she thought she was addressing, and who was sleeping with her, had not moved from the bed. Almost at the same time the child passed from the window into the room of her (my cousin's) sister A——, and the latter, as she afterwards declared, distinctly saw the figure of a child with dark hair standing by the side of a table in her room. She spoke to it, and it instantly disappeared. The 'little girl' was subsequently again seen, for the last time before I saw it, by my cousin's father, Dr. H——. It was in the early daylight of a summer's morning, and he was going up-stairs to his room, having just returned from a professional visit. On this occasion he saw the same child (he noticed its dark hair) running up the stairs immediately before him, until it reached his room and entered it. When he got into the room it was gone.

"Thus the apparition has been seen three times by the family, and once by me. I am the only one, however, that has seen its face. It has, also, never been seen twice in the same room by anyone else."

No refutation, explanation, or continuation of this mysterious matter appears to have been attempted as yet by anyone.

APPENDIX.

———◆———

MISCELLANEOUS.

LORD BROUGHAM.

IN the *Life and Times of Lord Brougham, written by Himself;* and published in 1871, is given the following strange story, which shall be repeated in the autobiographer's own words. "A most remarkable thing happened to me," records Brougham, "so remarkable, that I must tell the story from the beginning. After I left the High School (in Edinburgh), I went with G——, my most intimate friend, to attend the classes in the University. There was no divinity class, but we frequently in our walks discussed and speculated upon many grave subjects, among others, on the immortality of the soul, and on a future state. This question and the possibility, I will not say of ghosts walking, but of the dead appearing to the living, were subjects of much speculation; and we actually committed the folly of drawing up an agreement, written with our blood, to the effect that whichever of us died first should appear to the other, and thus solve any doubts we had entertained of the 'Life after Death.'

"After we had finished classes at the College, G—— went to India, having got an appointment there in the Civil Service. He seldom wrote to me, and after the lapse of a few years, I had almost forgotten him; moreover, his family having little connection with Edinburgh, I seldom saw or heard anything of them, or of him through them, so that all the old schoolboy intimacy had died out, and I had nearly forgotten his existence. I had taken, as I have said, a warm bath; and while in it and enjoying the comfort of the heat after the late freezing I had undergone, I turned my head round towards the chair on which I had deposited my clothes, as I was about to get out of the bath. On the chair sat G——, looking calmly at me. How I got out of the bath I know not, but on recovering my senses I found myself sprawling on the floor. The apparition, or whatever it was that had taken the likeness of G——, had disappeared. The vision produced such a shock, that I had no inclination to talk about it, or to speak about it even to Stuart; but the impression it made upon me was too vivid to be easily forgotten; and so strongly was I affected by it, that I have here written down the whole history with the date 19th December, and all the particulars as they are now fresh before me. No doubt I had fallen asleep; and that the appearance presented to my eyes was a dream, I cannot for a moment doubt, yet for years I had had no communication with G——, nor had there been anything to recall him to my recollection; nothing had taken place during our Swedish travels, either connected with G—— or with India, or with anything relating to him or to any member of his family. I recollected quickly enough our old discussion, and the bargain we had made. I could not discharge from my mind the impression that G—— must have died, and that his appearance to me was to be received by me as a proof of a future state."

This was on December 19, 1799. In October 1862, Lord Brougham added as a postscript:—

"I have just been copying out from my journal the account of this strange dream: *certissima mortis imago*. And now to finish the story begun about sixty years since. Soon after my return to Edinburgh, there arrived a letter from India, announcing G——'s death! and stating that he had died on the 19th of December."

THE REV. T. A. BUCKLEY.

LITERATURE, ghostly literature especially, is replete with stories of the fulfilment by the dead of *ante mortem* promises. Abroad, the recorded instances of this mysterious completion of the compact with the survivor are, apparently, more numerous than in the British Isles; but we know of none described more circumstantially, and yet with more conventionality, than a case mentioned in Newton Crosland's new *Theory of Apparitions*.

On the 30th January 1856, at the early age of thirty, died the Rev. Theodore Alois Buckley, author of *The Dawnings of Genius*, a work on the early lives of eminent men, and formerly one of the chaplains of

Christ Church, Oxford. He was a man of extraordinary
ability, but, says Mr. Crosland, "his life was unfortunate, and his death sad." When he was alive and
well at Oxford, about the year 1850, conversing on
the subject of ghosts one day with a mutual friend, Mr.
Kenneth R. H. Mackenzie, a gentleman who contributed
the chapter on "Chatterton" to the above-mentioned
work, the two friends entered into a compact that, whoever departed this life first, should, if permitted, visit
the other as an apparition; and the signal of communication was arranged to be the placing of a ghostly
hand on the brow of the survivor. On the night of the
2nd of February, about twelve or half-past twelve
o'clock, Mr. Mackenzie was lying in bed, watching the
candle expiring, preparing his mind for sleep, and *not
thinking of his departed friend*, when he felt placed
over one eye and his forehead a cool damp hand. On
looking up he saw Buckley in his ordinary apparel, and
with his portfolio under his arm, as in life, standing at
the bedside. The figure, as soon as it was recognised,
retreated to the window; and after remaining plainly in
sight for about a minute, disappeared. A few nights afterwards, the spectral Buckley again made his appearance,
bearing in his hand the exact image of a letter, which
Mr. Mackenzie at once identified as an old one that he
had casually picked up from his letter-box in the course
of the day. The letter was one that had been formerly
written by Mr. Buckley to his friend Mr. Mackenzie.

BURROUGHS.

In his account of "Apparitions," Aubrey relates some curious particulars of one that was believed to haunt Caisho Burroughs, eldest son of Sir John Burroughs; and if the antiquary's record, derived from his friend Monson, might be credited, it is one of the best authenticated stories of its class now extant. Sir John Burroughs, a high-spirited gentleman, who subsequently perished in the ill-fated siege of Rochelle, being sent by Charles I. as envoy to the Emperor of Germany, took with him his son Caisho. Subsequently Sir John made a tour through Italy, leaving Caisho at Florence to learn the language.

Whilst residing in the Tuscan capital, young Burroughs fell passionately in love with a beautiful courtesan, a mistress of the Grand Duke. At last their intimacy became so notorious that it came to the Grand Duke's ears, and he, it is alleged, grew so jealous that he formed the design of having Caisho assassinated. Warned by some of the English residents in Florence of the fate awaiting him, the young man hastily left the city, without even acquainting his mistress of his intended departure. When the Grand Duke found himself baulked of his anticipated vengeance on his rival, he vented his spite on his mistress, "in most reproachful language," and she, on her side, "resenting

the sudden departure of her gallant, of whom she was
most passionately enamoured, killed herself."

At the very moment that the unfortunate woman
expired in Florence, her apparition, so it is alleged,
appeared to her lover at his residence in London.
Colonel Remeo, a Member of Parliament, and after-
ward's an officer of Charles II.'s household, was sleeping
with young Burroughs, and he, also, is said to have
seen the apparition. This ghost, it is averred, reproached her lover for his conduct in flying from her so
suddenly, and leaving her exposed to the fury of the
Grand Duke. She informed him of her tragical fate,
and warned him that he should be slain in a duel.

Henceforth this spectre frequently appeared to
Caisho, even when his younger brother, after Sir
John Burrough's death, was sleeping with him. As
often as the apparition came, the unfortunate man,
unable to restrain his mental anguish, "would cry out
with great shrieking and trembling of his body, saying,
'O God! here she comes—she comes!'" These
visitations continued from time to time until Caisho's
death. He was killed in a duel, and the morning before his death the apparition appeared to him for the last
time. "Some of my acquaintances have told me," says
Aubrey, "that he was one of the most beautiful men in
England, and very valiant, but proud and bloodthirsty."

The rumour of this haunting of Caisho Burroughs
had spread so widely that it reached the King's ears.
Charles I. was so interested in the account, Aubrey
declares that he cross-examined Sir John Burroughs,

as also Colonel Remeo, as to the truth of the matter, and, in consequence of their report, thought it worth his while to send to Florence in order to make inquiries there. The result of the King's investigations in Tuscany was, the story states, that it was found that the unhappy woman had expired at the very time her apparition first appeared to her lover in London, when he was in bed with Colonel Remeo. Mr. Monson, Aubrey's authority for this marvellous account, was intimate with Sir John Burroughs and both his sons, and declared that whenever Caisho alluded to the affair he wept bitterly.

JOHN DONNE.

In Isaak Walton's life of the well-known Dean of St. Paul's is a very strange family legend, that is none the less worthy of quotation that it has been so often told. According to the old piscatorial biographer, Dr. Donne and his wife were living at one time in the house of Sir Robert Drury, in Drury Lane. The Lord Haye being about to depart to the Court of Henry IV. of France, on an Embassy from James I. of England, Sir Robert Drury resolved to accompany him to the French Court, and to be present at his audience there. No sooner had Sir Robert formed this resolution, than he determined Dr. Donne should be his companion on the journey. This desire having been made suddenly known to Mrs. Donne, who was not only in very bad health, but also expecting her speedy confinement, she was so distressed, and protested so earnestly against her husband's departure, saying that she had a presentiment that some ill would occur in his absence, that finally the doctor laid aside all thoughts of his projected journey, and determined to stay at home.

When Sir Robert heard of this he exerted himself to the utmost to alter Dr. Donne's determination; and the doctor, fearing that after all the many benefits he had received from his friend, he should be deemed unthankful if he so persistently declined to accompany him, told his wife so; who, therefore, with very great reluctance, at last gave way, and most unwillingly assented to her husband's departure. The visit was to last for two months, and was begun within a little while after Mrs. Donne's consent had been gained.

The party reached Paris safely. Two days after their arrival there, Donne was left alone in the room where Sir Robert and he, with some others, had dined. About half-an-hour after his departure, Sir Robert returned, and found Dr. Donne where he had left him, but in such a state of agitation, and so strangely altered in his looks, that he was perfectly amazed at him, and earnestly desired him to inform him what had happened during the short space of time in which he had been left. At first Donne was not sufficiently collected to reply, but after a long and perplexed pause, answered:

"I have seen a dreadful vision since I saw you. I

have seen my dear wife pass twice by me through this room, with her hair hanging about her shoulders, and a dead child in her arms; this I have seen since I saw you."

To this Sir Robert responded:

"Surely, Sir, you have slept since I saw you, and this is the result of some melancholy dream, which I desire you to forget, for you are now awake."

Dr. Donne's reply to this was:

"I cannot be surer that I now live, than that I have not slept since I saw you, and am sure that at her second appearing she stopped, and looked me in the face and vanished."

Nothing would alter Dr. Donne's opinion that he had had a vision, and the next day he was more than ever confirmed in his idea, affirming it with such a deliberate confidence that he finally persuaded Sir Robert that there must be some truth in the vision. Determined to learn the truth as speedily as possible, the knight sent a special messenger back to England, to learn how it fared with Mrs. Donne: whether still alive, and, if alive, in what state. On the twelfth day the messenger returned to Paris with the information that he had found and left Mrs. Donne very ill in bed, and that, after a long and dangerous confinement she had been delivered of a dead child; the date and hour of the child's birth having proved to have been, so it is alleged, identical with that at which Dr. Donne affirmed he had seen the apparition pass by him in the room.

SIR JOHN SHERBROKE AND GENERAL WYNYARD.

Of all the stories of apparitions extant, none, probably, has excited so much discussion as that of the Wynyard ghost. With variations of one kind and another it has been published in many dozens of works, and has been continually discussed at the mess dinners of our army in every part of the world. From time to time inquiries have been made about the circumstances in *Notes and Queries*, in the pages of which invaluable publication all the facts of the case have been gradually revealed. From the periodical referred to, and from other sources of credit, we have been enabled to compile a complete history of the affair.

In 1785, the 33rd Regiment, at the time commanded by Lieutenant-Colonel Forke, was stationed at Sydney, in the island of Cape Breton, off Nova Scotia. Among the officers of this regiment were Captain (afterwards Sir John) Sherbroke and Lieutenant (afterwards General) George Wynyard. These two young men are said to have been connected by similarity of tastes and studies, and to have spent together in literary occupation much of that vacant time which was squandered by their brother officers in those excesses of the table that, in those days at least, were deemed part of the accomplishments of the military character.

On the 15th of October of the above year, between

eight and nine o'clock in the evening, these two officers were seated before the fire in Wynyard's parlour drinking coffee. It was a room in the new barracks, and had two doors, the one opening on an outer passage, the other into Wynyard's bed-room. There were no other means of entering the sitting-room but from the passage, and no other egress from the bed-room but through the sitting-room; so that any person passing into the bed-room must have remained there unless he returned by the way he entered. This point is of consequence to the story.

As these two young officers were thus sitting together, Sherbroke, happening accidentally to glance towards the door that opened to the passage, observed a tall youth of about twenty years of age, but pale and very emaciated, standing beside it. Struck with the presence of a perfect stranger, he immediately turned to his friend, who was sitting near him, and directed his attention to the guest who had thus strangely broken in upon their studies. As soon as Wynyard's eyes were turned towards the mysterious visitor his countenance became agitated. "I have heard," said Sherbroke, "of a man's being as pale as death, but I never saw a living face assume the appearance of a corpse, except Wynyard's at that moment." As they looked silently at the form before them—for Wynyard, who seemed to apprehend the import of the appearance, was deprived of the faculty of speech, and Sherbroke, perceiving the agitation of his friend, felt no inclination to address it —as they looked silently on the figure, it proceeded

20

slowly into the adjoining apartment, and in the act of passing them cast its eyes with an expression of somewhat melancholy affection on young Wynyard. The oppression of this extraordinary presence was no sooner removed than Wynyard, seizing his friend by the arm, and drawing a deep breath, as if recovering from the suffocation of intense astonishment and emotion, muttered in a low and almost inaudible tone of voice, "Great God! my brother!" "Your brother!" repeated Sherbroke, "what can you mean, Wynyard? There must be some deception. Follow me." And immediately taking his friend by the arm, he preceded him into the bed-room, which, as I before stated, was connected with the sitting-room, and into which the strange visitor had evidently entered. I have already said that from this chamber there was no possibility of withdrawing, but by the way of the apartment through which the figure had certainly passed, and as certainly never had returned. Imagine, then, the astonishment of the young officers when, on finding themselves in the centre of the chamber, they perceived that the room was untenanted. Another officer, Lieutenant (afterwards Colonel) Ralph Gore, coming in, joined in the search, but without avail. Wynyard's mind had received an impression, at the first moment of his observing it, that the figure which he had seen was the spirit of his brother. Sherbroke still persevered in strenuously believing that some delusion had been practised.

At the suggestion of Lieutenant Gore, they took note of the day and hour in which the event had happened, but they resolved not to mention the occurrences in the regiment, and gradually they persuaded each other that they had been imposed upon by some artifice of their fellow officers, though they could neither account for the reason, or suspect the author, or conceive the means of its execution. They were content to imagine anything possible rather than admit the possibility of a supernatural appearance. But though they had attempted these stratagems of self-delusion, Wynyard could not help expressing his solicitude with respect to the safety of the brother whose apparition he had either seen or imagined himself to have seen; and the anxiety which he exhibited for letters from England, and his frequent mention of his fears for his brother's health, at length awakened the curiosity of his comrades, and eventually betrayed him into a declaration of the circumstances which he had in vain determined to conceal.

The story of the silent and unbidden visitor was no sooner bruited abroad than the destiny of Wynyard's brother became an object of universal and painful interest to the officers of the regiment; there were few who did not inquire for Wynyard's letters before they made any demand after their own, and the packets that arrived from England were welcomed with a more than usual eagerness, for they brought not only remembrances from their friends at home, but promised to afford the clue to the mystery which had happened among themselves. By the first ships no intelligence relating to the story could have been received, for they

20 *

had all departed from England previously to the appearance of the spirit. At length the long-wished-for vessel arrived. All the officers had letters except Wynyard. Still the secret was unexplained. They examined the several newspapers; they contained no mention of any death, or of any other circumstance connected with his family that could account for the preternatural event. There was a solitary letter for Sherbroke, still unopened. The officers had received their letters in the mess-room at the hour of supper. After Sherbroke had broken the seal of his last packet, and cast a glance on its contents, he beckoned his friend away from the company and departed from the room. All were silent. The suspense of the interest was now at its climax; the impatience for the return of Sherbroke was inexpressible. They doubted not but that letter had contained the long-expected intelligence. At the interval of an hour Sherbroke joined them. No one dared be guilty of so great a rudeness as to inquire the nature of his correspondence; but they waited, in mute attention, expecting that he would himself touch upon the subject. His mind was manifestly full of thoughts that pained, bewildered, and oppressed him. He drew near to the fire-place, and, leaning his head on the mantel-piece, after a pause of some moments, said in a low voice to the person who was nearest to him, "Wynyard's brother is no more!" The first line of Sherbroke's letter was, "Dear John, break to your friend, Wynyard, the death of his favourite brother." He had died on the day, and at the very hour, on which his friends had seen his spirit pass so mysteriously through the apartment.

Some years after, on Sherbroke's return to England, he was walking with two gentlemen in Piccadilly, when on the opposite side of the way, he saw a person bearing the most striking resemblance to the figure which had been disclosed to Wynyard and himself. His companions were acquainted with the story, and he instantly directed their attention to the gentleman opposite, as the individual who had contrived to enter and depart from Wynyard's apartment without their being conscious of the means. Full of this impression, he immediately went over, and at once addressed the gentleman; he now fully expected to elucidate the mystery. He apologised for the interruption, but excused it by relating the occurrence which had induced him to the commission of this solecism in manners. The gentle man received him as a friend. He had never been out of the country, but he was another brother of the youth whose spirit had been seen.

This story is related with several variations. It is sometimes told as having happened at Gibraltar, at others in England, at others in America. There are also differences with respect to the conclusion. Some say that the gentleman whom Sir John Sherbroke afterwards met in London, and addressed as the person whom he had previously seen in so mysterious a manner, was not another brother of General Wynyard, but a gentleman who bore a strong resemblance to the family. But, however, the leading facts in every account are the same. Sir John Sherbroke and General Wynyard, two gentleman of veracity, were together present at the spiritual appearance of the brother of General Wynyard, the appearance took place at the moment of dissolution, and the countenance and form of the ghost's figure were so distinctly impressed upon the memory of Sir John Sherbroke, to whom the living man had been unknown, that, on accidentally meeting with his likeness, he perceived and acknowledged the resemblance.

It may be added that the brother of General Wynyard, who died on the 15th of October 1785, was John Otway Wynyard, at the time of his death lieutenant in the 3rd Regiment of Foot Guards.

Colonel Gore, being asked many years afterwards by Sir John Harvey to give an account of the affair, so far as it came within his cognizance, testified in writing to the main facts of the narrative here given; and Sir John Sherbroke, forty years after the event, assured his friend, General Paul Anderson, in the most solemn manner, that he believed the appearance he had seen to have been a ghost or spirit, and this belief, he added, was shared by his friend Wynyard.

THE LUMINOUS WOMAN.

THE following startling relation was furnished to Robert Dale Owen by a clergyman of the Church of England, chaplain to a British legation abroad. Although the narrator's name is not given, Owen had the consent of the Rev. Doctor to communicate it in any case in which he might deem it would serve the cause to advance which his work, *Footfalls on the Boundary of Another World*, was written. It is not given now, for obvious reasons, but the story is too characteristic to be omitted, and shall, therefore, be given as nearly as possible in the narrator's own terms :—

"In the year 185– I was staying, with my wife and children, at a favourite watering-place. In order to attend to some affairs of my own, I determined to leave my family there for three or four days. Accordingly, one day in August, I took the railway, and arrived in the evening, an unexpected guest, at —— Hall, the residence of a gentleman whose acquaintance I had recently made, and with whom my sister was then staying.

"I arrived late; soon afterwards went to bed, and before long fell asleep. Awaking after three or four hours, I was not surprised to find I could sleep no more; for I never rest well in a strange bed. After trying, therefore, in vain again to induce sleep, I began to arrange my plans for the day.

"I had been engaged some little time in this way, when I became suddenly sensible that there was a light in the room. Turning round, I distinctly perceived a female figure; and what attracted my especial attention was, that *the light by which I saw it emanated from itself*. I watched the figure attentively. The features were not perceptible. After moving a little distance, it disappeared as suddenly as it had appeared.

"My first thoughts were that there was some trick. I immediately got out of bed, struck a light, and found my bedroom-door still locked. I then carefully examined the walls, to ascertain if there were any other concealed means of entrance or exit; but none could I find. I drew the curtains and opened the shutters; but all outside was silent and dark, there being no moonlight.

"After examining the room well in every part, I betook myself to bed and thought calmly over the whole matter. The final impression on my mind was that I had seen something supernatural, and, if supernatural, that it was in some way connected with my wife. What was the appearance? What did it mean? Would it have appeared to me if I had been asleep instead of awake? These were questions very easy to ask and very difficult to answer.

"Even if my room-door had been unlocked, or if there had been a concealed entrance to the room, a practical joke was out of the question. For, in the first place, I was not on such intimate terms with my host as to warrant such a liberty; and, secondly, even if he had been inclined to sanction so questionable a proceeding, he was too unwell at the time to permit me for a moment to entertain such a supposition.

"In doubt and uncertainty I passed the rest of the night; and in the morning, descending early, I immediately told my sister what had occurred, describing to her accurately everything connected with the appearance I had witnessed. She seemed much struck with what I told her, and replied, 'It is *very* odd; for you have heard, I dare say, that a lady was, some years ago, murdered in this house ; but it was not in the room you slept in.' I answered that I had never heard anything of the kind, and was beginning to make further inquiries about the murder, when I was interrupted by the entrance of our host and hostess, and afterwards by breakfast.

" After breakfast I left without having had any opportunity of renewing the conversation. But the whole affair had made upon me an impression which I sought in vain to shake off. The female figure was ever before my mind's eye, and I became fidgety and anxious about my wife. 'Could it in any way be connected with her?' was my constantly recurring thought. So much did this weigh on my mind that, instead of attending to the business for the express purpose of transacting which I had left my family, I returned to them by the first train ; and it was only when I saw my wife and children in good health, and everything safe and well in my household, that I felt satisfied that, whatever the nature of the appearance might have been, it was not connected with any evil to them.

" On the Wednesday following I received a letter from my sister, in which she informed me that, since I left, she had ascertained that the murder *was* committed in the very room in which I had slept. She added that she purposed visiting us next day, and that she would like me to write out an account of what I had seen, together with a plan of the room, and that on that plan she wished me to mark the place of the appearance and of the disappearance of the figure.

" This I immediately did ; and the next day, when my sister arrived, she asked me if I had complied with her request. I replied, pointing to the drawing-room table, 'Yes ; there is the account and the plan.' As she rose to examine it, I prevented her, saying, ' Do not look at it until you have told me all you have to say, because you might unintentionally colour your story by what you may read there.'

" Thereupon she informed me that she had had the carpet taken up in the room I had occupied, and that the marks of blood from the murdered person were there, plainly visible, on a particular part of the floor. At my request she also then drew a plan of the room, and marked upon it the spots which still bore traces of blood.

" The two plans—my sister's and mine—were then compared, and we verified the most remarkable fact, that *the places she had marked as the beginning and ending of the traces of blood, coincided exactly with the spots marked on my plan as those on which the female figure had appeared and disappeared.*

" I am unable to add anything to this plain statement of facts," remarks the narrator. " I cannot account in any way for what I saw. I am convinced no human being entered my chamber that night ; yet I know that, being wide awake and in good health, I *did* distinctly see a female figure in my room. But if, as I must believe, it was a supernatural appearance, then I am unable to suggest any reason why it should have appeared to me, I cannot tell whether, if I had not been in the room, or had been asleep at the time, that figure would equally have been there. As it was, it seemed connected with no warning nor presage. No misfortune of any kind happened then, or since, to me or mine. It is true that the host, at whose house I was staying, when this incident occurred, and also one of his children, died a few months afterwards; but I cannot pretend to make out any connection between either of these deaths and the appearance I witnessed. . . . But what I distinctly saw, that, and that only, I describe."

It is unfortunate that there is no evidence available as to whether this was the only appearance recorded of the apparition; or whether it was known to have ever been seen before or after the night on which the narrator of the above account beheld it.

THE RESULT OF A CURSE.

In Dr. Lee's *Glimpses of the Supernatural*—a collection of ghost tales and revivified mediæval legends—is given a marvellous narrative of the results of a curse, as, according to the reverend author, "fresh evidence of the existence of the supernatural amongst us, had we only eyes to see and ears to hear." We include the story in our collection as a fair specimen of the way in which such subjects are treated in our days, but must suggest that it would bear a greater air of *vraisemblance* were the names of some at least of the persons introduced given, or some more definite clue to the localities afforded. The story, as told by Dr. Lee, is this :—

"The younger son of a Nova Scotia baronet, under promise of marriage, betrayed the only surviving daughter of a Northumbrian yeoman of ancient and respectable family, nearly allied to a peer, so created in William the Fourth's reign. She was a person of rare beauty and of considerable accomplishments, having received an education of a very superior character in Edinburgh. After her betrayal, she was deserted by her lover, who fled abroad. The night before he left, however, at her earnest request, he met her in company with a friend, with the avowed intention of promising marriage in the future, when his family, as he declared, might be less averse to it.

"After events show that this was merely an empty promise, and that he had no intention of fulfilling it. A long discussion took place between the girl and her betrayer, in the presence of the female friend in question, a first cousin of her father. High words, strong phrases, and sharp upbraidings were uttered on both sides; until at last the young man, in cruel and harsh language, turning upon her fiercely, declared that he would never marry her at all, and held himself, as he maintained, perfectly free to wed whom he should choose.

"'You will be my certain death,' she exclaimed, 'but death will be more welcome than life.'

"'Die and be ——,' he replied.

"At this the girl, with a wail of agony, swooned away. On her recovery she seemed to gather up her strength to pronounce a curse upon him and his. She uttered it with deliberation, yet with wildness and bitterness, maintaining that she was his wife, and would haunt him to the day of his death; declaring at the same time to her relation present, 'And you shall be the witness.'

"He left the place of meeting without any reconciliation or kind word, and, it was believed, went abroad. In less than five months, in giving birth to her child, she died, away from her home, and was buried with it (for the child, soon after its baptism, died likewise) in a village church-yard near Ambleside. Neither stone nor memorial marks her grave. Her father, a widower, wounded to the quick by the loss of his only daughter, pined away and soon followed her to his last resting-place.

"Five years had passed, and the female cousin of the old yeoman, being possessed of a competency, had gone to live in London, when, on a certain morning in the spring of the year 1842, she was passing by a church in the West End, where, from the number of carriages waiting, she saw that a marriage was being solemnized. She felt mysteriously and instinctively drawn to look in. On doing so, and pressing forwards towards the altar, she beheld, to her astonishment, the very man, somewhat altered and weather-worn, who had caused so much misery to her relations, being married (as on inquiring she discovered) to the daughter

of a rich city merchant. This affected her deeply, bringing back the saddest memories of the past. But, as the
bridal party were passing out of the church, and she
pushed forward to look, and be quite sure she had made
no mistake, both herself and the bridegroom at one
moment saw an apparition of her relation, the poor girl
whom he had ruined, dressed in white, with flowing
hair and a wild look, holding up in both hands her
little infant. Both seemed perfectly natural in appearance and to be of ordinary flesh and blood. There was
no mistaking her certain identity. This occurred in
the full sunshine of noon, and under a heavy Palladian
porch in the presence of a crowd. The bridegroom
turned deathly pale in a moment, trembled violently,
and then, staggering, fell forward down the steps. This
occasioned a vast stir and sensation among the crowd.
It seemed incomprehensible. The bridegroom, said
the church officials in answer to inquiries, was in a fit.
He was carried down the steps and taken in the bridal
carriage to his father-in-law's house. But it was reported that he never spoke again ; and this fact is
mentioned in a contemporary newspaper account of the
event. Anyhow, his marriage and death appeared in
the same number of one of the daily papers.

"And although the family of the city merchant
knew nothing of the apparition, what is thus set forth
was put on record by the lady in question, who knew
the mysterious circumstances in all their details, which
record is reasonably believed by her to afford at once a
signal example of retributive justice and a marked

piece of evidence of the supernatural. Names, for various reasons, are not mentioned here. The truth of this narrative, however, was affirmed on oath by the lady in question," why or wherefore Dr. Lee does not state, " before two justices of the peace at Windsor, on October 3rd, 1848, one of whom was a beneficed clergyman in the diocese of Oxford, well known to the editor of this volume, to whom this record was given in the year 1857 (when he was assistant minister of Berkley Chapel) by a lady of rank who worshipped there."